LOON *Magic*

10th Anniversary COLLECTOR EDITION

LOON Magic

by Tom Klein

10th
Anniversary
COLLECTOR EDITION

Photography by Carl R. Sams II and Jean Stoick

NorthWord
NORTHWORD PRESS, INC.
Minocqua, Wisconsin

Acknowledgments

This book is now into its second decade. The *Loon Magic* story reads like fiction: A self-published book by a previously unpublished author sells by the tens of thousands and launches a highly successful nature publishing company. Only in Hollywood. Or only if some magic was working. There simply had to be magic involved. Nothing else could have united those words with over 150,000 readers. The loons did it! I'll take credit only as an interpreter for a very powerful mystique.

And any credit belongs equally to Pat Klein who worked side by side with me during those tough early years to bring the first *Loon Magic* copies off the presses. Without her, none of the magic could have happened.

Paul Strong contributed significantly, with "A Day in the Life of a Loon," as technical advisor on the 1990 edition, and again as a resourceful editor on this edition. The book is greatly enhanced by Paul's knowledge of loons and loon lore.

Words are important but this book's compelling loon portraits bring this magnificent bird to life. No one has better captured loons than Carl Sams and Jean Stoick, whose astonishing work graces these pages. They have devoted thousands of hours to the production of this book. Their love of loons goes way beyond professional responsibilities. They are both true believers in loon religion.

Finally, thanks to everyone who has internalized the message of *Loon Magic* and made life a little better for this symbol of wilderness and serenity.

© 1996 NorthWord Press, Inc.

Photography ©1996 Carl R. Sams II and Jean Stoick, except:
©1996 Art Wolfe, Inc. pages 10-11 and 22-23
©1996 DRK Photo: Johnny Johnson, pages 12-13, 16-17, 20-21
©1996 DRK Photo: Wayne Lynch, page 14
©1996 Tom and Pat Leeson, page 19

Book design, feather illustrations and maps by Kenneth Hey

NorthWord Press, Inc.
P.O. Box 1360
Minocqua, WI 54548

Printed in the United States

Library of Congress Cataloging-in-Publication Data

Klein, Tom
    Loon magic / by Tom Klein ; photographs by Carl R. Sams II and Jean Stoick.
        p.   cm.
        Includes bibliographical references.
        ISBN 1-55971-548-0 (hc)
        ISBN 1-55971-578-2 (sc)
        1. Loons.   I. Title.
    QL696.G33K54   1996
    598.4'42—dc20   95-38568

Dedication

To the memory of Sigurd F. Olson (1899-1982) who opened my mind and heart to the music of the wilderness, and to his son, Sigurd T. Olson, who helped me understand loons.

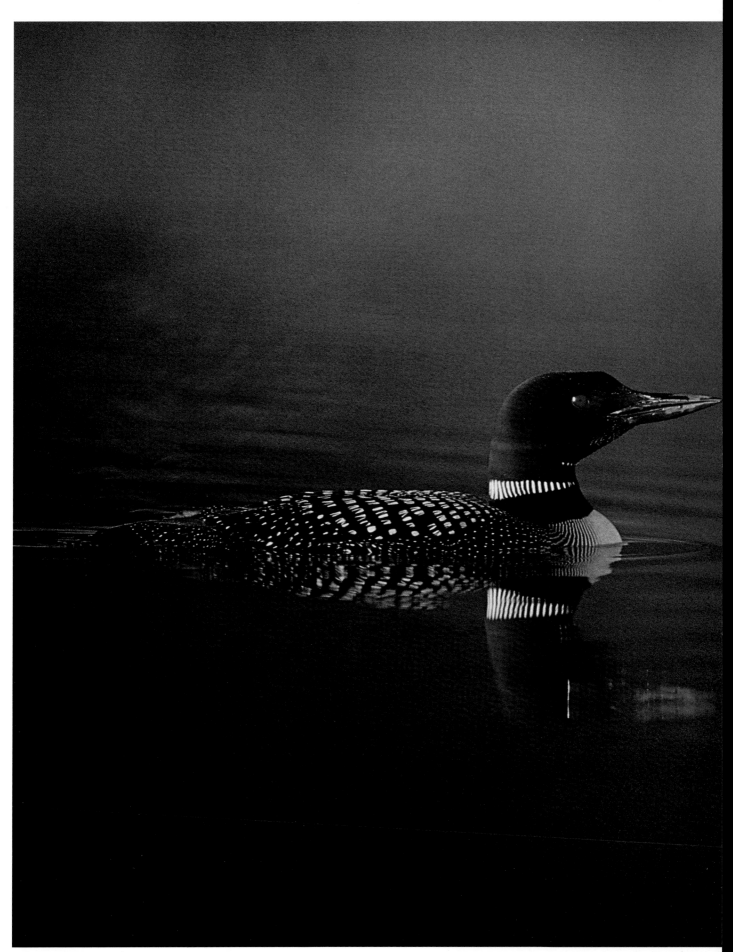

Reflection of a common loon.

The Lord did well when he put the
loon and his music in the land.

— *Aldo Leopold*

Foreword

It has been said that one's early childhood experiences are a basic force in molding what a person will be in later years. Loons have always been a part of my life. I can't remember when I first became aware of them but I have distinct childhood recollections of my parents stopping to watch or listen to a loon and hearing them say, "There's a loon!" or "Listen to the loons!" and always with a great sense of pleasure and excitement. No matter what the circumstances, paddling, portaging, picnicking or hiking, the presence of a loon always merited special notice and acknowledgment; and this from people who had no doubt seen thousands of loons over their years in the north!

I suppose that is why, in part at least, loons have become an indelible part of my being and why the lake country of Minnesota and Canada where I grew up is always synonymous with loons. This association is not privy only to me for I share it with almost everyone who has traveled and loved the lake country where common loons occur. While there is a certain degree of fascination inherent with all species of loons, it is the common loon which holds the greatest attraction and appeal for all. Its distinctive coloration, haunting wild calling, remarkable and often bizarre behavior patterns are all unique. No other species of loon exhibits these particular attributes or merits the status and attractiveness of the common loon in the minds of those who have come to know, love and respect this unusual north country denizen. These qualities occur, however, primarily on its northern summer ranges. On its wintering grounds its appeal to observers is greatly reduced or lost as the loons assume their winter plumage and a much more retiring comportment and demeanor.

To me, it is most significant that almost without exception, loons, wildness and wilderness are always considered concurrently. Although loons are at their best in true wilderness situations, they also occur in non-wilderness areas. However, in the minds of those who encounter loons, no matter where, the images, impressions and feelings of true wilderness automatically surface and strongly assert themselves. The loon's freedom, independence, and simplicity characterize the true spirit of wilderness.

Its wild, weird calling does more to create the indescribable feeling of being apart from civilization and being close to the primitive than any other natural phenomenon in the wilderness country.

The ancient impulses, urges, fears and wonder are much closer to the surface than most realize. In fact, an interesting paradox sometimes exists. While most people react positively and thrill to these primal feelings inspired by the sight and sounds of loons, some experience actual dread and fear. Of primary importance, however, is the close instinctive association with wilderness and its values, which characterizes in the truest sense the very spirit of wildness, freedom, independence, simplicity, mystery and exultation. Dr. Walter J. Breckenridge was most eloquent when he described his feelings: " . . . to me it expresses the essence of unrestrained wildness and seems to put the stamp of genuineness on a North Country setting like 'Sterling' does on silver. . . "

The wild calling of loons does more for me to create the sense of being apart from civilization and again being close to the primitive than almost any other phenomenon except perhaps for the howling of wolves. If the presence and calling of loons creates only these feelings for those who see and hear them it would be important enough; however, they also undeniably verify that wilderness is an actuality, and they punctuate it graphically with their presence.

For travelers and residents of the northern lake country, the frequent occurrence of loons creates a ready source of highly valued enjoyment. Unlike most wildlife, they are seldom wary or secretive. They are readily observed as they go about their daily routines, save perhaps for their nesting activities. It is not uncommon to see loons many times during the course of a day's paddle. Listening to the spectacular spectrum of calls and observing their wild, unpredictable behavior provide a true wilderness viewing opportunity rarely experienced with other species of wildlife.

Because loons are unquestionably an integral part of the wilderness idea, any knowledge that can be developed to shed more light on the management of wilderness lands and loons is vital to their continued well being. To this end, in 1950 I spent one of the most interesting and challenging years of my young life gathering basic data on the status and natural history of loons for a thesis. At that time, information concerning loons was scant and fragmentary at best, and almost everything I discovered was new and exciting. Since then much more has been done and increasingly sophisticated and comprehensive studies and investigations are under way over most of the loon ranges in North America. They are now providing critical information needed to better understand the loon's ecological niche.

Public awareness and appreciation of loons has become a full-blown love affair, increasing far beyond any early expectations, and has expressed itself in some unusual though perhaps predictable ways. The common loon has now become the official state bird for Minnesota; it is eagerly sought after as a subject for hosts of artists and photographers, and salable items featuring loons ranging from elegant silver jewelry to tee-shirts can be found in nearly every gift and specialty shop in the north country. The importance of the loon in this day and age can scarcely be denied.

Those who know the lake country of the north, as well as those who are only occasional visitors, have embraced the loon not only as an authentic symbol of wilderness, but as a vital component of wilderness itself. And now, we will have at our disposal a definitely delightful, infinitely usable, state-of-the art publication documenting the life and times of the common loon as we know it today. The loon has definitely come of age!

—Sigurd T. Olson

Loons require about one-quarter of a mile to become airborne.

No one who has ever heard the diver's music—the mournful far-carrying call notes and the uninhibited, cacophonous, crazy laughter—can ever forget it.

—Oliver Austin, 1961

Introduction

From Maine to Montana and Quebec to British Columbia, the fascination with loons keeps intensifying. Not even an endless parade of books, videos, CDs, T-shirts, playing cards, posters, notecards, windsocks, and every other trinket imaginable has satisfied this craving to be close to loons. Each year thousands of people become involved in loon population surveys, festivals, or fund raising activities. Tens of thousands avidly watch their lakes for the reassuring sight of "their" loons. And hundreds of thousands (maybe even millions) of boaters, fishermen, lakeshore residents, and campers enjoy the occasional sight and thrill to the frequent sounds of this beloved bird.

Over the past few years the loon has become the symbol for the northern experience— a mystique which draws thousands of urban refugees from the concrete caverns of New York, Detroit, Chicago, Milwaukee, Minneapolis, and all points south, north to loon country.

Loon Magic is a book for loon people. Not an ornithological textbook, it is intended to be an accurate and interesting look at loons. The product of careful research and review by many technical experts, *Loon Magic* explains scientific terms and concepts without using other scientific terms and concepts.

It is meant to be read, not studied. No scientific axes grinding, *Loon Magic* presents the loon with no preconceived notions or rules. The book's theme is simple: Loons are just loons; they do not mirror the minds or values of their lakeshore admirers.

While *Loon Magic* contains information about all five species of loons, by design and circumstance it focuses upon the common loon. By design because the common loon is the only loon of the contiguous states and southern Canada, and because it is the glamour bird of northern lakes. And by circumstance because so little is known about the "other four": the arctic, yellow-billed, red-throated, and Pacific loons.

While the research phase of *Loon Magic* involved tracking down every scientific article, thesis, essay, field guide, monograph and rumor connected with loons, this library work was a small part of the effort. Far more important were the discussions with dozens of field scientists and amateur loon watchers. The acceptance of information from non-scientists will, no doubt, be viewed with horror by some. So be it. I'll take the word any day of a lakeside resident who has seriously observed loons for twenty or thirty years over the opinion of a pressured graduate student whose commitment to loons usually encompasses only one or two summers.

But the most important ingredient in *Loon Magic*, the animating influence, was my own loon watching. Not studying loons . . . I'm not a scientist. Just watching. And enjoying. Ever since my first trip in the Minnesota-Ontario canoe country, loons have been, at least mentally, a constant companion. For me, loons have been important. For me, loon music is more than a pleasant distraction while fishing or paddling; it is often the prelude to a powerful spiritual experience.

Many people clearly recall their first experience with loons and people almost always remember the first time they heard loon music. I'm slightly embarrassed to admit I don't. While boyhood trips to northern Wisconsin produced a few loon encounters, nothing special happened. It wasn't until August of 1965 on the Minnesota-Canada border that loons grabbed my soul. With Bill Richtsmeier, a high school buddy, I drove to Moose Lake, a little north of Ely, to start a great Boundary Waters adventure.

We brought everything on that trip, including a six-pound tackle box, an ax, two machetes, two sleeping bags worthy of an arctic expedition, and a steel ammo case to protect our eight pounds of bacon. After a long day's paddle and portage, we made it to Louisa Falls at the bottom of Agnes Lake, just over the Canadian border. Shoulders bright red from the August sun and sore from the sharp bite of the thin Duluth pack straps, we settled into the campsite surrounded by a reassuring audio backdrop of falling water.

The loons on Agnes called that night, probably no louder nor more often than they do on any other August night. But the calling found the right spot. We sat by the campfire bewitched, anticipating two weeks of granite cliffs, water diamonds on the shimmering lakes, firm lake trout, spongy sphagnum moss and quiet evenings with the voices of the wilderness.

That night on Agnes we didn't know the difference between the tremolo, wail or yodel. And we didn't care. We just soaked it all in. It was a magical night. I haven't kept track of Bill over the passing years so I can't speak for him, but nothing has been the same for me since.

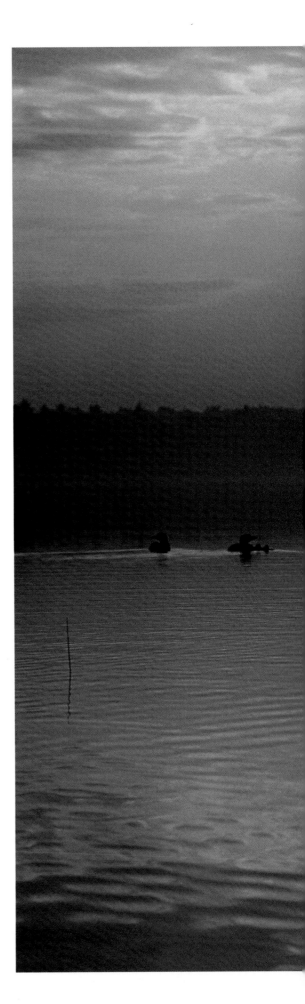

Common loon family on a golden pond.

Contents

Loon pair confronting a territory invader.

LOOKING FOR LOONS

Loon People

Loons are part of many people's religion. Julius Dinger, a real estate appraiser, summers at Hurd Lake, just north of his Eau Claire, Wisconsin home. That's where he got to know loons and where loons got to him. An admitted loon fanatic, Julius, when he dies, doesn't want hymns played. He wants a special service: "I suppose this will sound a little silly to most people, but when I pass away, the music I want at my memorial service is the call of the loon," says Dinger. Loon magic at work.

Ken and Chip Sorlien live on Squam Lake, the real golden pond, in New Hampshire's rugged lake country. A retired General Mills sales executive, Ken moved north from Boston just to watch the peaceful waters of Squam, but he watches much more now. As a volunteer coordinator for the elaborate loon protection effort on the lake, he spends thirty to forty hours a week watching Squam's loons and keeping track of the other volunteers. His efforts paid a personal dividend when a loon pair nesting on an artificial nest island right in front of his home turned an egg into a chick. Ken and Chip offered a 7:30 a.m. champagne toast from their pier. More loon magic.

Grace James lives with her husband, Charlie, in Milwaukee, but her soul is to be found on Stone Lake, a small but attractive northern Wisconsin lake. Grace has four children, but every summer her family expands by three or four members. The Stone Lake loons, you see, are hers. She watches them, talks to them and protects them. When an unsuspecting fisherman strays a little too close to the island where her loons always nest, Grace grabs the bull horn she keeps handy and shouts across the lake: "Keep away, don't you know loons are on that island?" It always works. Later she rows out and explains to the fisherman the special considerations nesting loons deserve. Once, when a red-tailed hawk swooped over an adult loon with two chicks, Grace raced out of her cabin frantically waving a towel to frighten away the potential predator. For her antics she has picked up the nickname "Loony Grace," but she doesn't mind. She lives in a world of loon magic.

These people have lots of company; the loon's spell has spread across the Northeast and Midwest. In Wisconsin, hundreds of people volunteer to monitor the loon populations on their lakes. In New Hampshire, nearly 3,000 people make contributions of time and money to the Loon Preservation Committee. In Michigan, volunteers of the Whitefish Point Bird Observatory are on Lake Superior's shore at dawn on chilling April and May mornings to count migrating loons.

Why? What is so enchanting about a stout black and white bird that likes to call when most people like to sleep? Part of the answer might be the distance loons and people have traveled together. In the film *A Quest For Fire*, set in the dawn of human origins, loon calls were used extensively in the sound track. It was a forgettable film but it had one memorable scene depicting a band of primitive humans stopping to listen to that call so familiar yet so haunting. No one knows if a half a million years ago the loon's call was the same sound that echoed last summer around Squam in New Hampshire or Saganaga in Minnesota. But it could have been.

If the call of the loon does go back to our first days as humans, the strong feelings of *déjà vu* many people experience when hearing loon calls would be more understandable and the pull of loon magic a bit less mysterious. Writer and wilderness philosopher Sigurd F. Olson often wrote about *racial memory*, the ability of a person to recall, however vaguely, the common thoughts, feelings or experiences of ancestors from thousands of years ago. The romantic poets of the nineteenth century understood the concept. So do people who accept the concept of reincarnation.

Like the call of the loon, the howl of the wolf has this power to take people back. In an article on wolves for *Smithsonian* magazine, novelist David Nevin detailed his profound response to a wolf howl: the recognition " . . . went far back, it flowed from that pool of inherited knowledge we all carry from the past. I'd have known it anywhere." Cynics will attribute such insights to harmless fantasy or delusion; empirically minded scientists might, with a condescending nod, toss the idea of racial memory into a class of phenomena which can neither be proved nor disproved.

LOONS IN NATIVE AMERICAN CULTURE

But the idea intrigues Keewaydinoquay, an Ojibwa who teaches ethnobiology at the University of Wisconsin-Milwaukee. Kee (she prefers her Ojibwa name) recalls that loons were an important part of her childhood on Beaver Island, a small island in Lake Michigan off the northeastern shore of Wisconsin. She would communicate with loons by offering *kaneck*, a blend of sacred herbs, which she placed on the shore. Loons would come to share and accept her offering. A bond was formed.

Over a lengthy breakfast interview, Kee told me a powerful story, *Brave is Mahng is Loon*, about the origins of the Ojibwa. In the story, the loon was not just another bird, but the first act of creation when the very voice of the Creator echoed across the void and became embodied in a gray and black shadow, the spirit of the loon. Later, Sun threw light on the shadow, giving Loon his striking white markings. Loon loved Anishinabe, the first man. It was Loon who saved Anishinabe when, while swimming, his long black hair became entangled in logs.

And so the magic began a long time ago. It's easy to imagine how Kee's story developed: a bright campfire reflected in the eyes of an ancient people alive

Common loon performing the tremolo call.

with creativity and wonder, a people curious about their origins and their relationship to the natural world. A vibrant tremolo call halted the conversation, moved it in new directions . . . .

The legend reflects the special relationship between loons and the Ojibwa. In the Ojibwa language, *mahng* is the word for both brave and loon. In the "Song of Hiawatha," Longfellow praised Hiawatha with a reference to loons:

> *From the red deer's flesh Nokomis*
> *Made a banquet to his honor.*
> *All the village came and feasted,*
> *All the guests praised Hiawatha,*
> *Called him Strong-Heart, Soan-ge-taha!*
> *Called him Loon-Heart, Mahn-go-taysee!*

Mahn-go-taysee, translated by Kee as "thou art a loon-hearted one," is about the finest compliment an Ojibwa can pay another person.

The very first accounts of the chemistry between loons and people were not written by Longfellow, nor told by Native American storytellers; they can be seen only on the granite out-croppings of the Canadian Shield, north of the Great Lakes. Crude pictographs of loons still grace some of those rock faces. Even after hundreds or thousands of years, these red images, made with hematite and fish oil, cling to the rocks. Little is known of their origins; no oral traditions interpret them or offer a clue to the identity or motives of their makers.

Anthropologists know only that some people lived in the region about 8,000 years ago, following the edge of the great ice sheets. Later, about 5,000 years ago, a group known as the Old Copper Culture people inhabited the Upper Great Lakes and left copper mines and tools as testimony of their presence. Native Americans, defined only as the Early Woodland Culture, used the area until about the birth of Christ and left burial mounds, pottery and pipes. Then we start getting into "recorded history." The first Europeans entered the north country in the early 1600s. Any of these groups or none of them could have painted loons on granite cliffs. We just don't know. But with eloquent silence, these paintings remind us simply that moose, canoes, abstract deities and loons were part of the lives of a mysterious people.

Far more is known of the Ojibwa people who moved into the Upper Great Lakes region in the early seventeenth century. The Ojibwa, like most Native American tribes, structured their society through a system of clans. The clan was patrilineal: your father's clan became your clan. According to Delores Bainbridge, an Ojibwa storyteller living in Ashland, Wisconsin, the five great clans of her tribe—the Loon, Crane, Bear, Marten and Fish clans—came out of the waters at the mouth of the St. Lawrence River.

According to William Warner, author of *A History of the Ojibway Nation*, the head of the Loon Clan was known for wisdom, honesty and bravery. In her comprehensive study of Ojibwa music, Frances Densmore uncovered songs of the loon which were sung by warriors preparing for battle. If a loon were heard calling on the eve of the warpath,

it was considered an omen of victory.

Loon legends span the continent. While some are obscure—like the story from eastern Canada of Tatler, a loon who served as the eyes and ears of the Creator, Gloosaph—others are well known like the Tsimshian Indian legend of the loon's necklace. Stories of a loon woman are known in several Indian cultures. The Cree of northern Canada believed the loon's call was the cry of slain warriors calling back to the land of the living.

In the Pacific Northwest, a legend from the east side of the Olympic Peninsula related the story of an Indian boy who disobeyed his mother by swimming in a lake inhabited by evil spirits who turned the boy into a loon. The boy returned to his home but could speak only in the harsh cries of a loon and was chased away by his mother, an obvious

Older chicks become too big for a comfortable ride.

lesson on the dangers of disobedience. Many Indian loon legends have similar practical objectives.

Probably no native peoples have more references to loons in their folklore than the Eskimo. Tuutlick, the most frequent Eskimo name for the common loon, turns up in dozens of Eskimo legends, including the Bering Strait Eskimo story of Soolook, a boy blinded by his evil witch-doctor mother. One day Soolook followed the call of a loon to a small lake where the loon restored his sight. Thanking the loon, Soolook spoke for generations of Eskimos when he said, "The spirit of one's good friend, the loon, shall always be the favorite spirit of one's children and their children's children." The existence of over thirty different Eskimo names for the four species of loons speaks to the importance of loons for the Eskimo. Well into the twentieth century, loons were part of the culture and commerce of the Eskimo. For the Nunamiut Eskimos, the loon had a variety of uses. It was used for food and valued as a source of fat; the bill of the yellow-billed loon was used for headband decorations and the skin of the neck, which is very tough, was used to make boots and parkas.

In 1910, Bernhard Hantzsch traveled to Baffin Island where he observed substantial numbers of common and Pacific loons and a few red-throated loons. His journal, however, details the extensive robbing of loon nests by Eskimos, which resulted in the collapse of local loon populations. Hantzsch offered an editorial note on the practice: "But as such recklessness is natural to primitive man, and as restriction of hunting through game laws is out of the question here, Nature herself must see to the management of her highest creation." For other Eskimos, though, the loon was sacred. One group in Northwest Alaska upheld a strict taboo against the killing of any loons.

Ceremonial masks similar to this one were used centuries ago by Eskimos. The food in the loon's mouth may have symbolized a hunter's wish for abundant game and the concentric hoops and grooves may have represented the stars and heavens.
Illustration based upon museum artifact at the Alaska State Museum, Juneau.

Fishing floats shaped like loons were used by Eskimos to buoy the end of gill nets which were set at right angles from the shore.
Illustration based upon museum artifact at the Alaska State Museum, Juneau.

Many Eskimo tribes venerated the loon in their art. Most museum collections of Eskimo art contain loon images. The Bering Sea Eskimos devised elaborate loon masks and carved loon decoys for use as fish net floats. Excavations of prehistoric Eskimo villages near Point Hope, Alaska uncovered loon heads carved out of walrus ivory.

The pervasive occurrence of the loon in the art and oral traditions of Native Americans across the North American continent is vivid testimony to the magnetism of this bird of the north and to the roots of the loon magic which still grips northern people.

NEW LEGENDS UNFOLD

Like staring into a campfire or watching a river flow, listening to loons has a hypnotic effect which transcends time. It has a power at the edge of rationality. Fifty years ago a woman spent just one summer on Lake Winnipesaukee in New Hampshire where the loons worked their spell. Last year she made a financial contribution to the Loon Preservation Committee, commenting that she remembered the "wonderful calling at night" and just wanted to help. Nearly 10,000 others have expressed similar feelings by contributing to private loon organizations in nine states and one province. Something is going on here.

In the early twentieth century Charlton Ogburn, Jr. wrote *The Meaning of Birds*, an intriguing essay. No mystic or spiritualist by any means, Ogburn nevertheless found just the right words to describe the power of birds: "Birds are translators for us, the intermediaries between the vast world beyond us and our own emotions, expressing in their notes, in tones within our spiritual register, the nature of our common setting. . . " Amen.

As translators, loons are multi-lingual: they spoke to the early Cree, Ojibwa and Inuit and they speak to people today. Loons spoke very clearly to Joe Anderlik. A retired paper company executive living in Arlington Heights (a Chicago suburb), Anderlik heard the loon's call as a boy. He even remembers the year—1929. It was a sound he would never forget, a sound which would draw him back to the north country many times. Now, instead of stolen days up north, Anderlik spends every summer at his lake home near Lac du Flambeau in northern Wisconsin. He begins his daily routine at four in the morning when he goes to his workbench and starts carving—you guessed it—loons. He loves every minute of his work and his carvings show it.

Having watched many people fall for loons, he sees a definite pattern: "People come up north from the city and hear this strange bird. This creates a lodestone. They carry the memories, often for years. Eventually they start spending more and more time up north. Pretty soon, they're living up here. Once they fall in love with loons, it's forever."

There are thousands of people like Joe scattered around the Northland. It's difficult to separate their love for loons and their love for the place loons happen to be. It could be that loons reinforce for people their image of the north country. The similarity of some of the northern lakes of Maine and Minnesota or of New Hampshire and Wisconsin is remarkable; all loon country exudes that rugged northern beauty. But maybe the question is moot, loons and loon country being one, symbol and substance, player and stage—a captivating creature in a magical land.

Water droplets cling to feathers after a dive.

Performing the "wing flap" to dry feathers.

The study of birds is to me like the study of man. It demands more than one faculty, and the end is not so much the elucidation of great laws, such as we may expect to derive from examination of the physical universe, as the delineation of character.

—Charlton Ogburn, Jr., 1915

Family Album

THE CLASSIFICATION OF BIRDS

Phylum . . . superclass . . . subspecies . . . genus . . . suborder . . . superfamily . . . subclass . . . order . . . kingdom . . . The classification of birds is a playground for ornithologists. If your primary interest is loons, however, you're in luck. Nearly every bird book begins with loons, the oldest living birds. Their classification is simple with no suborders, superclasses or even subspecies to clutter their listing.

Taxonomists, scientists specializing in the classification of plants and animals, use only eight categorical levels to sort out the common loon:

Kingdom: Animalia—all animals including man
Phylum: Chordata—animals with spinal cord
Subphylum: Vertebrata—animals with solid backbone
Class: Aves—all birds
Order: Gaviiformes—the loon group
Family: *Gaviidae*—the only family of loons
Genus: *Gavia*—the group of five loon species
Species: *immer*—one of five loon species

The scientific name for any bird simply combines the genus and species names. For example, *Gavia immer* is the common loon, which is one of five distinct species of the family *Gaviidae*. The loon's family tree is bare: unlike most orders of birds, the order Gaviiformes has only one family, the Gaviidae. If your passion were small perching birds, you would encounter the order Passeriformes, holding no less than twenty-nine families including the thrush family with 306 species and the finch

Pacific loons tolerate little disturbance on their breeding territory.

family with 436 species. With loons, it's one family and only five species.

The classification system is a straightforward method of keeping birds organized. It provides sharp, if somewhat arbitrary, boundaries for the complex and often confusing natural order by establishing a clear hierarchy from the general to the specific. The bird classification system works somewhat like the United States election system, with birds and voters organized at many levels. While the most general level for voters is the nation and for birds the class, voters are then divided by states and birds by orders. (The names of all bird orders end with the suffix "-iformes.") Beyond the state level, voters are organized by counties and birds by families. Counties have a smaller unit, the city, and bird families have a more specific grouping, the genus. Finally,

voters are classed within the city by precinct and birds are classed within the genus by species, the most specific level of classification.

WHAT'S IN A NAME?

The generic name for loons is *Gavia,* from which order and family names are derived. Old bird books used *Gavia* for both loons and sea smews, a Eurasian merganser which only rarely wanders onto the North American continent. Since smews resemble loons neither in appearance nor habit, it is odd that loons carry *Gavia* as half of their scientific name. Loon fanciers can take some pleasure, though, in the sure knowledge that loons are far more famous than smews.

The species name *immer* is Scandinavian. Its root, the Swedish word e*mmer,* meaning the blackened ashes of fire,

The name game ended in 1950 when the International Commission of Zoological Nomenclature gave the common loon its current, and presumably final, scientific name.

The bird's popular or common name "loon" has been around a long time. Most bird books list two possible sources: the English word *lumme*, meaning lummox or awkward person, and the old Scandinavian word *lom,* meaning lame or clumsy. In both cases the point is clear. As any veteran loon watcher knows, loons can be ridiculously clumsy and almost helpless on land. The *Century Dictionary*, however, has a different etymological approach. Its editor believed loon to be a corruption of the Provincial English word *loom*, meaning the "track of a fish," which probably described the wake a fish makes while swimming just under the surface.

Of the five species of loons, the four of the far north—the Pacific, arctic, yellow-billed and red-throated loons—carry proud, descriptive names. But is the other loon really "common"? To most, it's a spectacular bird. The name may be unfair, but the common loon is in the good company of the common egret, the common merganser, and the common sandpiper. With all the truly great bird names like royal tern, great egret, golden-crowned kinglet or magnificent frigate bird, there should have been one more exciting name to help out the common loon. Considering there are least bitterns, lesser goldfinches, and even parasitic jaegers, it could have been worse. Perhaps the number of "other" names for the common loon have been a response to this injustice. The common loon has flown under such interesting names as the great northern diver (the European name), the ring-necked loon, the black-billed loon, the ember goose, and the walloon. By any name, the common loon is a special bird.

How Old is Old

Loons are the first birds on the American Ornithologists Union's (AOU) *Check-list of North American Birds,* and by no coincidence. The check-list is a phylogenetic ranking, a listing of birds from the lowest, most primitive orders, to the highest, most recently evolved orders. While L. L. Snyder, Curator of Ornithology for the Royal Ontario Museum of Zoology, calls loons an "old and distinguished group of birds which have changed very little," the exact age of the loon species is open to speculation. A bit of bird history is required to help place the loon in perspective. The first known player on the avian stage was *Archaeopteryx,* dating back about 140 million years. Fifty million years later, about the time *Tyrannosaurus* rex dominated the landscape, the genus *Hesperornis* entered the scene. In 1870, Professor March of Yale University found fragments of this ancient bird in western Kansas. Drawn from fossil remains, artist's renderings of *Hesperornis* look remarkably like present day loons, but Hesperornis was about six-feet long and probably flightless. While scientists

is a fitting reference to the common loon's contrasting black and white plumage. *Immer* is also the contemporary Norwegian word for loon. Several researchers, though, point to the Latin *immerus*, meaning submerged, as another possible source for *immer*.

The common loon has not always had *Gavia immer* as its scientific name. The ten-volume *Century Dictionary,* edited by William Dwight Whitney in 1899, contains a description of the common loon with two scientific names, *Colymbus torquatusor* and *Colymbus glacialis.* Although it refers to ice, the second option has a pleasant warmth. For years, scientists kept changing their minds about the proper place for loons in the bird world. The 1917 edition of *Birds of America* edited by Gilbert Pearson placed loons in the order Pygopodes with the company of auks and grebes.

contend *Hesperornis* was not a direct loon ancestor, the editors of *The Audubon Society Encyclopedia of North American Birds* do note that it was "in form and habit much like a loon of today." So loon-like birds go back about ninety million years.

A much smaller bird, and certainly a loon relative, has been described by Robert Storer. Writing in the bird journal *Auk*, Storer postulates that loons separated from primitive gull-like stock between the late Cretaceous period and early Eocene epoch, roughly forty to eighty million years ago. While no fossils of loons from that era have been discovered, a loon fossil *Colymboides minutes* was studied by Storer. Found in France, this twenty-million-year-old bird was only ten to twelve inches in length and, according to Storer, probably flew more frequently than today's loons. Not all birds have such ancient lineage. The larks came along less than ten million years ago and tanagers are real newcomers, having appeared just ten thousand years ago.

LOONS AND GREBES

Early ornithologists believed the loon to be closely related to the grebe. Classed as a family of twenty worldwide species (including six in North America) within the order Podicipediformes, grebes share many traits with loons. Flying with legs straight out and neck hunched down, grebes have a similar profile. And like loons they are waterbirds with well-developed diving abilities. Grebes also demonstrate a few behaviors typical of loons, such as shared nest building and incubation, backriding of chicks and the running start before flight. Despite these many similarities, however, grebes are very different birds. Much smaller in size, grebes have partially webbed lobed toes, while loons have fully-webbed feet. Grebes are quick divers, but reach depths of only twenty feet, compared to a loon's dive of over 100 feet. There are also many physiological differences such as the number of neck vertebrae and arrangement of plumage which differentiate the two groups. Loons and grebes may share some lakes, but they do not share the same branch of the family tree.

Dr. Charles Sibley is one of the most well known scientists who study the classification of and family connections of birds. His research in the 1960s and early 1970s allowed him to establish relationships based on the similarities between proteins found in the egg whites of birds. Instead of grebes or other birds with similar lifestyles, Sibley found that loons shared a common ancestor with a group of birds known as tubenoses which includes albatrosses and petrels. Their next closest relatives are penguins and frigate birds. Loons themselves are very similar to one another with the red-throated being the most specialized.

THE FIVE SPECIES OF LOONS

If a population of birds or animals becomes geographically isolated by glaciation, mountain formation or other large-scale natural processes, an opportunity for speciation is created. Small changes in distinct geographical groups can lead, over thousands of years, to the development of a new species. Loons have had plenty of time (millions of years) and plenty of room (most of the northern part of the northern hemisphere) to allow for the development of isolated populations. Why five species of loons emerged instead of two or twenty is academic. We do know that of about 8,000

Red-throated loons are seldom seen far from salt water.

species of birds, five are loons—the common, arctic, red-throated, Pacific, and yellow-billed. Or do we?

There has been discussion regarding subspecies of the common loon for many years. Bird books as late as Frank Chapman's 1939 *Handbook of Birds in Eastern North America* list a common loon subspecies, *Gavia immer elasson* (the "lesser loon"), defined by a smaller size alone. While there is considerable geographical size variation for the common loon, the scientific community now recognizes only one common loon, *Gavia immer*.

The arctic and Pacific loons were thought to be just one species, the arctic, until 1985 when the AOU recognized them as distinct species. Arctic loons are found primarily in Eurasia while Pacific loons are found in North America.

ARCTIC LOON
Gavia arctica
PACIFIC LOON
Gavia pacifica

Until recently, ornithologists have recognized four species of loons: common, yellow-billed, arctic, and red-throated. Recent evidence from Russian scientists, however, suggests that the birds we have called arctic loons are really two species—the arctic loon (*Gavia arctica*) and the Pacific loon (*Gavia pacifica*). Based on this new classification, all of the "arctic loons" in North America are really Pacific loons. While little is known of the differences between these species, one distinctive characteristic, apparent only during the breeding season, is the color of the iridescent head feathers. The arctic loon's head looks green while the Pacific loon's appears purple.

The Pacific loon is probably not as closely related to the common loon as the yellow-billed. However, the Pacific and common loons are not so evolutionary divergent as to prevent occasional interbreeding. Apparent hybridization between Pacific and common loons has been reported at least twice in scientific literature. In 1973, Ian Robertson and Mark Fraker were conducting environmental studies for the Gulf, Imperial, and Shell Oil Companies in Canada's Yukon Territory. They observed a family of loons consisting of an adult common loon, an adult Pacific loon and two chicks. Both adults were in breeding plumage and gave calls appropriate for the respective species. They watched the family for most of the summer. While they had no scientific proof that the chicks were a common-Pacific cross, there seemed to be little chance of any other possibility.

Unlike the yellow-billed loon, the Pacific loon differs

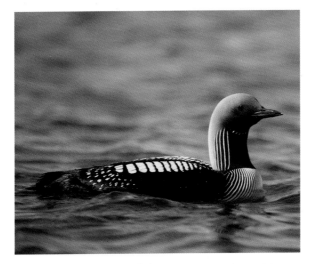

The head of a breeding Pacific loon appears a pale purplish gray.

from the common loon in many ways. Pacific loons breed throughout the tundra and taiga regions of Alaska, the Yukon and Northwest Territories. It is also found breeding in northeastern Saskatchewan, northern Manitoba, northwestern Ontario, the Belcher Islands and northwestern Quebec. When Ralph Palmer defined its breeding range in 1962, Alberta and British Columbia were not included. E. O. Hohn recorded a breeding Pacific loon in Alberta in the early 1970s and more recently, the Pacific loon has been found nesting in two areas in northern British Columbia. Two pairs of Pacific loons have been seen nesting on subalpine lakes in west coastal British Columbia. Apparently some Pacific loons like U.S. coastal waters. *American Birds* magazine contains a report of 200 Pacific loons spending most of the summer near the south jetty of the Columbia River in Oregon.

Arctic loons nest across northern Europe and Asia including the British Isles, Scandinavia and Russia. Like the other loons, arctic and Pacific loons winter primarily in coastal areas. Arctic loons can be found as far south as Spain in the northeastern Atlantic and also occupy the Mediterranean, Black, Caspian and Aral Seas. Arctic loons nesting in Siberia are probably the ones wintering in the eastern Pacific from northern Russia south to China.

Pacific loons winter off the North American Pacific Coast from northern Sonora, Mexico to southern Alaska. Pacific loons are seen in small numbers, but frequently on freshwater lakes and reservoirs in southern California, Arizona and New Mexico. Each year, at least one Pacific loon seems to show up in Duluth-Superior harbor to spend part or all of the winter in western Lake Superior.

Arctic and Pacific loons nest on lakes that receive relatively little human disturbance over most of their breeding range. In a few areas they share their nesting lakes with people. Graham Bundy found arctic loons successfully raising young on lochs in northwestern Scotland frequented by fishermen. In the city of Anchorage, Alaska nongame wildlife biologists from the Alaska Department of Fish and Game have reported Pacific loons nesting within the city limits, making Anchorage the largest city in North America with nesting loons.

Like the other loon species, Pacific loons apparently are unable to recognize their own young from another loon's chicks. One pair of Pacific loons in Alaska really had a case of misidentification. Kenneth Abraham, a summer employee of the U.S. Fish and Wildlife Service, observed a mated pair of Pacific loons tending a brood of five spectacled eider ducklings.

The loons and a pair of eiders had nested only ten meters apart on a small island in the lake. Abraham did not see what happened to the adult eiders or the loon eggs. After watching both pairs incubate their own eggs, he was surprised to find the eider ducklings tended by the Pacific loon adults. The loons and the ducklings accepted each other well. The loons protected the ducklings from predatory gulls and even let the ducklings ride on their backs. Although eider ducklings are capable of catching their own invertebrate meals, they were happy to accept free handouts from their "adopted" parents. Pacific loons typically catch and feed the same kind of aquatic insects that eider ducklings catch on their own.

Arctic loons have been studied extensively in Europe, and Pacific loons have received a fair amount of research attention in North America. Two studies in particular established much of the baseline data on the ecology of Pacific loons. From 1967 to 1969 Rolph Davis studied Pacific and red-throated loons on the western coastal plain of Hudson Bay in the Northwest Territories as part of his Ph.D. program at the University of Western Ontario. In 1974 and 1975 Margaret Petersen, then a Master's student at the University of California-Davis, studied Pacific and red-throated loons near the Bering Sea in western Alaska.

These two studies did not reveal anything about the nesting ecology of Pacific loons strikingly different from that of common loons. In fact, it was the similarities that were striking. Although smaller than the common loon and nesting on more northern lakes, the Pacific loon seems to be a close counterpart of the common loon. Like the common loon it lays two eggs, incubates the eggs for 28 to 30 days and raises the young on the nesting lake, obtaining all of the food for the chicks from the nesting lake. Thus, except for the obvious physical differences and some different calls, Pacific and common loons are quite similar.

Pacific loons and red-throated loons occasionally share the same lakes, but red-throated loons are careful to keep their distance from the larger and more aggressive Pacifics. Maybe red-throated loons know something that a Canada goose found out the hard way.

Two of Rolph Davis' student colleagues at the University of Western Ontario were studying Canada geese in the same areas as Davis' loon study. One day in June 1967 they observed an aggressive encounter between a male Canada goose and a Pacific loon that left the goose dead. Inspection of the dead bird revealed a six-inch-deep puncture wound in the chest that struck the pulmonary artery and the wing. They guessed that the loon must have sunk the entire length of its bill into the goose's breast.

The year to watch Pacific loons must have been 1967. That year Martin McNicholl, now the director of the Long Point Bird Observatory in Ontario and the Ontario Lakes Loon Survey, observed some strange behavior of a pair of Pacific loons. While checking nearby nests of arctic terns and herring gulls, McNicholl noticed a Pacific loon nest unattended by either adult. From time to time he did see a Pacific loon flying over the lake, apparently "checking" the unattended eggs in the nest. This happened almost always on calm days. McNicholl suspected that the adults were feeding in nearby Hudson Bay (about a third of a mile away) and were doing so only on calm days which are preferred for feeding. He explained their behavior by hypothesizing that it may have been advantageous for both adults to feed providing that the eggs were "checked" periodically to deter potential predators. The "checking" behavior may have resulted from a conflict between the urges to feed and incubate the eggs.

Except for its alarm call, which is very similar to a common's tremolo, the vocalizations of the Pacific loon are unique. They are usually described as guttural with a wide range of wails, shrieks, squeals and yelps. After listening to Pacific loons for several months in Alaska, one researcher compared their call to the bark of a dog, while another compares the call to the cackle of a hen. When disturbed, the Pacific loons can emit a high pitched squeal. According to Gabrielson and Lincoln, Pacific loons on their breeding grounds are "among the noisiest of all waterfowl." They quote one naturalist who found the wail heart-breaking and added, "If ever a species enjoyed spreading sorrow through the bird world it is this loon." Looking at the dramatic breeding plumage of the Pacific loon, it is difficult to relate such beauty with sorrow. Probably to other Pacific loons the vocalizations are sweet music—it's all in the ear of the listener.

RED-THROATED LOON *Gavia stellata*

The red-throated loon is the most widely distributed loon, ranging throughout northern Eurasia and in the tundra areas of northern North America from Alaska to Quebec, including the maritime areas of northeast Canada, Newfoundland and Iceland. It breeds as far south as northern British Columbia. In the late 40s and 50s, it was reported to nest on the north shore of Lake Superior but none are found there today. In 1956, an adult red-throated loon was seen with its two downy young off a Wisconsin point in western Lake Superior, but there are no southern breeding records since that time. In Alaska and the Canadian arctic regions, the red-throated is the most numerous of the loon species. In *Birds of Alaska*, the red-throated loon is described as breeding on "any suitable habitat found in Alaska." It winters on both the Pacific and Atlantic Coasts and occasionally on the Great Lakes, particularly Lake Michigan. In Europe, the red-throated loon winters over a wide area including the British Isles, the Mediterranean, Black and Caspian Seas and off the coast of Japan.

While red-throated loons are not commonly seen by most American bird watchers, keen-eyed eastern Wisconsin residents along the shore of Lake Michigan have the rare opportunity to see red-throateds in their impressive breeding plumage in early April. From Milwaukee to Green Bay, small groups of red-throated loons stop over within viewing distance of shore for a week to ten days. A few red-throateds are even seen on inland lakes for a day or two as they wing their way north to Canada.

Every family has its black sheep, its second cousin that just doesn't fit in with the rest of the clan. The red-throated loon or red-throated diver is the odd ball of the loon family. The common, arctic, Pacific and yellow-billed loons are more similar to each other than they are different. L. L. Snyder of The Royal Ontario Museum calls the red-throated the "least 'loonish' of the loons."

Some of the differences are obvious. Size, or lack of it, sets the red-throated apart from the other loons. The smallest Pacific and arctic loons weigh around five pounds, while the largest red-throateds weigh around four pounds. Its body length (24 to 27 inches) and wingspread (42 to 45 inches) are not that much smaller than the other four species, however. This may account for the red-throated loon's ability to take off from water without the long run needed by the other species. In fact, the red-throated loon can take off from land or water directly by springing into the air.

Most of the red-throated's breeding habits are similar to those of other loons. Incubation length is typically 27 to 29 days. The young can fly by seven weeks or so, which is four weeks less than the time needed for common loons to fly. The nest is crude and built at the water's edge.

Even the choice of nesting lakes is different. Red-throated loons typically nest on small lakes on the tundra. These lakes often are acidic (naturally) and contain few or no fish. The adults typically fly to nearby large lakes or the ocean to feed while the other loon species establish nesting territories on lakes which provide them with most or all of the food they need for themselves and their young.

This different strategy causes red-throated loons to be very efficient in their food-gathering technique. Because flying to and from nesting lakes to catch food for the young is energy-expensive, adult red-throated loons carefully choose the size of the fish they fly back with. In a study conducted in the Queen Charlotte Islands of British Columbia, Ted Reimchen and Sheila Douglas from the University of Alberta found that the adults made an average of eleven flights per day from the nesting lakes to the ocean. Each flight took about sixty minutes. The length and weight of the fish brought to the chicks varied predictably through the prefledging period. Young loon chicks were brought small (about one gram in weight), shallow-bodied fish like sand lance and gunnel. As chicks matured, larger and deeper-bodied fish like herring, smelt and cod were

brought. Older chicks were fed large (over 20 grams), deep-bodied sea perch almost exclusively. This strategy was based on at least two factors. Young chicks do not need as much food as older chicks, thus the smaller fish. But the limiting factor on fish size was the ability of the young to swallow the fish. Extremely young chicks were sometimes offered fish they couldn't swallow, but older chicks could swallow all fish brought by the adults. Older chicks need about 200 grams of fish per day. Because the adults were limited in their feeding activity by the number of feeding flights they could make in a day, they brought back the heavier sea perch to feed the older chicks. Small fish were almost never brought because it would have been energetically inefficient.

Reimchen and Douglas found that they were able to differentiate between the male and female of one pair by

The yellow-billed loon nests in grass-lined depressions on tundra lakes and ponds.

counting the number and spacing of vertical white lines on the back of the neck. The female had six or seven white lines and the male ten lines. This allowed them to calculate how much time each sex spent on different activities during the chick rearing period. Predictably, the female spent more time catching food for the chicks while the male spent more time defending the territory from other red-throated and common loons. When alone, the female would only be aggressive toward other red-throated loons while the male would defend against any intruders.

Like the other four loon species, red-throated loons typically defend a nesting territory from other members of the same species. However, red-throated loons have been observed nesting in colonies in Iceland and Finland. On one small lake in northern Finland, thirty pairs nested on an island with the nests only a few yards apart. The red-throated's habit of feeding away from the nesting territory no doubt predisposes it to colonial nesting when nesting sites are scarce.

Unlike the other loons, the red-throated has aerial displays advertising for mates and ownership of territory. Prior to nesting, the loons frequently fly high into the air, calling often and circling. If the birds are already paired or a single is joined by another, the pair glides downward toward the territory with the wings held in a V-position.

Other displays are similar to those of the other species although modified slightly and distinctively red-throated. Although the red-throated loon has been observed taking off directly from land or the water, most red-throated loons need 50 to 150 feet of wing flapping and feet paddling to gain enough acceleration to become airborne (decidedly shorter than the hundreds of yards usually needed by the more heavy-bodied common and yellow-billed loons).

A Swedish zoologist has provided one of the most interesting accounts of red-throated loon ecology. Magnus Enquist studied territorial behavior of red-throated loons. He became intrigued with how rapidly skuas (large, gull-like predatory birds of the polar regions) found and depredated loon nests. Even though skuas do not harass incubating loons, they watch patiently for a temporarily uncovered nest. Since the large eggs of a loon are a high-protein food source, skuas have developed foraging strategies that maximize their chances of obtaining a loon egg dinner.

Using loon dummies and fake nests with gull eggs painted to look like loon eggs, Enquist demonstrated that skuas searched shoreline areas where loon nests are most likely to be and also checked the location of known loon nests to see if the nest was unattended by the adults. Fake nests near the water's edge were depredated by skuas much more quickly than nests farther inland. Fake nests on which a papier-mâché loon was placed for a day before exposing the eggs were depredated even more quickly.

The presence of an extremely aggressive and intelligent predator like the skua puts pressure on red-throated loons to stick close to the nest during incubation. Those birds that leave their nests uncovered for as little as an hour are likely to find an empty nest upon returning.

Robert Bergman and Dirk Derksen studied red-throated loons off Storbersen Point in northern Alaska, an area where both red-throated and Pacific loons nest. The researchers found that the two species did not socialize. While the Pacific loons spent most of their time on the larger freshwater ponds, the red-throated loons flew to the coasts where the arctic cod provided table fare. They watched red-throated loons make repeated trips from nest sites on freshwater ponds to the Beaufort Sea carrying fish crosswise in their bills. Bergman and Derksen also noted that the red-throated loons preferred island nest sites, selecting islands eighty-eight percent of the time. The nest sites were often used for more than one year. Of twenty-seven nest sites, nineteen were used in consecutive years. The researchers found that nesting success for red-throated loons was much greater for the traditional sites than for first-time sites.

A team from the University of North Dakota studying yellow-billed loons just west of Prudhoe Bay in northern Alaska had occasion to watch red-throated loons nesting in the same general area. As with the red-throated loons near Storbersen, these loons also regularly flew to the ocean to fish because the small tundra lakes which the red-throated loons nested on usually did not have adequate food supplies. The researchers did witness some red-throated thievery. When they could get away with it, red-throated loons would sneak into lakes owned by the much larger yellow-billed loons to fish until discovered.

Studying red-throated loons on the island of Unst, the northernmost of the Shetland Islands off Scotland, Graham Bundy uncovered habits similar to those exhibited by Alaskan red-throated loons. He observed twenty-four pairs living in freshwater lochs. Averaging about two acres in size, these small Scottish lakes provided little food, forcing the red-throated loons to feed almost exclusively at sea. Bundy determined the incubation period to be 24 to 29 days. The young red-throated loons had restless wings. Bundy watched the first loon leave the lochs at the tender age of only 39 days; the oldest bird to leave was 48 days old. By contrast, young common loons cannot fly to their own waters until they are about 80 days old.

While any bird can make a mistake, one pair of red-throated loons made a dandy. For several days in the summer of 1934, R. A. and Hazel Johnson watched a pair of red-throated loons sit faithfully on their nest. These Quebec birds were nesting well into August before the Johnsons ended the game. The loons might have sat a long time. The Johnsons found a spiral-shaped sea shell about the size of a loon egg in the nest. It had failed to hatch.

According to most bird books, the red-throated loon is a quiet bird, but some researchers dispute that contention. Red-throated loons certainly were not quiet in 1887 when Edward W. Nelson visited Alaska; he heard red-throated calls ringing "out over the marshes twenty-four hours a day during the breeding season." He also attempted a spelling of their most common call, "Gr-r-ga, gr-r-ga, ga, gr-r."

With migration routes along both the Atlantic and Pacific coasts, red-throated loons are more common in winter along the northern Atlantic Coast where gatherings of a hundred or more are not unusual. Migrants have been observed far inland as well, making the red-throated the one of the "other four" loon species which most often turns up on amateur birders' life lists.

The red-throated loon's scientific name, *stellata*, is Latin meaning "starred," referring to the white speckling of the winter plumage. Other common names for the red-throated loon are equally descriptive, including "little loon," uninspired but accurate; "pegging-awl loon," a reference to the loon's bill which resembles awls used in shoe making; "pepper-shinned loon," referring to the speckling on the plumage by the bird's legs; "the sprat loon," a reference to the small herring called sprat which are a favorite red-throated prey; and "the rain-goose," a name given by the residents of the Shetland Islands who believed the red-throated loon's calling predicted stormy weather.

Away from its breeding territory, the red-throated loon seldom calls.

Yellow-billed loons are the least abundant of the five loons that are found in North America.

YELLOW-BILLED LOON *Gavia adamsii*

The yellow-billed loon could be called the king of the loon family. Its weight of 10 to 14 pounds is nearly three times the weight of the average red-throated loon and twice the weight of the Pacific loon. Found in Eurasia (where it is known as the white-billed loon) from Finland to Siberia, and in North America, from northern Alaska to the west side of Hudson's Bay, the yellow-billed loon is truly a bird of the far north.

The breeding range of the yellow-billed loon is northern and western Alaska and arctic Canada east to the Melville Peninsula. It nests on lakes, large ponds, and occasionally on large, slow-moving rivers primarily north of the tree line. In Eurasia it nests possibly as far west as northern Finland, east all the way across Siberia. While it is occasion-

ally seen in summer on Baffin Island and near Great Slave Lake, it does not breed in these areas. Yellow-billeds winter in North America primarily along the Pacific coast of Alaska but are seen occasionally as far south as northern Baja, California. In Eurasia it winters along the Pacific coasts of China, Japan and Korea, and in the Atlantic Ocean along eastern Greenland and south to southern Europe.

The North American population apparently follows two major migratory routes, one coastal and one overland. The birds breeding in western Alaska migrate along the coast of Alaska and go around the Alaskan Peninsula. The birds breeding east and northeast of Great Slave Lake follow an overland route from south coastal Alaska and Northwest Canada to northeastern Alaska and the Northwest Territories.

As with the other loon species, yellow-billed loons can

plumage is very similar to a common loon's, with slightly lighter markings on the head and neck. The bill, even in winter, is much lighter in color and provides the best identification tag, except in the case of young yellow-billed loons which cannot be easily distinguished from the young of the common loon. The nests of the yellow-billed aid in identification. They are constructed of mounds of mud and are much larger than the nests of common loons.

The short ice-free season in the breeding range of this species does not allow for renesting attempts if first nests fail. Spring migrants arrive before ice-out on their breeding lakes and wait on earlier thawing rivers. First nests are established soon after ice-out which can be as late as late May. A month of incubation and ten to twelve weeks for fledging leave little time to spare since ice starts to form as early as mid-September.

The breeding range of the yellow-billed loon overlaps only slightly, if at all, with the common loon in northeast Alaska and northwest Canada. It is likely in the regions of overlap that the yellow-billed occupies lakes on the treeless tundra while the common loon occupies lakes in forested areas. For all practical purposes their breeding ranges are separate, but cross-breeding by the two species has been recorded.

Because of their similar physical and vocal characteristics and their separate breeding ranges, many scientists have argued that they are the same species or that the yellow-billed loon is a subspecies of the common loon. Recently the AOU has ruled that the two species constitute a super-species, which literally translated means that they would probably interbreed and produce fertile offspring if they were brought together in nature.

Despite its seemingly unlikely location, Alaska may have been the place where yellow-billed loons evolved from common loons. There, some places stayed free of ice while glaciers up to a mile thick covered most other parts of North America. Although strictly conjecture, a small population of loons may have been able to return to inland lakes in Alaska to nest and raise young during what must have been incredibly short and cool summers. This geographic isolation and the need for the nesting loons to adapt to new conditions may have led to a new species. Their larger size may have been a response to natural selection for large size in northern regions, and the yellow bill and larger spots and neck bars may have been characteristics that evolved in isolation and now discourage interbreeding.

The calls of the yellow-billed are harsh yet analogous to some of the common loon's calls. There is an equivalent of the wail and the yodel, and a variation of the tremolo that is even wilder and more raucous than that of the common loon. Despite published reports that yellow-billed loons call less frequently than the common, one researcher, Jeri Schwerin of Duluth, Minnesota, believes yellow-billed loons are very vocal birds. The remoteness of their breeding

turn up in strange places. One appeared in the Duluth-Superior harbor in 1987, one of just two sightings in Minnesota birding records. Even more surprising, a yellow-billed in 1986 spent over two weeks in the waters of northern Illinois' Rock River. The yellow-billed loon is near the top of many avid birders' wish lists and they keep their eyes peeled for this rare treasure. Over the last two decades, yellow-billeds have been spotted during the winter in northern Mexico, South Dakota, and Oklahoma among other places outside of its normal wintering range.

Except for its large size and its pale yellow, slightly upturned bill, the yellow-billed is nearly a carbon copy of the common loon, but close inspection of yellow-billed loons shows much wider white bands in the necklace and larger but fewer white markings on the back. The winter areas, she contends, accounts for their unearned reputation as quiet birds.

Bryan Sage studied the yellow-billed loon in arctic Alaska in 1969 and 1970. He reported that the breeding distribution of this species is entirely north of the Arctic Circle, where it nests in treeless tundra on low-rimmed freshwater lakes of forty acres or larger. He referred to the bird as an "exceedingly wary species when nesting." Sage found some overlap in distribution of the yellow-billed with the common and Pacific loons.

No accurate estimate of yellow-billed loons has ever been made. In North America, Alaska probably has the largest population which likely numbers only in the few thousands. The vast tundra across northern parts of Eurasia may harbor many more. However, based on their limited breeding range and large territory requirements, yellow-billeds are clearly the least common loons.

In March 1989, the tanker *Exxon Valdez* became grounded and spilled 11 million gallons of crude oil in Prince William Sound in southern Alaska. At least 5,000 common, Pacific, red-throated, and yellow-billed loons winter in this area and approximately 40,000 loons may migrate through and stop over there. Initial reports indicated that yellow-billed loons were affected more than other species. By July 1989, eighty-six yellow-billed loon carcasses had been recovered and identified. There was a good deal of concern over what effects this might have on what was known to be a relatively small breeding population.

Dr. Rebecca Field of the Massachusetts Cooperative Fish and Wildlife Research Unit, her graduate student Judith Wells, and Michael North of the Bureau of Reclamation studied a small nesting population of yellow-billeds in the Colville River delta on Alaska's north coast where North had been studying loons previously. Although most of the territories were occupied by breeding pairs, only about half of the pairs attempted to nest that year compared to other years, suggesting that some of the territories were occupied by new breeders not yet ready to nest. They could not be sure that loons from that area were wintering in Prince William Sound, but their research suggests that yellow-billed populations may have suffered both in the death of adults and juveniles from the oil spill and from subsequent years of lowered reproductive success. Syracuse University biologist Judy McIntyre's study of yellow-billed loons along Alaska's North Slope following the spill suggested that the oil spill did not affect breeding populations there as densities were equal to or greater than those reported on earlier surveys.

The yellow-billed loon was named *Gavia adamsii* in honor of Edward Adams, an English surgeon-naturalist, who served in a nineteenth century voyage to the Arctic. Presumably he saw a few yellow-billed loons to earn the honor.

COMMON LOON *Gavia immer*

The common loon is the well-known loon of North America, inhabiting a breeding range from Alaska and Canada down to the northern tier of states. It also breeds in Greenland and Iceland where about 300 pairs summer. These Icelandic birds winter off the coasts of Western Europe. It has captured the interest of many scientists and the hearts of thousands of lakeside admirers. It deserves a closer look.

Large Arctic loons ride low in the water.

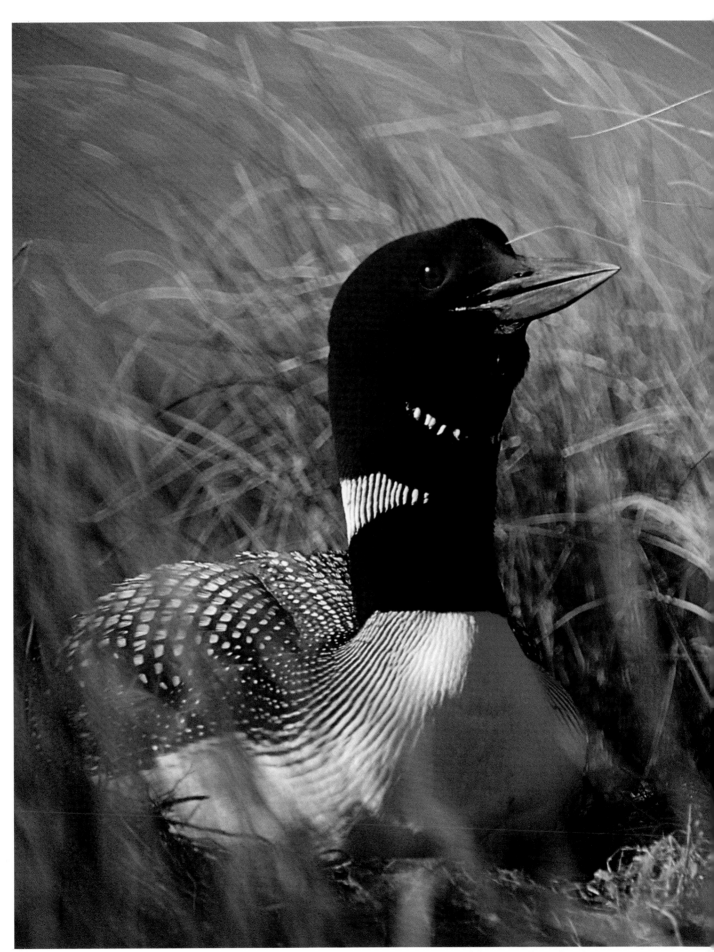

Common loon performing "wail call" to its mate from the nest.

*The loon is a paragon of beauty.
Alert, supple, vigorous—one
knows himself to be in the presence
of the master wild thing when he
comes upon a loon on guard in his
native element.*

—W. L. Dawson, 1923

A Close Look

In appearance, voice, behavior and physiology, the common loon is a fascinating bird. It is distinctive from its daggerlike beak right down to its feet—they are enormous and seriously understudied. In thousands of pages of research papers on loons, there are only casual references to the feet, usually noting simply that the feet are webbed and large. Large doesn't do justice to the loon's primary means of aquatic locomotion.

Loon devotees might want to take matters into their own hands and measure the feet of a few mounted specimens. If they did, they would find the average loon foot to be about five inches long by three inches wide. If real loon fanatics traveled to Concord, New Hampshire and visited the offices of the New Hampshire Audubon Society, they would be rewarded. A monster loon is on display there with feet nearly six inches long and a full four inches wide. (Pull out a ruler and take a careful look at four inches.) The loon is an avian bigfoot; a proportionate human shoe size would be about 45 triple R.

SWIMMING AND DIVING

While loon's feet are fully webbed with three toes, they are not what scientists call perfect swimming feet, a distinction reserved for birds like the cormorants and pelicans which have totipalmate feet (four toes joined by webs). Not perfect maybe, but the loon's feet do the job well. In the 1917 edition of *Birds of America*, contributing editor Edward Howe Forbush compared the dive of the loon to a bolt shot from a crossbow, and described their quickness as "truly astonishing."

Part of the loon's quickness is due to basic anatomy. The bird's torpedo shape, with leg muscles blending into a streamlined body mass, helps to give the loon amazing aquatic freedom. On a quiet, glassy lake surface, loons swim effortlessly, as if friction were not a physical property. Swimming on the surface with the ease of an otter, a loon bobs slightly as the big feet push alternately. Moving and at rest, loons ride low in the water with the water line just below the top of the white breast feathers, maybe two inches from the dramatic necklace. Underwater, a loon's body appears to be flattened from top and bottom, taking on the shape of a flying saucer. As it kicks its feet alternately or both at once, a loon literally slices through its watery milieu.

Early naturalists thought loons to be "underwater flyers" like auks and puffins, species that use both feet and wings for propulsion below the surface. Contemporary scientists have refuted this with numerous observations of "feet only" swimming.

Film sequences now show that "feet only" is the most common mode of underwater swimming. However, rare footage of loons using their feet and wings has been taken also. Scientists believe that the wings may be used when loons are seriously frightened and may be a reversion to the method young chicks use. Sigurd F. Olson, who in the 1950s did pioneering loon research at the University of Minnesota often observed chicks trying to use their wings in diving attempts. With their buoyant down feathers, chicks need a lot of help to get down under.

How deep do common loons really dive? This simple question still sparks heated discussion among loon experts, professional and amateur alike. Olson interviewed Lake Superior fishermen who claimed they found loons in their gill nets which had been set at depths of 240 feet. While such reports are too numerous to ignore, they are also hard to swallow. Fishermen are not generally known for their veracity. At 200 feet the pressure is six times the normal sea level pressure, far more than most air-breathing animals can tolerate. Having unique half-bird/half-fish attributes, the loon is not like most animals. If any top-side creature could function at 200 feet, the loon is the one. Loons are not deep-dive champions. Another black and white bird, the penguin, can dive to 800 feet and stay submerged for about twenty minutes.

How long loons stay underwater is a related question. Probably every loon watcher has watched a loon dive and never come up. While observing loons on a small bay of Burntside Lake near Ely, Minnesota, I was amazed once when I "lost" my loon. While timing feeding dives, I watched the loon submerge. About five minutes later, I started to think I was timing a record dive. Ten minutes later, I was worried about the loon. Fifteen minutes later, I realized that the only record at stake was my gullibility. Loons are sneaky. They can surface quickly and dive again with barely a trace of broken water, and with their rapid underwater movements, they also cover great distances in a short time.

The scientific literature does have references to extended dives. In 1913, F. R. Jourdain reported several cases of immersion of ten minutes and one case of a wounded loon which stayed submerged for fifteen minutes, but these were extreme cases involving birds in a state of panic. When pushed to the edge of survival, many animals display extraordinary toughness, and loons are particularly tenacious. In his 1924 book, *Birds of the Lake Umbagog Region of New Hampshire*, William Brewster described the

strength of a wounded loon: " . . . the heavy bullet passed directly through the middle of the neck, about three inches above the body, partially shattering some of the vertebrae and cutting the jugular vein, yet she [the loon] dove twice . . . going each time a long distance."

Most dives are quite brief. P. K. Kinnear, a British researcher watching common loons feeding on the ocean wintering range near Tronda, off the Shetland Islands, estimated the median dive at ninety seconds but did record several dives of up to five minutes. Carter, another British researcher, estimated the median feeding dive to be about twenty seconds. Of 258 dives, Carter recorded only three over one minute with the longest ninety seconds. Sigurd Olson estimated an undisturbed loon's average feeding dive at about forty seconds and timed no dives over three minutes. The length of dives is

A chick hugs close to its parent for camouflage.

affected by several variables, but particularly the availability of prey. Why dive to a hundred feet when most prey, small fish and minnows, are usually near the surface?

The questions of depth and length of dives are illuminated by "Dewar's Rule," a rule-of-thumb estimate of time required for diving birds to get under water. The rule, proposed by John M. Dewar in 1924, states diving birds need twenty seconds for the first six feet of a dive and ten seconds for each additional six foot increment. The journey to 200 feet would take a loon about six minutes. Of course the loon has to get back to the surface which would require probably an additional three or four minutes, placing a loon at the very edge of any reported immersion times. Animals rarely subject themselves to such danger, especially when so little is at stake. While loons certainly dive to depths in excess of 100 feet,

their dives to 200 feet, supported only by the claims of commercial fishermen, should be viewed with healthy skepticism.

While the maximum depths and durations of dives are not well documented, the physiological mechanisms the loon utilizes to make extended dives are fairly well understood. Over a hundred years ago, W. H. Slaney advanced the theory that diving birds could change their specific gravity (the weight of an object divided by the weight of an equal volume of water) by expelling air from their body cavities. His contemporaries studying divers believed birds like the gallinule remained underwater by grasping vegetation with their feet. Slaney was right. To prepare for dives, loons expel air from their lungs and air sacs inside their bodies and compress their dense and waterproof plumage tightly, forcing out air trapped between the feathers. With these simple air reduction techniques, loons can sink into the water without noticeable effort, suggesting that loons have a specific gravity, or density, very near that of water.

Just getting rid of unwanted air does not make a bird a great diver; several other important physiological adaptations help the loon earn its nickname of "the great northern diver." Fifty years ago noted ornithologist Erwin Stresemann described the loon's skeleton as completely lacking pneumaticity. While typical bird bones have an interior spongelike construction with lots of air spaces (a light-weight skeletal construction ideal for organisms adapted for flight), the loon is not typical; it is built for diving first and flying second. Since any air within the body cavity, even in the bones, would compromise diving abilities, the evolutionary path for the loon went the way of water and favored the development of many solid bones in the skeleton, which made diving much easier but flying a little tougher.

Loons also have ribs with overlapping spurs called, oddly enough, uncinate processes which form a type of lattice preventing the rib cage from collapsing from water pressure during deep dives.

Another significant adaptation of loons is their ability to dive with minimal oxygen. While underwater, loons derive needed oxygen from the oxyhemoglobin and oxymyoglobin stored in the blood and muscles. According to A. W. Schorger, the dark color of the flesh of diving birds, including loons, is due to the presence of these respiratory pigments. In addition, the loon's circulatory system helps by reducing the heart rate.

The loon's vital body organs have an unusual tolerance for low levels of oxygen. In the textbook *Avian Biology*, edited by Donald Farner and James King, this phenomenon is described as a system which rations available oxygen preferentially to tissues particularly susceptible to damage from oxygen deprivation. Farner and King report a 90 percent metabolic reduction during experimental submergence of some diving ducks. While such tests have not been performed on loons, it is likely that similar metabolic reductions occur. Like most birds, loons normally have a high metabolic rate which is reflected in their body temperature of about 102° F.

AGE

With their internal motors running at such high speeds, it's surprising loons live as long as they do. While definitive answers await additional banding research, most scientists believe the common loon is "long-lived." While

an arctic loon was recovered 28 years after banding and a red-throated loon in Sweden was found 23 years after banding, no common loons of that age have been recovered, even though about 1,500 have been banded. In 1988, however, Judy McIntyre reported that a loon she banded in 1970 was sighted alive, making the oldest known common loon 18 years old. Yet, biologists estimate the life span of the common loon at 15 to 30 years.

Many familiar birds live much longer. Wild Canada geese often live over 20 years. Golden eagles in the wild can reach 30, while eagles of several other species have survived 50 years of captivity. Herring gulls, thought by some to be distantly related to loons, can live 20 years, and some captive gulls have reached 40. If a common loon is found wearing a 30-year-old band, few people will be surprised.

SIZE

The common loon is a large bird. In most bird books, the weight range is listed as 7 to 9 pounds. Weighing a number of loons from Alberta, Canadian Wildlife Service researcher Kees Vermeer found their average weight to be 8 pounds. The largest male weighed nearly 11 pounds and the largest female weighed just over 8 pounds. The U.S. Fish and Wildlife Service weighed eight loons killed by botulism. Found in Lake Michigan, these birds weighed in from 8 to just under 13 pounds. Dave Evers has weighed hundreds of adult loons in the last few years and has found that weight differences between males and females is consistent with males weighing more in 94 percent of the cases. While males are larger, the difference is slight and does not provide an accurate method for field identification.

There is substantial evidence for a geographical size gradient. The smallest loons reside in Minnesota, North Dakota and Manitoba, averaging about 9 pounds. Much larger common loons live in the Northeast, averaging about 12 pounds. Baffin Island is home to the largest loons.

Because their bodies are compact and dense, loons are deceptively heavy. While the bald eagle appears to be much larger than the loon, eagles weigh 8 to 12 pounds, just slightly heavier than the average common loon. Sandhill cranes, with wingspreads of seven feet, have an average weight about the same as the common loon.

The length of common loons ranges from 28 to 35 inches. Thirteen adult loons from Minnesota had an average length of 29 inches.

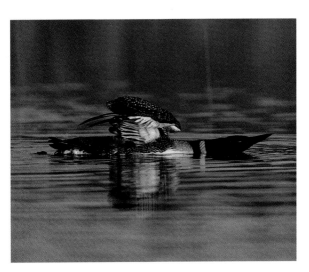
Loons roll and kick while preening.

FLIGHT

Even with a broad wingspan of up to 58 inches, common loons still have small wings for such a heavy bird. Olson compared the loon's wing area with its weight and found the ratio to be 1 to 2 compared to a nearly 9 to 1 ratio for the golden crowned kinglet, a small songbird of northern forests. While this doesn't mean that it is eighteen times easier for the kinglet to get off the ground, it does reveal the loon's flying handicap. In his book *Birds of the World*, Oliver Austin underscored this point by observing that loons have the "... least wing surface in proportion to their body weight of any flying bird." In 1957, researcher D. B. Savile graphically described the loon's flight: "The common loon is a flying anachronism. It has an appallingly high wing load and very inefficient wing form . . . it takes off only with great difficulty, after a long run and climbs shallowly."

How long is that run? While loons sometimes need up to a quarter mile of aquatic runway, they can be more efficient. In his classic *Handbook of North American Birds*, Ralph S. Palmer reports common loons taking off after a 20-yard run. While wind is a factor, it is not needed (contrary to loon folklore) to get the birds off the water. One calm summer day in northern Wisconsin, I watched a pair of loons take off from a small lake, marking the distance with prominent landmarks. Later, using detailed maps of the lake, I estimated the distance from the first "step" to breaking contact with water at about 80 yards. There are probably many variables involved here, but the individual loon's capability is, no doubt, the most important one.

Getting off the water, however, does not get a loon safely away from the lake. The ascent of a loon's flight is quite gradual, often forcing the bird to circle a lake to get over the treetops. On many small lakes, loons fall into routine flight patterns, curving around part of the lake and heading over the trees at a fairly predictable spot.

Loons in flight cut a distinctive hunchbacked silhouette with their head and feet lower than the rest of their body. Their flight also produces a distinctive sound as air rushes under their wings and around their streamlined bodies. Loon watchers with a keen ear can often detect a loon passing overhead before sighting it.

On a canoe trip in Ontario's Quetico Provincial Park, my wife, Pat, and I were on the water at dawn on a foggy morning when a pair of loons flew toward us just a few feet off the water. About fifty feet from the canoe, they flared slightly to our left and passed us at eye level only fifteen feet from the canoe. In twenty years of camping and canoeing in loon country, I had never been so close to flying loons, or so awed by any natural sight or sound. The wings cutting through the air created a sound much louder and more dramatic than the whistling of mallard wings or that of any other bird I've heard. Unlike those of other large birds like geese, cranes or herons, a loon's wing beats are very rapid, about 250 beats per minute.

The speed of flying loons is surprisingly fast. While most bird books still list the common loon's flight speed at 60 mph, contemporary researchers place the speed substantially higher. New York biologist Paul Kerlinger has estimated ground speeds (taking into account following winds) of 93 mph during spring migration and 108 mph during fall migration. The average air speed (not counting the help of wind) was 75 mph. A physician flying his airplane near Charlotte, North Carolina had his small plane at nearly full throttle while watching a loon pull away. He estimated the loon's speed at 100 mph.

Arthur Cleveland Bent, in his *Life Histories of North American Diving Birds*, was superbly expressive describing the loon's flight:

> The lines are perfect; the strong neck and breast, terminating in the long sharp bill, are outstretched to pierce the air like the keenest spear; the heavy body, tapering fore and aft, glides through the air with the least possible resistance; and the big feet, held close together and straight out behind, form an effective rudder. The flight of a loon is decidedly distinctive; such a rakish craft, long and pointed at both ends, could not be mistaken for anything else.

It's obvious Bent did not have a graduate school committee looking over his shoulder; his rich prose is a rarity in scientific literature.

A loon's transition from air to water is nearly as exciting as that from water to air. Described by Olson as graceful, perfect seaplane touch-downs, loon landings begin with a long set-wing glide before their landing gear drops to drag the water for a short distance and end with full braking with their breasts. If there is a wind, loons, like all waterfowl, will land into it.

Not all landings are picture perfect. Some loon watchers have witnessed total wipeouts. Paul Strong, formerly a biologist with the Sigurd Olson Environmental Institute of Northland College and Director of Wisconsin Project Loon Watch, has seen some dandies with wings, legs and neck going in several directions at once. Coming in as fast as they do, even minor landing errors can provide comic relief. Loons often dive immediately after landing, perhaps to check the area for danger. After a quick underwater exploration, loons surface and usually perform a couple of wing flaps before settling down.

MOLTING

Feathers do not last a loon's lifetime: they simply wear out with use. The striking plumage of the adult loon requires constant care and periodic replacement of old feathers. Molting, the annual or biannual process of natural feather loss and replacement, is usually related to the breeding cycle. Most ducks, after hatching their eggs, go through a complete molt, including flight feathers, which provides new feathers for the fall migration. While biologists believe molting is hormonally controlled, they have not isolated the precise control mechanism. Many birds undergo head and body molt during nesting season and a flight feather molt after migration. For other birds, like the red-wing blackbird, both the extent and the timing of the molt vary by region. Since the variations seem endless, most scientists suspect there is not a common molting scheme among birds.

During his study of common loons on lakes in the northern Minnesota canoe country, Sigurd Olson carefully observed the common loon's molting process. He noticed the earliest signs of the molt in late August. By then he found patches of breast and back feathers on the water. Because the ends of the feather shafts were concave instead of pointed, he knew the feathers were pushed out by new ones. He watched loons molt first at the base of the bill, the chin and forehead and later on the back. In early September he noted only one gray-faced bird, but by mid-September nearly all the loons showed some signs of molt. By late September most birds were in complete winter plumage. When Olson paddled out of his wilderness study area in early October, he saw no loons in the black and white breeding plumage. At this time the adults, now in winter plumage, were difficult to distinguish from their young.

The exact time of the fall molt appears to vary. In Maine, Paul Strong has observed loons in breeding plumage as late as December. In New Hampshire loon plumage typically starts to change in late October and early November. Rawson Wood, one of New Hampshire's most avid loon watchers, cannot recall seeing any birds in breeding plumage after November. Most Wisconsin loon watchers, even those living on lakes with resident loons, rarely see a loon in winter plumage. Even birds leaving Wisconsin in late November, when most lakes freeze, are clearly black and white. It is possible, but not likely, that all of the late-leaving loons are the young-of-the-year and that adults in breeding plumage all leave much earlier.

According to ornithologist Gene Woolfenden, the common loon's wing molt takes place in late winter on coastal waters. His evidence is a number of loons found without wing feathers during February on Florida beaches. This delayed wing molt, Woolfenden suggests, relates to the degree of parental care loons provide their young. To feed and protect their chicks, loons need to be mobile and consequently need their wing feathers. Protecting their territory is vital to a loon and covering up to 200 acres of water often demands flight. If the flight feathers were replaced after the young were fairly independent, migration of the adults could be greatly delayed and loons would then face the possibility of an early freeze and premature death. Evolution doesn't work that way; loons play it safe, keeping their wing feathers through the fall migration.

Another factor in the delayed molt is the energy cost of replacing large flight feathers. Depending upon the species, the energy cost of molting is anywhere from five to thirty percent of total daily energy demand. Molting plus concurrent caring for young would place considerable stress on parent loons. According to Woolfenden, immature loons spend two or three winters on the coast before returning to northern waters. During their adolescence on the coast, they replace their wing feathers in late summer or early fall, not in winter as the adults do. Since these immature loons have no young to provide for, nor ice-covered lakes to worry about, there is no reason for them to delay their molt.

Red-throated loons are the exception to the adult loon delayed wing molt rule. They have a complete post-nuptial molt in summer. Because the red-throated loons do not face the same "ice-in" danger (they can lift right off the water, not requiring a long running start) they can afford to wait until ice cover is nearly complete before heading south. Common loons, as well as Pacific and yellow-billed loons, do not have that luxury.

CARE OF FEATHERS

To date no enterprising graduate student has counted the feathers on a loon, but researchers have estimated the number of feathers on some birds. We know at least one whistling swan had 25,216 feathers and one house sparrow 3,500. The loon probably falls somewhere in between the two in the feather count.

Whatever the number, the feathers of the loon in large part account for the bird's celebrity status. The stark simplicity of the black and white design give this ancient bird a modern look. Unlike loons, many bird species have separate dress codes for males and females. Usually the plumage differences, as with ducks or pheasants, are permanent, but some birds like the scarlet tanager or indigo bunting have seasonal differences. Creating much confusion for researchers, loons have identical, not just similar, breeding plumage. One loon is as beautiful as the next, which makes field identification of individuals very tricky.

To keep their feathers looking good, loons spend a lot of time preening. Removing external parasites and distributing oil from a gland at the base of the tail, preening is vital for survival. A few avian species, including some parrots, pigeons, and herons indulge in reciprocal preening. This "you scratch my back and I'll scratch yours" behavior is most common with pairs that spend a lot of time together at the nest site. Except for the short periods when trading incubation duties, loons are alone at the nest, and they are solo preeners. In winter, loons spend about twenty percent of their daylight hours preening and performing other maintenance activity. During molt periods additional time is invested in feather care. Surprisingly, preening can be exciting to watch.

Five-week-old chick preening its belly feathers.

I once spent a full day watching a pair of adults and an immature loon on a northern Wisconsin lake which was small enough to allow observation from a single position. (A twenty-power spotting scope and tripod helped.) The birds went about their rather routine feeding, resting and preening activities until mid-afternoon, when the immature bird went totally berserk in an orgy of preening. The loon repeatedly rolled on its back, kicked its legs in the air, splashed with its wings and all the while preened aggressively. The show lasted two hours but included a few well-deserved rest breaks. Meanwhile the adults were also preening vigorously but without the theatrics of rolling on their backs. After the performance I went to the windward shoreline. With a stiff wind blowing, I didn't have long to wait before a trail of feathers hit the beach. This was serious preening. Apparently such wild preening behavior is not limited to the common loon. Near Point Barrow, in northern Alaska, Jeri Schwerin observed yellow-billed loons preening with the same roll-on-the-back intensity.

A Curious Creature

Common loons are a curious lot. Even during the era when loons were favored targets, Bent noticed that common loons could not resist the impulse to investigate. He found it was "an easy matter to toll [attract] one within gunshot range by remaining hidden and waving some suspicious object." I've tested Bent's theory on several occasions and discovered that loons have not learned much over the past sixty-five years: they are still gullible. Once I brought two adults and a chick within a distance of ten feet from shore by waving a spruce branch and giving a ridiculously inept version of the "hoot" call. Two less-than-quiet dogs were at my feet and even their low growling did not suppress the loons' powerful curiosity.

Yellow-billed loons are equally curious. In 1943, A. M. Bailey made an expedition to arctic Alaska where he encountered yellow-billed loons willing to check him out when he loudly yelled "yoo hoo" and frantically waved a cloth. In the dark days of the turn of the century, when loons were shot for sport, this instinct to know what's going on in their territories probably shortened the lives of many loons.

The Red Eye

A look at the common loon is not complete without reference to the bird's dramatic red eye, a feature shared by the other four species of loons. Without the ruby eye, fewer artists would be inspired to capture the loon on canvas. Always a source of romantic mystery, the loon's bright red eye raises the obvious question—why red? The way to approach the question is through a better question—why is the loon's eye not some other color? According to biologist Denny Olson who conducted research on light penetration of water at the Minnesota Zoo, red may be a lesser evil which was selected by default. Scientists have known for some time, he explains, that water filters out the red, orange

and yellow end of the spectrum first, allowing the blues and violets to penetrate deeper into a lake.

Because a loon's eye reflects red light back to us, it looks red. By reflecting red light, a loon's eye eliminates red light before it enters the eye; in effect, it does the same thing as the water—it eliminates red. If a loon's eye were blue, it would filter out the only light available for deep water fishing. Beyond fifteen feet or so there is no red anyway, so why not have an eye that filters out red? Any other color would remove even more light, making fishing tougher. A small but perhaps important added advantage of the red eye could be the camouflage effect of an eye that appears gray at depths of fifteen feet or deeper, which would not reflect back to alert prey fish. Olson's theory is attractive but it doesn't explain why the loon's eye turns

Common loon stretching its wings.

brown in winter and why immature loons don't have eyes nearly as red as adults. It is possible the red eye is related to breeding status. But don't tell any artists.

A NAMELESS STAR

Because enjoying loons is usually part of larger experiences, it's difficult to summarize the attraction of the common loon. Writing in the June, 1947 issue of *The Living Wilderness*, Olaus J. Murie, one of the founders of the Wilderness Society and an enduring wilderness philosopher, captured with sublime understatement the importance of loons:

We returned to camp in the evening. The wind was dying down as the sun sank below the trees. The sky was saffron when the moon climbed into view and a large bright star dropped its reflection with that of the moon on the still, darkening water while from out in the lake arose the exuberant yodeling of loons. We stood in the deepening dusk, reverently. I did not want to speculate on what star that was. A man-made name would be an intrusion here. I wanted only to look and feel and listen, while the saffron tint faded, the shoreline shadows darkened, the moon and that glorious star gradually took over their place of prominence in the night. Long after we had crept into the tents and lay quiet and contented in our sleeping bags, we listened to the wild serenading of the loons.

Scientists continue to debate the function of the loon's red eyes.

A pair of loons nested in Quittacus Pond, Lakeville, Massachusetts, about fourteen miles from my home, in 1872, but the eggs were taken and both birds were shot; none have nested in this section of the state since. The same story is true of many other New Hampshire lakes where the insatiable desire to kill has forever extirpated an exceedingly interesting bird.

—Arthur Cleveland Bent, 1919

Status & Distribution

HISTORICAL PERSPECTIVE

Little is known about the distribution of loons prior to European settlement. While references to loons are frequent in Native American legends, geographical or population determinations based upon these references are speculative at best. It is probably safe to assume that in the presettlement era common loons bred over much of the Northeast, Midwest and Pacific Northwest of the United States and nearly all of Canada except the arctic regions. In Canada common loons have been so plentiful for so long that little attention has been paid to them. Historical information on Canadian populations is non-existent. It is also probably safe to assume that loons in seventeenth century America were at or near their maximum biological carrying capacity in most of their range. Although some Indian tribes harvested loons for food, others protected the loon as part of their religious traditions; human-caused mortality of loons was minimal.

The southern edge of loon country started to move north in the late eighteenth and early nineteenth centuries. In that time the shooting of loons was considered great sport. William Brewster described well the attitude toward loons by observing in a 1924 publication: " . . . it was customary to shoot at them [loons] whenever opportunity offered." Many people looked for the opportunity. "That was an era," explains Jeff Fair of New Hampshire's loon recovery program, "in which our society had gunpowder and the time to play with it, but too little environmental understanding or conscience to realize the effects of such behavior."

In 1912, Edward H. Forbush described in detail recreational loon shoots in Buzzards Bay and Manomet Bay, Massachusetts. On a breezy spring day, these popular loon shooting spots would be filled with boats carrying hunters eager to measure their wing shooting skills by their success in hitting fast-flying loons. Most of the loon mortality in this era probably resulted from the thousands of less public incidents: a bored duck hunter wondering if the old story about loons being faster than bullets were true . . . a sport fisherman thinking the loons on his pond were stealing trout . . . market hunters firing indiscriminately at any group of waterbirds. Whatever their method or motive, the shotgunners changed the loon's distribution and status. Even as far north as Maine loons began to disappear. By the 1920s on Maine's Lake Umbagog, loons were scarce.

By the time systematic natural history surveys were conducted, the loons' southern limit had already been transposed some distance to the north. But at the turn of the century loons were still more common than they are today. In the 1895 volume of *The Ornithology of Illinois*, Robert Ridgeway described the common loon as a " . . . common winter resident on larger waters throughout the state," which nested "in the northern portion."

In the 1917 edition of *Birds of America*, T. Gilbert Pearson listed the common loon's breeding range as the area "south to parallel 42°." This designation included northern Illinois; the northern half of Iowa; all of Wisconsin, Michigan, Minnesota, the Dakotas, Montana and Washington; the northern fringe of Pennsylvania and Connecticut; and all of the Northeast. Bent's 1919 *Life Histories of North American Diving Birds* put the breeding line in roughly the same place, but referred specifically to central Pennsylvania, northeastern Indiana, northeastern Illinois, northern Iowa, and northeastern California to describe the southern edge of the common loon's breeding range. Loons were still relatively abundant, prompting Bent to comment that "nearly every suitable lake within the breeding range of the species has its pair of loons, or has had it, and many lakes support two or more pairs."

The Migratory Bird Treaty Act of 1918 helped to hold the line. The provisions of the act controlled the previously unregulated harvest of waterbirds, but some biologists think the law came too late; the damage to the loon's reproductive capacity, especially in the East, had already been severe. And many of the blessings of the twentieth century, such as massive habitat destruction, chemical contamination, and oil spills were yet to come.

THE COMMON LOON TODAY

Over the decades since Bent described the loon's breeding range many problems more serious for loons than bird shot have emerged. Lakeshore development has had probably the most devastating consequences. Except in northern Maine and in the large federal tracts in northern Minnesota, lakes without a necklace of summer homes are hard to find these days. The post World War II economic boom, coupled with a new interest in the outdoors, fueled an all-out assault on our northern lakes.

I learned this history lesson in July, 1959 during my first fishing trip to northern Wisconsin. I was twelve years old and could think of little else but muskies as long as an oar. There were no superhighways then from my home

town of Sun Prairie, Wisconsin, to the Lac du Flambeau fishing paradise in Vilas County, nearly three hundred miles north. With no extra lanes or bypasses, it seemed to take forever to drive through Wausau, a modest city even now.

What I had expected to find and what I found when I arrived in the "north" were quite different. My childhood fantasies of wild country brimming with fish and wildlife collided violently with the reality of countless lakeside developments, backwoods intersections cluttered with a bewildering array of resort and supper club signs, commercialized Indian ceremonials and ubiquitous bait shops hyping minnows "Guaranteed to Catch Fish or Die Trying." For northern Wisconsin, the decade of the 50s was the beginning of the end for authentic wilderness. No one was counting loons then, but as nest sites became beaches, boat docks or picnic grounds, loons were gradually pushed to remote lake corners until the necklace of whitewashed cabins became a noose choking off the last breath of wildness. Yet, loons did not disappear from all of Wisconsin's northern lakes. Many adapted to their new neighbors, and a sizable population still calls Wisconsin home. But the lakes are different now, and life for the remaining loons is . . . well, who can say?

This pattern of lakeshore development on northern lakes was similar in most loon states. In some areas of the Northeast, the lot sizes were larger and more homes sported redwood or cedar siding, but the overall effect was the same: loons had to share their lakes with many more people. While hard data on loon populations between 1950 and 1980 are limited, it is clear that during that period loon numbers in most of the United States declined substantially. Speaking at a loon conference in 1979, Richard Plunkett confirmed what many lakeshore observers believed when he noted that "Available data from Minnesota, Wisconsin, Michigan, New York, Vermont, New Hampshire, Massachusetts and Maine suggest a northward shrinkage of the historically occupied breeding range of the common loon."

Declining loon populations at the time of that first major conference on the status and conservation of loons were about to turn the corner. Over the next fifteen years, common loon populations rebounded in many areas and loons started summering and nesting on lakes in states or in parts of their range where they hadn't been seen for several decades. Where intensive surveys were being conducted, total numbers of loons, breeding pairs, and chick production increased. In other areas, a general trend was noted by state wildlife biologists and avid birders.

In Wisconsin, for example, nesting pairs of loons were recorded in central counties and in a few southern reaches of the state. Michigan's loon survey documented not only an increase in total loon numbers, but similar nesting records in central and southern counties of the lower peninsula. In 1985, Pennsylvania's state ornithological journal

Common Loon

Pacific Loon

Red-throated Loon

Yellow-billed Loon

Breeding Range   Wintering Range

contained a report of loons nesting on the Penn Forest Reservoir in 1981 and 1983, the first time in many years that Pennsylvania could brag of nesting loons. In 1977, Peter Vickery reported a nesting pair of loons in Connecticut. Common loons even found suitable nesting lakes in the primarily agricultural state of Iowa in the 80s and 90s. In the Pacific Northwest, speculation of nesting loons in Oregon was high and in Washington state, the common loon began a slow comeback.

While populations rebounded and ranges expanded slightly, loss of habitat, deterioration of water quality, disease, and oil spills on coastal wintering areas continued. What seemed to be happening was that loons were learning to live with changes in their environment and public awareness of the loon's plight caused people to change their behavior. Loons in the 1980s and 90s proved that they can exist with people, but both the loons and the people have to work at it. The people especially.

OFFICIAL STATUS

Officially, the common loon is not an endangered species in either the United States or Canada. Unlike the California condor, the peregrine falcon, or the Kirtland's warbler, the common loon is not on the U.S. Department of Interior's "List of Endangered Wildlife." The federal designation process for *endangered species* requires that the species be "in danger of extinction throughout all or a significant portion of its range." The same holds for federally *threatened species*; the species must be "likely within the foreseeable future to become endangered throughout all or part of a significant portion of its range."

The key word is significant. Loons are in serious trouble in parts of their United States' range, but not in a large enough percentage to fit the endangered or threatened criteria; therefore, the special protections and funding programs of the U.S. Endangered Species Act are not available for loon management efforts. In 1984, the U.S. Fish and Wildlife Service did nominate the common loon for a new "List of National Species of Special Emphasis," but Congress did not accept the nomination. It is, however, currently on the U.S. Fish and Wildlife Service's list of "nongame migratory birds of special management concern." In reality, the common loon has no special status which directs special attention or funding to its conservation at the federal level. With the exception of occasional funding support for research projects, it is treated like any other migratory nongame bird.

At the state level there has been a lot of attention directed toward common loon management and many states have provided special designations. For example, it has been declared by state legislation an endangered species in Vermont, a threatened species in New Hampshire and Michigan. In Wisconsin, the loon is on the state's "Watch List," indicating that a close monitoring of the species is

needed. The picture of loons in the United States today is a mosaic with pockets of plenty like northern Minnesota, Maine, or Alaska, states with marginal populations like Vermont, and states like Wisconsin with fairly comfortable numbers.

In Canada, the common loon is protected by federal law, but it enjoys no special designation or protection even though the loon is featured on the Canadian dollar coin known affectionately as the "loonie dollar" and just recently appeared on the country's twenty dollar bill. In 1994, the common loon was voted Ontario's official provincial bird and the loon will soon be an option on Ontario license plates.

The markings of adult male and female loons are similar.

CANADA

Canada is the heart of the common loon's range. With uncounted lakes—Quebec has around a million, Ontario about a quarter million—Canada has plenty of loon habitat. Found in every province, the common loon is absent only from the High Arctic, the open plains of the prairie provinces, and the heavily settled parts of southeastern Ontario. With most of Canada's vast breeding range sparsely settled by humans, the country offers a large number of lakes suitable for nesting and chick rearing.

Hard data about the numbers of common loons in Canada are scarce. The only comprehensive study of loons has been the Breeding Bird Survey but that has been limited to areas with roads. Because much of the loon's breeding range is in areas without roads, population estimates are difficult to obtain. Historical records are scarce or absent. Although protected by federal law, individual provinces haven't seen the need to give loons special designation.

Since Canada has so many loons, a different perspective is operative. To ask a Canadian wildlife manager about loon population is roughly equivalent to asking a U.S. manager about the status of chickadees or robins. You would probably get a funny look and a bemused "we don't have any data" answer. The absence of solid data for much of Canada should be viewed not as a sign of indifference regarding a much loved Canadian bird but as a signal that populations are comfortable and most likely stable.

YUKON AND NORTHWEST TERRITORIES

The common loon breeds throughout the Yukon Territory except at the northern tip and is a fairly common breeder in southern parts of the territory, where it breeds on lakes both above and below timber line. In the Northwest Territories it breeds throughout much of the MacKenzie and Keewatin Territories, but is absent from most of the High Arctic islands in the Franklin Territory, except southern Baffin Island. The northern limit of the tree line delineates the boundary of common loon breeding. It is common in Nahanni National Park, but is absent beyond the timber line in the Thelon Game Preserve. It also breeds on islands in James Bay. All four North American loon species are known to breed in The Northwest Territories.

James King, a U.S. Fish and Wildlife Service Biologist, covered for many years the Yukon and Northwest Territories while conducting duck and goose breeding surveys. He counted loons also. While the Yukon had fairly sparse loon counts, the Northwest Territories were loaded. His rough estimate for the Yukon Territory was 500 common loons. For the Northwest Territories, his estimate (based on 240 survey transects) was 137,000 common loons.

BRITISH COLUMBIA

The common loon is widespread in British Columbia, breeding nearly everywhere in the province. The south-central portion seems to be the provincial center of abundance. Loons breed commonly on Vancouver Island and the Queen Charlottes, but are scarce on coastal islands north of the Queen Charlottes. The common loon has been classified as an uncommon to fairly common summer visitor throughout the province based on a recently completed book on the birds of British Columbia produced by the British Columbia Provincial Museum.

Spring migration peaks in late April and early May and the passage of birds is relatively fast. Flocks are often seen on large lakes and protected bays, inlets, and harbors off the coast. Non-breeding summer birds are often seen in flocks of usually less than fifty in coastal bays and on some lakes. Autumn migration occurs from early September through November with the peak in the first half of October. Winter birds are widely distributed along the coast and on some inland lakes that stay ice-free. Flocks numbering less than twenty birds are the norm. Major coastal wintering areas include the northern end of the Strait of Georgia, off the Frasier River delta, and at the east end of the Juan de Fuca Strait. Larger lakes in the vicinity of Oliver, Osoyoos, and Vernon are preferred wintering sites when open.

A province-wide population estimate is not available although there are at least 512 lakes with records of breeding loons. There have been local population declines in the past, but Breeding Bird Survey data for areas west of the Rocky Mountains showed no decrease in population. It seems likely that the current loon pairs in eastern Washington State and the historical populations in Washington and Oregon were linked to the breeding population in British Columbia.

PRAIRIE PROVINCES

The status of the common loon in Alberta, Manitoba, and Saskatchewan has not been well documented. It is thought to breed throughout the entire non-prairie portions of the region. The aspen parklands and pockets of forested areas allow it to extend its range south into the prairie. Common loon numbers seem to have declined in more populated areas of these provinces.

Saskatchewan has over 90,000 lakes in the northern part of the province alone and according to officials at the province's Parks and Renewable Resources Department, most lakes have two or three breeding pairs. The Federation of Alberta Naturalists has completed a breeding bird atlas for their province. The common loon is a fairly common breeding bird across the central portion of the province where there are the greatest concentration of lakes. Wildlife officials in Alberta estimate about 3,000 common loons inhabit the province. There are no estimates for Manitoba, but the large number of lakes in the province suggests that thousands of loons probably live there.

ONTARIO

Loons have been studied intensively in Ontario where the Canadian Lakes Loon Survey, coordinated by the Long Point Bird Observatory, has been collecting data since 1981. Since around 1991, this effort has been expanded into other Canadian provinces, but the majority of the work continues to be in Ontario. Since the focus of this survey has been the effects of lake acidification on common loons, distribution and population numbers are not well documented. Studies do clearly show, however, that the common loon breeds throughout most of Ontario particularly in the Precambrian (Canadian) Shield area. It formerly bred in the heavily settled southern part of the province, but is absent or a sparse breeder there now. The dividing line for good loon habitat in Ontario runs roughly from North Bay to Sault Ste. Marie. To the north and northwest of this line, loons seem to inhabit virtually every lake except for areas close to Hudson Bay.

Peter Croskery, formerly the fish and Wildlife supervisor in Ontario's Ministry of Natural Resources Ignace Office, has conducted common loon surveys in northwestern

Ontario. He considers the loon population there to be very healthy, perhaps even in excess of its natural carrying capacity. He views the large numbers of nonterritorial loons on many Ontario lakes as evidence of "surplus stock," waiting to fill any vacant territory. Croskery cited as a case in point, one lake of 6,000 acres which has fifty breeding pairs and as many as seventy-five extra loons. He estimates the population in his district at about forty loons per 100 square miles, a figure he believes can be generalized to most of northwestern Ontario.

Near Hudson Bay, prime loon habitat starts to fade. The roughly 100,00 square miles of Hudson Bay lowlands probably do not support as many loons as the areas around Ignace according to Harry Lumsten, a wildlife researcher based in the Ministry's Maple Office. One survey conducted to monitor goose populations turned up only fourteen loon nests over a 150 square mile area.

Trends in Ontario's common loon population can not be determined at present. However, its disappearance from southern Ontario and some evidence that shoreline development, recreation, and lake acidification affect breeding performance suggest that populations may decline in the future. Overall the situation looks good. The common loon was found in the second most number of squares in northern Ontario during recent breeding bird

A parent often protects a chick under its wing.

atlas studies and in central Ontario population densities of nearly thirty-eight breeding loons per 100 square miles have been recorded.

QUEBEC

Quebec has around one million lakes and an uncounted but large number of common loons. A government study put the total of 35,000 pairs with 12,000 in New Orleans (north of 52nd parallel), 7,000 in midnorth Quebec (50th to 52nd parallel), and 16,000 in the Laurentian and Appalachian Mountains south of the 50th parallel. Common loons also winter in small numbers off Quebec's Atlantic Coast.

While population trends for common loons in Quebec have not been determined, it seems likely that they may be declining in some areas. Shooting by Inuit and Cree tribes in New Quebec averaging about 4,600 per year, lake acidification, and water level fluctuation caused by intensive hydroelectric power undoubtedly negatively affect populations.

MARITIMES

Common loons breed in New Brunswick, Nova Scotia, Labrador, and Newfoundland. Common loons were reported to have been breeding birds in Prince Edward Island, but there has not been a confirmed breeding record there since 1900. There are no estimates of loon numbers for Nova Scotia, Newfoundland, and Labrador, but Canadian biologists conducted surveys and made estimates in the early 1990s in New Brunswick. A province-wide breeding bird survey in Nova Scotia provides some information about the status of loons there if not an estimate of numbers.

In New Brunswick, the provincial breeding population of adults is around 3,000 and appears to be increasing. Most of the nesting activity is in the southwestern part of the province and there is very little in the northeast. Loons

are nesting and raising young successfully on some highly acidic lakes, but the long-term prognosis for these lakes must be watched. There are an estimated 300 to 400 subadult common loons that summer off the coast every year. This area is one of the few known concentrations of summering subadults in North America. Water level fluctuations and recreational disturbance are negatively affecting some breeding pairs, but appear to be localized problems. A much greater problem province-wide is the accidental drowning of loons in commercial fishing nets in both salt and fresh water. Rudy Stocek, from the Maritime Forest Ranger School, reported that approximately two-thirds of the known mortality of adults loons is from entanglement in nets.

Tony Erskine, a renowned Canadian Wildlife Service biologist for many years, organized province-wide breeding bird surveys for the Maritimes. Confirmed breeding locations for common loons ranged all across Nova Scotia and there are probably more loons there than in New Brunswick. Overall, he believes that loons occupy most of the areas they did before European settlement. However, he estimates their numbers to be one-third to one-half below those historical levels.

UNITED STATES

With the exception of Alaska, the northern United States forms the southern fringe of the common loon's breeding range. Once found nesting plentifully as far south as Iowa and Indiana, the common loon is now restricted for the most part to only the top northern tier of states,

The parent loon slips silently into the water so as not to draw attention to the nest site.

plus Wyoming and Massachusetts.

A great deal is known about the status and distribution of loons in the U.S. State surveys have been conducted in every state with nesting loons except North Dakota. Small populations and limited distributions in most states have allowed biologists to make reasonable estimates of population numbers which in total approximate 21,000 adult loons. Historical data from early ornithological surveys give some indication of past numbers and distribution. Additionally, private loon organizations have sprung up in nearly every loon state and public education, population monitoring, and research projects are ongoing. The loon movement is booming.

ALASKA

Official State Classification: *None*

HISTORICAL PERSPECTIVE:

All four North American species have been common in Alaska. Unfortunately, few records have been kept. The frequent references to loons in Inuit legends indicate loons have been around for centuries.

PRESENT POPULATION:

Alaska has lots of loons. Surprisingly, a fair number of population surveys of loons have been done in various parts of the state. However, there were no official population estimates for Alaska until 1991 when Nancy Tankersley from the Alaska Department of Fish and Game and Anne Ruggles, a graduate student at the University of Alaska, estimated a minimum of 12,691 common loons, 3,354 yellow-billed loons, 23,639 red-throated loons, 121,130 Pacific loons, and fewer than 100 Arctic loons summering on Alaska's three million lakes.

PROSPECTS:

Dan Gibson of the University of Alaska Museum in Fairbanks believes loons are "doing well" and will continue to do so. Even the highly publicized North Slope oil developments will probably not affect population levels, according to Gibson, because these developments involve only a fraction of Alaska's coasts, a habitat loons only use casually anyway.

As has been the case in every area with humans and loons, common loons seem to be decreasing in number in the heavily settled and used area around Anchorage. The Alaska Department of Fish and Game is now conducting a loon watch program. Presently, there is some concern that some suitable lakes are not being used and that recreation activities may be reducing their reproductive success.

PRIVATE LOON ORGANIZATION:

The Nongame Wildlife Program of the Alaska Department of Fish and Game coordinates an Alaska Loon Watch program out of its Anchorage office. The program enlists the support of volunteers in population monitoring, education and management programs.

WASHINGTON

Official State Classification: *Sensitive Species as of 1992*

HISTORICAL PERSPECTIVE:

It has been assumed for decades that loons were once fairly common nesting birds in Washington. The most recent volume on birds of Washington (1953) states that the common loon "is a fairly common breeding species in Washington, both east and west of the Cascades, though few details of its nesting within the state have been published." However, this optimistic report does not appear to be very accurate. There have been only sporadic reports of loons nesting in the state since 1900 until recently.

PRESENT POPULATION:

Surveys conducted in the 1980s started to reveal a few nesting pairs. More intensive surveys conducted by the State wildlife agency and by incredibly enthusiastic volunteers of the Loon Lake Loon Association have revealed around eight nesting pairs which produce around ten chicks a year.

PROSPECTS:

There seem to be a fair number of suitable lakes for loons in Washington. However, they will probably remain vacant unless there is a strong immigration from Canada which seems unlikely. The best hope is that the existing pairs raise young successfully for the next few years and that some of the young return as breeding adults.

PRIVATE LOON ORGANIZATION:

Despite the paucity of loons in the state and the absence of nesting loons on Loon Lake, there is a Loon Lake Loon Association. The Association sponsors educational programs, several fund-raising events, and an annual "loon watch." Artificial nesting islands have been placed on Loon Lake to try to encourage the few loons that stop during spring migration to stay and nest.

OREGON

Official State Classification: *None*

HISTORICAL PERSPECTIVE:

Parts of Oregon and northern California may have harbored nesting loons, but early records are rare and it is difficult to determine the historical status of loons in these areas. There are many reports of loons summering in Oregon in the 1900s, with nesting presumed but never confirmed. If the loon was a breeding bird in Oregon in this century, it was certainly extirpated by 1950. Records suggest that wintering loons have been common along the Oregon coast all through this century. Common loons are also seen frequently on some inland lakes during spring migration.

PRESENT POPULATION:

Char Corkran, an ecologist with the Northwest Ecological Research Institute, thinks there may be a few loons nesting in or near the Bull Run watershed in the Mt. Hood National Forest in northern Oregon. She has located an apparent territorial pair on one reservoir, but no nesting has been confirmed.

PROSPECTS:

Increasing numbers of spring and summer sightings of common loons may be tied to the creation of large reservoirs and fish stocking activities on some high elevation lakes. Like Washington, there seems little chance that Oregon will have a substantial nesting loon population soon.

PRIVATE LOON ORGANIZATION: None

IDAHO

Official State Classification: *Species of Special Concern*

HISTORICAL PERSPECTIVE:

The common loon was probably never abundant as a nesting bird in Idaho. Sightings during migration date to 1890 and have been reported regularly since then. Records of nesting birds have been rare since the turn of the century. Loons have been reported nesting on lakes in the Panhandle, west-central, central and southeastern parts of the state. The most recent reliable report of nesting dates to 1963 in the Bruneau area of western Idaho.

PRESENT POPULATION:

Current information indicates that the common loon has been eradicated as a nesting bird in Idaho. From 1985 through 1987, researchers canvassed the state without discovering a single nest. While no breeding pairs were observed, many non-nesting loons that apparently spent all or most of the summer in Idaho were seen. The most recent nesting attempt was observed by Dr. Charles Trost of Idaho State University. He saw a loon pair attempting to nest on a lake in 1984 in southeastern Idaho, but the nest failed when a water level drawdown caused nest abandonment. No other nesting attempt has been recorded since the 1963 observation.

Chicks are alerted to impending danger by their parents.

PROSPECTS:

Although no nests have been reported recently, state and federal wildlife officials are optimistic about loons returning as nesting birds. The Wyoming and Montana populations border Idaho and if future nest success in those areas occurs, young loons returning as adults may find some Idaho lakes to their liking and begin to nest there. There are many Idaho lakes ideal for loon nesting.

The Idaho Department of Fish and Game is currently using film of loons on television as advertisements for its non-game program. With the large amount of statewide interest and support, if and when the loons return, there will be plenty of habitat and public support that should lead to their population recovery.

PRIVATE LOON ORGANIZATION: None

Montana
Official State Classification: *Sensitive Species*

HISTORICAL PERSPECTIVE:

Early naturalists' records indicate loons were present in small numbers on remote Montana lakes. Don Skaar, former coordinator of the Montana Loon Study, believes loons may have occupied as many as ninety lakes in the state.

PRESENT POPULATION:

Don Skaar and others have been collecting data on common loons since 1982. The statewide summer population is estimated to be 173 adults. Approximately sixty pairs are known to nest each year. The population has not increased substantially over the past few years and is considered to be stable. Most of the nesting lakes are in northwestern Montana in Glacier National Park, and the Flathead and Kootenai National Forests.

PROSPECTS:

The Montana loon population probably will not change greatly unless some disaster occurs. There is a lot of recreational use of the lakes on which loons nest, but there seems to be a delicate stability for now. A management plan for loons in Montana has been completed and partially implemented.

PRIVATE LOON ORGANIZATION:

The Montana Loon Society (MLS) coordinates a group of volunteers who survey the loon population, launch artificial nesting islands, and conduct public education programs. The MLS works with the state wildlife agency and the U.S. Forest Service to protect known nesting pairs. Protective floating signs around nests have had a significant positive effect on the number of chicks hatched and the continued use of these signs is seen as essential on many lakes.

Wyoming
Official State Classification: *None*

Although lacking official designation, the loon is one of sixty birds and mammals assigned "priority one species in need of special management" based on the Nongame Bird and Mammal Strategic Plan completed in 1987.

HISTORICAL PERSPECTIVE:

There is no historical information on loons for Wyoming. It is likely that they were nesters in the northwestern part of the state before European settlement. In the late 1980s, there were at least ten nesting territories in Yellowstone National Park and a half dozen or so nesting pairs on lakes just south of the Park. Terry McEneaney, a wildlife biologist in the Park, has compiled information on loon numbers there since 1987. During that period, the number of adult loons in the Park has ranged from 34 to 51, the number of nest attempts in a year has ranged from 9 to 15, and the number of chicks raised to flight stage has ranged from a low of 2 to a high of 17.

PRESENT POPULATION:

A small nesting population continues to exist in and around Yellowstone National Park in the northwestern corner of the state. State and federal biologists along with volunteers have been monitoring these pairs and searching other potentially suitable habitat. There are probably fewer than 100 adult loons in the state in the summer. In 1994, around 50 were in the Park on 21 different lakes on which 12 had nesting pairs. Only three of seven lakes with a past history of nesting outside the Park had nesting birds. Some loons may be nesting on lakes in the Wind River Mountains at extremely high elevations. Wyoming loons may set the high elevation records for nesting in the United States. One pair of Park loons on Riddle Lake, which rests at an elevation of 7,900 feet, raised two young in 1986. Wyoming gets its share of migratory loons, especially in the spring. Over a hundred loons are seen at one time occasionally on Yellowstone Lake and the unofficial record is nearly 2,000 on Flaming Gorge Reservoir in April 1989. These birds are probably heading for nesting areas in Montana and the Canadian Prairie Provinces. Loons trickle through in tens and twenties in the fall suggesting that Wyoming is part of a traditional inland migratory route.

PROSPECTS:

The state population is small, but all of the nesting pairs occur on fairly remote lakes surrounded by public lands. Lori Hunter, nongame biologist for the Wyoming Department of Game and Fish, thinks the loons are "in pretty good shape" and that there may be some additional pairs and some suitable vacant habitat. The population is unlikely o grow and expand its range quickly because of its small size and because it is the southernmost tip of a fragmented population of loons occurring in the Rocky Mountains. State and federal interest seems high. The Wyoming Game and Fish Department and Yellowstone National Park officials have developed a management plan for loons.

PRIVATE LOON ORGANIZATION: None

NORTH DAKOTA

Official State Classification: *None*

The common loon has been designated a "Watch Species" by the Endangered Species Committee of the North Dakota Chapter of The Wildlife Society.

HISTORICAL PERSPECTIVE:

North Dakota is the answer to the trivia question asking which northern tier state seems the most unlikely to have a breeding population of loons. Loons and North Dakota just don't sound right together, but loons have found a small pocket of loon heaven in a predominantly prairie state.

Records of loons in North Dakota date back to 1895. Loon populations in the state were probably never great and were restricted to extreme northern areas.

PRESENT POPULATION:

According to Randy Kreil, Zoologist for the North Dakota Natural Heritage Inventory, loons are limited to the Turtle Mountains area in Bottineau and Rolette Counties near the Canadian border. In the late 1980s, the State contracted a survey with a local biologist who knew the Turtle Mountain area. The count of adults turned up about what they expected. North Dakota has around 50 breeding pairs of common loons. No information on productivity was gathered. Since that time, no surveys have been conducted.

PROSPECTS:

The common loon doesn't get much attention in North Dakota where the majority of species in peril are prairie dwellers. According to Kreil, the habitat for loons in the Turtle Mountains is fairly secure and there is no reason to think that the loon population will grow or decrease substantially in the near future. Because the Turtle Mountains are somewhat isolated from the rest of loon breeding range in the United States and Canada, however, any problems loons have could take a relatively long time to repair.

PRIVATE LOON ORGANIZATION: None

MINNESOTA

Official State Classification: *State Bird*

No management designation has been given to the common loon.

HISTORICAL PERSPECTIVE:

Minnesota is one state where the common loon is common. In the 1932 edition of Birds of Minnesota the loon was listed as breeding throughout the state, but the editor, Thomas S. Roberts, suggested loons were "formerly more abundant than at present when every clear water lake was the home of a pair or more of noisy loons. Its steady decrease has been due, in great part, to the fact that this large bird has been the favorite target of the man with a gun."

The Land of 10,000 Lakes has probably hosted over 10,000 loons for many years. A survey in the 1980s by the Minnesota Department of Natural Resources tallied 1,367 adults and 503 chicks on just 437 lakes and officials extrapolated a statewide total of 10,700 loons. However, no statistically sound survey and population estimate was conducted until 1989 when the Minnesota DNR's Nongame Wildlife Program and the Sigurd Olson Environmental Institute's LoonWatch program collaborated on the first ever statewide loon survey.

Over 600 volunteers were recruited to search for loons on nearly 800 lakes 500 acres or less in size and trained biologists counted loons from airplanes on 126 lakes larger than 500 acres. The random sampling of lakes by size class and county allowed a statistically valid estimate of 11,626 adults. Although chicks were counted, no sound estimate could be made of the statewide numbers. Surveyors reported at least one adult loons on half of the lakes checked. Lakes with loons tended to be in the west-central, north-central, and northeastern parts of the state. Minnesota loons seem to prefer lakes between 150 and 500 acres with nearly two-thirds of the surveyed lakes in that size class with at least one loon.

PRESENT POPULATION:

Now that Minnesota has a good estimate of the total number of loons, they are turning their efforts toward following trends in six different parts of the state. In 1994, they initiated a long-term monitoring effort again using volunteers and professional biologists.

PROSPECTS:

The large size of the loon population and the numbers of loons on federal and state lands insure at least short-term security for Minnesota's loons. Minnesota should continue to be the land of the loon for many more years. The state's nongame wildlife office has given considerable attention to loon management and Minnesotans take loon protection seriously. There continues to be concern about mercury contamination especially in the northeastern part of the state.

PRIVATE LOON ORGANIZATION:

LoonWatch, a program of the Sigurd Olson Environmental Institute of Northland College, conducts public education and loon protection programs and works cooperatively with state and federal agencies on loon management problems.

WISCONSIN

Official State Classification: *Watch List*

HISTORICAL PERSPECTIVE:

The 1903 volume *Birds of Wisconsin* by Kumlien and Hollister listed the common loon as a common breeder northward from the southern tier of counties. The authors referred to two southern Wisconsin lakes, Lake Koshkonong near Madison and Delavan Lake near the Illinois border, as locales for breeding loons. At the turn of the century, loons were abundant in northern Wisconsin.

The first comprehensive survey of loons in the state was done in 1976 and 1977 by Gary Zimmer, a graduate student at the University of Wisconsin-Stevens Point. He visited every lake over thirty acres in the northernmost twenty counties. He found 976 adult and 222 young loons on 538 of the 2,019 lakes. He estimated the population to be 1,300 adults and 258 young.

Since 1978, LoonWatch, a program of the Sigurd Olson Environmental Institute of Northland College in Ashland, has collected data on summer loon populations. In 1985, they conducted a random sample survey and estimated a summer population of approximately 2,300 adults and 626 young. Further analysis of specific lakes surveyed in 1976 and 1985 revealed a positive trend. Three lakes known to produce young in 1976 did not have any loons in 1985 while nineteen lakes without any loons in 1976 had both adults and chicks in 1985. Additionally, there were reports of loons nesting in the southern two-thirds of the state where they had been absent for many years.

PRESENT POPULATION:

Wisconsin is on a five-year survey cycle. In 1990, the statewide survey was conducted and revealed 2,790 adults and 725 chicks. The population seems to be increasing steadily and chick production is good. Expansion of nesting into central counties and a few southern counties is still occurring.

PROSPECTS:

The recent increase in numbers, expansion of range of the loon population and the strong citizen's protection program suggest a secure population for the present. Increased shoreline development and recreation on the northern lakes may cause local declines, however, and the level of mercury in many loons is cause for concern. LoonWatch and the Wisconsin DNR have embarked on a long-term study to determine the correlation between mercury levels in loons and reproductive success.

PRIVATE LOON ORGANIZATION:

LoonWatch, in cooperation with the Wisconsin Department of Natural Resources, conducts an annual population survey, sponsors a wide variety of public education activities, and administers a modest research program.

MICHIGAN

Official State Classification: *Threatened*

HISTORICAL PERSPECTIVE:

Historical records of the common loon in Michigan are meager. From the few existing records, it appears that the loon nested statewide up until the early part of this century. Since that time, the breeding range has been shrinking to the north and numbers have decreased.

Jim Hammill of the Michigan DNR began systematic surveys of lakes in the Upper Peninsula in 1983. Only one in twelve apparently habitable lakes was occupied by loons.

He estimated 100 nesting pairs in the western and central Upper Peninsula. Bill Robinson, a professor at Northern Michigan University has organized a survey of a sample of the more than 11,000 inland lakes. Focusing on the lakes with known histories of loon nesting and lakes with suitable habitat features, he estimated the Michigan loon population in 1988 to be 275 nesting pairs with 40 pairs on Isle Royale, 139 in the Upper Peninsula, and 96 in the Lower Peninsula. This was an increase from the 225 nesting pairs estimated for 1985. Reproductive success rates were high compared to other states with large loon populations.

PRESENT POPULATION:

The 1994 Michigan loon population was estimated at

Performing a wing flap after successfully driving away a rogue loon.

295 territorial pairs, 190 of which nested. They produced 180 chicks and raised 133 of them to the flight stage. The number of territorial and nesting pairs continues to increase slowly and chick production seems to be increasing although it is variable annually.

PROSPECTS:

The population increase is good news. However, the amount of vacant suitable habitat is alarming and indicates that either chicks or adults are not surviving long enough to fill in the available space. There is some concern that adult loons are flying to the Great Lakes and being killed in commercial fishing nets. Human disturbance on nesting lakes is increasing in many areas, especially in the lower

peninsula. Fortunately, the loons nesting on lakes within National Forest, National Parks, federal wildlife refuges, and state-managed reserves are partially protected from these problems. The Michigan DNR established a Common Loon Recovery Team which drafted a recovery plan in the late 1980s. The interest shown by the DNR and federal agencies in loon research and management is encouraging.

PRIVATE LOON ORGANIZATION:

The Michigan Loon Preservation Association, a project of the Michigan Audubon Society conducts educational programs and works with state and federal agencies in man-agement and survey efforts. Also, The Nature Conservancy has conducted a Loon Registry program designed to identify lakes with nesting loons and implement loon protective programs through a network of volunteers.

NEW YORK

Official State Classification: *Species of Special Concern*

This classification refers to a species for which a risk of endangerment has been documented.

HISTORICAL PERSPECTIVE:

There are few records documenting early loon populations in New York. Loon researcher Judy McIntyre believes loons probably once nested on most of the Adirondack lakes as well as on all or most of the Finger Lakes. Robert Arbib compiled information from scientific documents, ornithologists, bird clubs, and conservation officers and published the first specific account of loons in New York in 1963. He listed over ninety lakes where pairs had been recorded and estimated the statewide population at 240 breeding pairs restricted to the Adirondack region.

The New York State Department of Environmental Conservation conducted two loon surveys in the 1980s. The total population was estimated at 800 to 1000 adults including 216 to 270 nesting pairs. The large number of nonbreeding adults and the relatively high reproductive rates suggested that the population was growing.

PRESENT POPULATION:

No statewide surveys have been done in recent years. State wildlife officials believe that the loon population is stable with numbers similar to those from the late 1980s.

PROSPECTS:

The future of loons in New York is tied quite closely to the acid rain issue. Over 200 Adirondack lakes are now fishless and consequently devoid of loons. Based on a study done by Karl Parker of the State University of New York at Syracuse, loons can adapt in a limited fashion to lake acidification and the subsequent loss of fish. However, it is clear that a lake without fish will soon become a lake without loons. Development and recreational pressures may also increase in the Adirondacks and cause some further problems for loons. Fortunately, there is a great interest in loons by the people of the state.

PRIVATE LOON ORGANIZATION:

The Audubon Society of New York conducts educational programs on loon protection.

MASSACHUSETTS

Official State Classification: *Species of Special Concern*

The loon is also on the "Rare Wetlands Wildlife" list which means that no activity can be undertaken that would have short or long-term adverse effects on nesting loons.

HISTORICAL PERSPECTIVE:

The noted ornithologist Edward Howe Forbush stated that "probably the common loon once bred in suitable locations throughout Massachusetts." By 1925, he considered them extirpated from the state after being unable to learn of any nesting locations in the early 1900s.

Quabbin Reservoir, a 25,000 acre lake used as the source of drinking water for metropolitan Boston, was constructed and filled by 1946. Loons were suspected to be nesting there on and off over the next several years. Meanwhile, nesting was documented on a nearby lake in 1943. Finally, in 1975 nesting was confirmed on Quabbin.

PRESENT POPULATION:

In 1994, there were 11 territorial pairs in the state, 7 of which nested and produced 7 chicks.

PROSPECTS:

The prospects for Massachusetts are good, but humble. After twenty years, the population seems to be limited in its probability for further growth. According to Brad Blodget, state ornithologist for the Division of Fisheries and Wildlife, there seems to be plenty of suitable habitat for loons on surface water reservoirs closed to boating, but they are not being filled. The relative isolation of this population and the low number of chicks produced each year may be the reason for such slow growth and range expansion.

PRIVATE LOON ORGANIZATION:

The Massachusetts Audubon Society, the Massachusetts Division of Fisheries and Wildlife, and the Metropolitan District Commission jointly sponsor a conservation and management program.

VERMONT

Official State Classification: *Endangered*

HISTORICAL PERSPECTIVE:

While there are no solid historical baseline population estimates for loons in Vermont, early naturalists reported loons breeding on most of Vermont's larger lakes. Records clearly indicate loons nested on Dunsmore and Bomoseen Lakes and Mallets Bay of Lake Champlain, all lakes where no loons have nested for at least thirty years. In 1978, the Vermont Institute of Natural Sciences (VINS) staff and volunteers surveyed sixty-eight lakes and found only sixteen active loon nests. Only 56 adults were seen.

PRESENT POPULATION:

VINS has surveyed Vermont lakes for loons each year since 1978. The number of nesting pairs reached a high of 19 in 1982, but dropped to a low of 8 the next year. Since the decline, the breeding population has gradually recovered at the rate of about one new breeding pair per year and has stabilized since 1989 at 13 to 16 pairs. In 1994, 13 pairs attempted nesting and 16 chicks survived to flight stage. The 1994 statewide loon count was 83 adults,

14 juveniles, and 11 immatures. Almost all of the lakes used by loons in Vermont are in the northeastern corner.

PROSPECTS:

There are a number of lakes with suitable loon habitat that are vacant at present. There has been a disturbing number of lakes that have been used only one, two or three years by nesting loons. Chris Rimmer, coordinator of the VINS loon project, is cautiously optimistic that the Vermont loon population will stay stable or increase slightly. It is unlikely that Vermont will ever have a large and secure loon population.

PRIVATE LOON ORGANIZATION:

The Vermont Institute of Natural Sciences, in cooperation with the Vermont Fish and Wildlife Department, conducts an annual loon survey, participates in research, and sponsors public education programs on behalf of loons. VINS is developing a formal loon recovery plan in hopes of ensuring the long-term viability of Vermont's common loons.

NEW HAMPSHIRE

Official State Classification: *Threatened*

HISTORICAL PERSPECTIVE:

While estimates of former loon populations are not precise, loons once nested on at least twice as many lakes in New Hampshire as they do today. A 1977 survey of sixty-eight lakes with historical records of loon usage turned up only thirty-two with loons, a fifty-three percent decline. Winnipesaukee, the state's largest lake, has a history of supporting 30 to 40 pairs but supported only ten pairs in 1978.

The New Hampshire Loon Preservation Committee conducted the first statewide survey in 1976 and recorded a total population of 271 loons. There were 93 territorial pairs on fifty-eight lakes which produced fifty-one fledged chicks.

PRESENT POPULATION:

If there is any state that knows where its loons are, it's New Hampshire. The Loon Preservation Committee (LPC) has continued to count loons statewide and it would be a fair statement that fewer than five percent of the loons that ever land on a New Hampshire lake during the summer go unnoticed.

In 1994, LPC biologists and hundreds of volunteer loon counters recorded a record number of adults—462, chicks raised to flight stage—91, and the total loon population—557. Additionally, record high numbers of territorial pairs—190—laid claim to New Hampshire's golden ponds and lakes. There were 135 lakes with loons in the state and a few lakes are added to the list every year.

New Hampshire boasts very high chick survival rates (between 75 and 90 percent) in part because of the doting of their parents, but in equal part because lake residents are extremely watchful and protective.

PROSPECTS:

Despite slowing a bit in recent year, the state's loon population continues to increase suggesting that there is still room for a few more loons in the Granite State. The population also continues to expand which is a sign that loon chicks hatched and raised in previous years may be coming home and setting up new territories. New Hampshire's lakes are heavily developed and used, but the overwhelming success of the LPC's public education and management programs, the strong support for population restoration by the citizenry of the state, and the growth of the loon population over the last two decades suggest that the still rather small loon population will be secure for some time to come.

PRIVATE LOON ORGANIZATION:

The Loon Preservation Committee of the New Hampshire Audubon Society conducts public education programs, constructs and monitors the use of artificial nest islands, censuses the loon population, works with hydroelectric power companies to reduce water level fluctuations during the nesting period, and is participating in regional research projects. It was the first private loon organization and through its founder, Rawson Wood, provided strong leadership in the national loon protection effort.

MAINE

Official State Classification: *None*

HISTORICAL PERSPECTIVE:

Common loons once nested throughout Maine and may have occupied many of the 2,700 lakes over ten acres in size. The Maine Audubon Society and the Maine Department of Inland Fisheries and Wildlife began surveying the loon population in 1977 and 1978. Seven hundred ninety-eight lakes were surveyed and loons were found on 439. There were 1,146 loon pairs, and 336 chicks. Loons were found in every county in the state, but the 1978 survey, which looked at the heavily populated southern region, indicated that loons were sparse in the southern counties and near areas with large human populations. The 1977 study concluded that "it appears that the loon population is stable enough to dismiss the immediate welfare of the species in Maine," despite some apparent declines in the southern counties.

PRESENT POPULATION:

The Maine Audubon Society, in cooperation with the Maine Cooperative Fish and Wildlife Research Unit at the University of Maine and the Department of Inland Fisheries and Wildlife, has conducted aerial and ground counts of loons since 1984. Two statewide estimates have been made since that time, but only of the adult population. The 1984 results yielded 3,531 adult loons and the 1990 results were 3,949. From Bangor south (the southern half of the state), a randomly stratified sample of lakes has been surveyed from the ground each year since 1986 with the exception of 1988. The number of adults has varied between 1,649 and 2,251 and the number of chicks between 163 and 368. Overall, the population seems to be stationary with no real evidence of a decline or increase.

The number of adults estimated in the statewide surveys puts Maine behind only Minnesota in the lower forty-eight United States.

PROSPECTS:

Maine is one of the few remaining areas in the eastern U.S. with large tracts of wild land. Currently, there is a development boom occurring in the state. Prime shoreline real estate is going quickly. Sally Stockwell, Maine Audubon's loon project coordinator, reports that the speculation that much of the privately owned timber lands in the northern half of the state would be sold and that financially strapped forest landowners would sell off shoreline lots on undeveloped lakes has not come to pass in most places. The southern half of the state continues to be a prime recreational area for the population centers of the East. Fortunately, lake protection is gaining momentum in the state. Private and state organizations and local governments are beginning to plan lakeshore use. It seems likely that Maine's loon population will decline in the face of continued lakeshore development and recreational use. However, the current stability of both the adult population and chick production, the large size of the population, and the remoteness of some areas in the state will protect Maine's loons from immediate danger for a while.

PRIVATE LOON ORGANIZATION:

The Maine Audubon Society runs the Maine Loon Project which conducts public education programs and an annual loon count. Additionally, they work with town and state governments on lake protection activities. In recent years, they have conducted and participated in cooperative research projects.

A solitary loon on a peaceful evening.

Crayfish are among the loon's favorite foods.

*I have laid aside business, and
gone a-fishing.*

—Izaak Walton, 1653

Making a Living

In 1919, Arthur Cleveland Bent, the serious scientist with the lively prose, deftly captured the fishing prowess of the common loon: "This loon feeds largely on fish, which it pursues beneath the surface with wonderful power and speed. The subaqueous rush of the formidable monster must cause consternation among the finny tribes."

The underwater hunting skills of loons obviously impressed Bent. Many sport fishermen were similarly impressed and probably wondered and worried about the diet of the loon. In his study of diving birds, Bent described the fisherman's worst nightmare: "Even the lively trout, noted for its quickness of movement, cannot escape the loon and large numbers of these desirable fish are destroyed to satisfy its hunger." Bent quickly noted, however, that loons and trout had coexisted for thousands of years before the arrival of modern fishermen. He was satisfied that it is not "fair to blame this bird, which is such an attractive feature of the wilds, for the scarcity of trout."

Many fishermen of Bent's era shot loons as competitors, and even pushed for bounties on loons, but Bent answered their charges with a comment remarkably sensitive for the time: "We are too apt to condemn a bird for what little damage it does in this way, without giving credit for the right to live." Bent was a man ahead of his times, but the slaughter of loons continued.

In today's more enlightened era, few loons are shot by selfish fishermen, but Bent was right about trout—loons do have a taste for them. Trout of considerable size apparently are fair game for common loons. In New York's Adirondack region, three common loons were found in trap nets. Analyses of the loons' stomachs by state biologists revealed the presence of metal tags which are routinely attached to stocked brook trout.

Since the size of the trout when tagged and the date of release were known, it was possible for officials to estimate the size of each trout when it met a loon for lunch. Some of the trout were estimated at eighteen inches—big brook trout by anyone's standard. An eighteen-inch brook trout would

Loons periscope down into water before diving for fish.

weigh nearly two pounds, not a bad meal for an eight-pound loon. While no one actually saw these loons consume trout, it is unlikely the loons could have picked up the tags in any other way. A study from Michigan supports the New York evidence. A Michigan biologist, G. R. Alexander, analyzed the stomachs of a dozen loons. He concluded their diet consisted of eighty percent trout, ranging in size from six to twelve inches. Loons in Ontario's Algonquin Park also dine on trout. One common loon found there had tags from twenty-five trout in its stomach.

However, loons should not be characterized as aquatic gourmands, feasting only upon the finest game fish. To the contrary, they are highly opportunistic aquatic hunters and will eat whatever is handy. If they live on trout lakes, they will eat trout, but most likely they will find other prey more abundant

and easier to catch. Since more typical loon prey (such as sucker or perch) is rarely tagged, evidence of eating fish other than prime game fish like trout is not readily available.

In many ways the loon/trout issue is like the wolf/deer debate. While wolves eat deer, they do not eat enough to threaten the deer population. In a similar fashion, loons are not serious competitors for the sport fisherman. Since they feed on almost anything that swims, loons take relatively few game fish. Some scientists, in fact, believe loons might actually improve sport fishing by removing large numbers of rough fish.

A BALANCED DIET

Although loons do eat a lot of fish, they also sample a wide variety of other prey items. In his *Handbook of North*

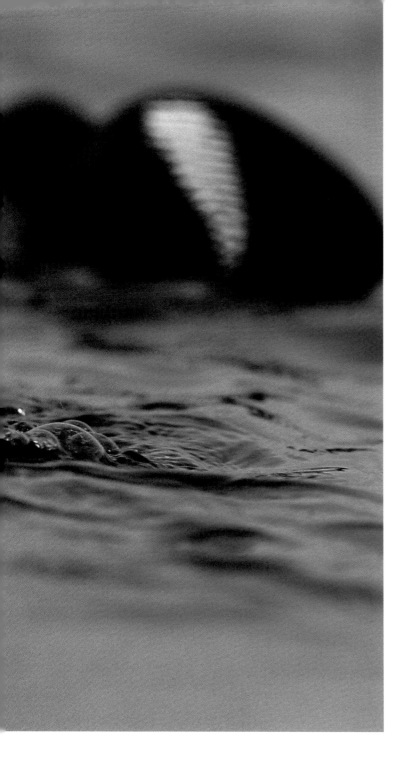

loons), suckers (five), and minnows (three). Other prey found included black crappie (two), walleye (two), northern pike (one), black bass (one) and pumpkinseed sunfish (one).

The extent of the loon's adaptive feeding behavior is impressive. In a 1945 study of British Columbia lakes, J. A. Munro discovered some common loons living throughout the summer on lakes containing no fish. Yet, he saw healthy loons in breeding plumage. Upon inspection of the stomachs of four loons, Munro found only mollusks, amphipods (small invertebrates) and insects. Freshwater clams are at least occasionally on the menu. Way back in 1896, a young loon in New Brunswick was on the menu for a clam. It was found with a clam attached to its tongue and inside the clam was most of the young loon's bill which had been torn off.

Loons, especially chicks, can be vegetarian, eating a variety of aquatic greens. One juvenile loon found in Minnesota had a gizzard completely full of vegetable matter. Rob Alvo's recent studies in Canada found that sixty-five percent of the food fed to chicks which were 4 to 15 days old was vegetation, but the percentage fell to four percent by the time the chicks were seven weeks old when fish made up the remainder of the diet.

Less is known about the loon's salt water diet, but at a minimum herring, sea trout, rock cod, flounder and various crustaceans and mollusks are on the menu. Loons spending time in Maine's coastal waters apparently sample the local cuisine just like the millions of tourists who flock there every year. Several loons hanging out in historic Boothbay Harbor (the ocean not the town) in March and April have been reported eating lobsters, bringing them to the surface and picking them apart. The price they had to haggle at the local fisherman's co-op was unknown. As in freshwater, availability is probably a more important factor than flavor. Whether loons are on salt or fresh water, they spend a lot of time fishing. They always capture live prey. In his many years on loon waters, Olson never observed a loon eating a dead fish. Once I tried to feed a pair of curious loons some dying and dead minnows. Even though the loons were only thirty feet from my canoe and were aware, I'm sure, of the minnows hitting the water, they didn't take the bait. While some captive or injured loons have been known to eat dead fish, wild loons like to catch their own dinners.

BIG APPETITES

Mark Blackbourn, director of The Northwoods Wildlife Center in Minocqua, Wisconsin, had a lot of experience with captive loons. He has handled sixty injured loons and returned fifty of them to northern Wisconsin lakes. Feeding loons while they recuperate from a variety of injuries has been a challenge for the clinic's staff. Blackbourn quickly learned that loons do not like to be fed, but need to capture their own minnows. To keep captive loons healthy and happy, Blackbourn constructed a small pond about twenty feet long and three feet deep. Keeping a loon in live minnows

American Birds, Ralph S. Palmer estimates the common loon's diet at eighty percent fish. In fresh water these fish are typically perch, suckers, bullheads, sunfish, smelt, and various minnows. Some non-finned items like frogs, salamanders, crayfish and leeches are also on the loon's menu. An examination of one loon found dead on Squam Lake in New Hampshire turned up only a collection of crayfish in its stomach.

In his Master's thesis on loons, Sigurd Olson summarized the results of analyses of twenty-seven stomachs taken from loons throughout the upper midwest. The information revealed not just what loons ate, but also how they ate. Of the twenty-seven stomachs, twenty contained only one species of fish. Apparently when loons find a good thing they stick with it, feeding—at least for awhile—exclusively on that species. The most common prey items were yellow perch (ten is no small task. A recovering loon typically would capture and eat eight dozen four-inch minnows per day, supplemented by a dozen or more crayfish. During daylight hours, the loons either fed or preened, with occasional naps on shore. (Contrary to conventional loon wisdom, Blackbourn has also observed non-nesting wild loons preening and sleeping on shore, even well after the nesting season.)

Blackbourn's report of loons eating a hundred minnows a day will not surprise research biologists. The loon's food requirement, at least during the nesting season, is enormous. Jack Barr, a biologist from the University of Guelph in Ontario, estimates that a pair of loons with two chicks will consume over a ton (2,310 pounds to be exact) of fish during the fifteen-week chick-rearing period.

There have been many reports of "greedy" loons. In 1927, a loon near Erie, Pennsylvania was found dead with a fifteen-inch pike-perch (walleye) in its throat. In a 1929 article, Edward Howe Forbush mentions loons on Nantucket Bay swallowing flounders five inches from belly to dorsal fin. Bent also saw flounder-loving loons, including one loon which had fifteen flounders averaging four inches in length in its gullet, in addition to a stomach nearly full of a partially digested fish. To handle such large prey, loons have developed a rather elastic esophagus. These are, however, examples of unusually large prey and loons more typically feed often, but on small prey. According to Jack Barr, the average weight of prey is only three-quarters of an ounce.

No avian gluttons, loons just have to keep up with a high level of energy expenditure. For most birds, just maintaining their body temperature requires a large number of calories. Birds generally eat relatively more for their weight than do other animals. The golden eagle consumes over a pound of food a day—fifteen percent of its body weight. The pelican devours about four pounds of fish a day—half of its weight. Ever watch a hummingbird? They feed almost constantly and consume more than their body weight every day.

FISHING TECHNIQUES

Generally, loons swallow their prey under water, but there are a few reports of loons coming to the surface with food. A fish brought to the surface is manipulated until it can be swallowed head first. Exceptionally large fish don't go down all at once. Loons are sometimes seen with the slowly disappearing tail end of a fish hanging out of the bill. Sigurd Olson once watched a loon on Como Lake, near St. Paul, capture small panfish and bring them to the surface to tear apart. Since the dorsal fin on sunfish is quite large and has extremely sharp points, loons would have a hard time swallowing such spiny prey. Tearing of prey is not the norm for loons and rarely seen. Loons do occasionally "bill" their prey into submission before swallowing.

Loons feed by sight alone and do not need cues of sound or odor, but do require relatively clear water to forage efficiently. Barr points out that as water clarity diminishes, loons start bottom feeding and fill up on slow-moving crayfish. Because of their sight-hunting methods, loons do not feed at night.

Studies across the United States and Canada indicate a positive relationship between water clarity and occupancy by loons. While loons need relatively clear water to feed effectively, other factors may outweigh clarity in determining where loons live. Loons reside on crystal clear lakes with visibility to the bottom and on tea-stained bog lakes in Canada on which it is difficult to see to the tip of a canoe paddle barely under water.

The loon's superb diving abilities and opportunistic tendencies have created problems for commercial fishermen on Lake Superior. Fishermen there use pond nets, large net enclosures with a lead or opening which funnels into the net. Since there is no cover over the net on the water's surface, Lake Superior's loons and cormorants quickly discovered that while fishing in the open lake may be good, fishing within these large pond nets is even better. While loons may not actually kill many trapped fish (most are too large), they do chase them into the sides of the net where many fish gill themselves in the net mesh and die. There is some spoilage which causes an economic as well as a time loss for commercial fishermen. Stories of fishermen carrying shotguns to deal directly with the problem are still common.

Sigurd Olson interviewed ten commercial fishermen on the Minnesota side of Lake Superior. While all had caught loons on their setlines baited for trout, one fisherman claimed to have caught forty loons in one day on a 200 hook setline. Many fishermen thought the loons had "learned" to spot the setline floats. Understandably, these fishermen did not have a deep appreciation for loons. While most wanted a bounty on loons, their wish was never realized. The sea lamprey entered the big lake in the early 1950s and settled the issue by destroying nearly all the trout in Lake Superior. With no trout to catch, the fishermen didn't need to worry about a few loons in their setlines; they went out of business or changed their target species and their fishing techniques. Then in 1961 the common loon prevailed over such beautiful birds as the wood duck, the scarlet tanager and the belted kingfisher to become the Minnesota State Bird. The loon, as they say, had arrived.

Some Michigan loons still are threatened by commercial fishing nets. Nets on both Lake Superior and Lake Michigan inadvertently capture hundreds of loons every year. While no hard evidence is available to prove the theory, some biologists suspect that Michigan's depressed loon population may be the result of adult loons from inland lakes flying to the Great Lakes to feed where many are being caught in commercial fishing nets.

This young loon managed to swallow a sunfish, with coaxing from its parents.

The haunting call of the loon is a true wilderness experience.

If perchance you have never had the good fortune to hear the mournful cry of the common loon, you have missed the full enjoyment of the wilderness. Like the howl of a timber wolf, the bugling of a bull elk and the singing of a humpback whale, the mournful cry of the loon is unique.

—*George Harrison, 1983*

Wilderness Music

More than unique, loon music is primitive, reaching into obscure recesses of the human mind. For some people, loon calls might reach down a little too deeply. A few years ago, a resort owner in northern Wisconsin told me the story of a Chicago couple who spent just one night in a lakeside cabin and checked out early the following morning. The loons just "got to them," he said. Apparently they felt more secure in the jungles of the Loop.

GETTING TO PEOPLE

Loon vocalizations *get* to a lot of people. There is something about loon music that unleashes the poet in many people. Despite his lofty reputation as a philosopher, Henry David Thoreau was often a stiff, pedantic writer, producing endless paragraphs about the number of nails in his cabin. But when Thoreau writes about loons, he becomes a hopeless romantic. In *Walden*, he describes a loon's call:

> *The loon uttered a long-drawn unearthly howl, probably more like that of a wolf than any bird; as when a beast puts his muzzle to the ground and deliberately howls. This was his looning, perhaps the wildest sound that is ever heard here, making the woods ring far and wide.*

Thoreau's Walden Pond is quiet these days, except for the laughter from the popular swimming beach and the occasional squealing of car tires. It is not a place for loons or poets.

Writing in a 1924 National Audubon Society leaflet, Arthur Norton captured the spirit of the loon with poetic prose worthy of Byron or Shelly:

> *The loon manifests uneasiness before a storm . . . maybe its savage spirit is stirred to depths of exultation by the turmoil of wind and wave for, with the rising gale, the bird becomes especially noisy, sending its powerful voice echoing across the water with great frequency. Like the spirits of old legends, it seems never to sleep, but to be*

ranging these realms both day and night,
sending abroad wild, loud notes at all hours.

Is he talking about the serene loon swimming on your lake? A "savage spirit?" Is loon music then a key which unlocks hidden doors of the psyche? That would explain why even very proper birders such as Oliver Austin get a little carried away. In writing his authoritative *Birds of the World*, Austin was all business, except for two pages devoted to loons. There he found space for a personal tribute to loon music:

> *It embodies the very spirit of far places, of forest-clad lakes where the clear air is scented with balsam and fir . . . no one who has ever heard the diver's music, the mournful farcarrying call notes and the uninhibited, cacophonous, crazy laughter, can ever forget it*

Even in 1899 the call of the loon had not gone unnoticed. In his definition of loon for the *Century Dictionary*, William Whitney added an editorial note: "The wild actions of the loon in escaping danger and its dismal cry suggest the idea of insanity; hence the common American simile 'as crazy as a loon.'" Times certainly have changed: few today would term loon music "dismal."

Even fewer people try to forget the loon's extraordinary calls. Loons have entertained generations of lakeshore visitors and have inspired a measure of national pride. In his book *Birds of Ontario*, L. L. Snyder described loon calls in language brimming with nationalistic feeling: Loon calls are " . . . as characteristic of our northland as bold rocks and blue waters, and as effective in inducing Canadian nostalgia as the odor of evergreens, or the taste of blueberries."

The calls are arresting yet mysterious. Despite years of listening, Sigurd Olson believes loon calls remain the "least understood attribute of the loon." By varying slightly the four basic call types, he believes loons create an "almost endless repertoire" of wilderness music. That's the gospel according to Olson.

According to Framingham State College biologist William Barklow, however, loon calls can be understood. And if anyone can understand loon vocalizations, it's Barklow, who has spent seven years studying and recording loon calls. Loon lovers should thank Barklow for his detailed doctoral dissertation, "The Functions of Variations in the Vocalizations of the Common Loon," and the record album, *Voices of the Loon*, a superb collection of loon recordings published in 1980 by the North American Loon Fund and the National Audubon Society.

Not content with just listening to loon calls, Barklow literally disassembled them. Using high tech equipment, Barklow produced audiospectrographs, sort of acoustical fingerprints or voice prints of loon calls. Also known as sonograms, audiospectrographs are made when a stylus transfers frequency patterns to a moving belt of paper.

With such a visual representation, loon calls can be analyzed with a discrimination far exceeding that of the human ear. These "images" of calls can also be fed into a computer for more detailed analysis and comparison with other loon calls.

While some people might worry about technology stealing some of the romance of loon music, they should recognize that these techniques allow scientists to hear more of the music and probe more deeply into loon communications. This research is giving loon devotees a deeper appreciation of the complexities of loon language without removing the magic.

LOON LANGUAGE

Long before Bill Barklow carried his microphone into the backcountry of northern Maine, the four basic loon calls had been clearly identified. In his 1919 study of loons and other divers, Arthur Cleveland Bent quotes William Underwood's description of common loon calls:

> *First, a short, cooing note, often heard when there are several loons together; second, long drawn-out note, known among the guides as the night call; third, the laughing call, which is familiar to everybody who has ever been in loon country; and fourth, another call which is not often heard, known among the guides as the storm call. The last is a very peculiar and weird performance which the guides regard as a sure sign of a coming storm.*

Without the aid of any tape recorders or other listening devices, Underwood had described quite accurately the hoot, wail, tremolo and yodel. His comment about the yodel being a storm call has not, however, stood up well through the years. Neither the yodel nor any other loon call predicts the weather any better—or worse—than the evening news.

While loon language does rest upon these four basic parts of loon speech, it also embraces a few extra pieces of vocabulary. Often calls are accidentally or deliberately (who knows?) combined to create additions to the loon lexicon. Fusions of the tremolo-wail and tremolo-yodel are frequently heard, delighting listeners and confounding researchers. Are these confused or clever loons? If the tremolo call implies a tendency to flee and the wail a need to establish contact, as several researchers suggest, does then the tremolo-wail reflect a deranged or even schizophrenic loon mind? Probably not. People change their minds, why not loons? Scientists believe that the combination calls represent vocal expressions of conflicting stimuli, similar to the fight/flight syndrome.

Further complicating loon linguistics are the frequent reports from many sober loon listeners of "different" calls. Even people who have memorized the Voices of the Loon album have heard loon calls which simply do not fit any call type or combination type. Give Barklow a few more years with his technological ears to settle the questions. In the meantime loon listeners can learn a lot by tuning in the four basic calls.

THE TREMOLO

Reacting to the common loon's tremolo call, writer John McPhee reflected, "If he were human, it would be the laugh of the deeply insane." It's probably this call which drove the Chicago tourists out of their lakeside cabin. But getting a tremolo call on paper is like catching a brook trout with bare hands—it may be fun to try but one should not expect much for dinner. Barklow called the tremolo "a relatively slow frequency modulation with a superimposed modulation of amplitude." Then he got technical. It's a good thing we have the *Voices of the Loon* album and the opportunity to hear many thousands of the real callers. To appreciate the tremolo or any other loon call you simply have to hear it.

While any motivational inferences about the tremolo are just informed guesses, Barklow and others have developed some well-supported theories. After several years of attempting to put loon calls and behaviors together, Barklow has defined the tremolo as the loon's all purpose call which can signal alarm, annoyance, worry or

A tremolo signals danger to chicks and mate.

greeting. Isolating three different types of tremolos, Barklow suggests the tremolo could provide a graded system of communication between loons. The lower frequency calls reflect a low level of anxiety or intensity while the high frequency tremolo calls reflect a sense of urgency. Barklow has designated these simply Types 1, 2 and 3 with Type 1 being the lowest and Type 3 the highest level of intensity.

According to Barklow, the ability to modify the "meaning" of a single call is rare in birds or other animals. Apparently loons can send very different messages by increasing the duration and frequency of the tremolo. The longest and most complex of the tremolo calls, the Type 3 call, is usually reserved for occasions of extreme alarm or anxiety.

In Barklow's view, all three tremolo types usually signal a tendency to flee. Usually the tremolo is coupled with behavioral responses such as a dive, a run on the surface or a take-off. The presence of people often elicits the tremolo, especially when boaters or fishermen approach too closely. University of Stockholm scientists, Sverre Sjolander and

Greta Agren, documented quite well this disturbance-tremolo association. From a distance they observed people encountering loons. In ninety-four consecutive human disturbance situations, loons gave a tremolo call; no other calls were heard.

Mated pairs frequently use a tremolo duet when a disturbance threatens their young. When given "in stereo" on opposite sides of the intruder (like fishermen in a canoe) it can be very distracting and could potentially confuse less mentally gifted predators. This beautiful tremolo duet is also used in early spring to apparently reinforce pair bonds and advertise territorial rights.

But the tremolo isn't reserved just for human encroachment. Millions of years before Homo sapiens appeared, the tremolo call echoed across ancient lakes. Loons often use the tremolo to communicate while flying; in fact, the tremolo is the only call loons typically give while in flight. Loons are selective in their use of, the tremolo when flying over lakes; Barklow noticed that loons flying over loon-less lakes were usually silent. Keeping track of when flying loons used the tremolo, Barklow heard tremolos only one of nine times a loon flew over a loon-less lake, but twenty-two of twenty-four times a loon flew over a lake holding loons.

Other situations which provoke the tremolo include, according to Barklow, the return of a loon's mate, social activities such as group displays, and chorusing with other loons. Attempting to relate the various tremolo types with particular loon behaviors, Barklow discovered that the Type 2 or middle ground call is the most versatile, accounting for over half of all tremolo calls. With the help of audiospectrographs, Barklow could even see subtle differences within call types. Some Type 2 calls reflect greater or lesser intensity. A low frequency Type 2 call might mean "let's get out of here" while a high frequency Type 2 might mean "let's get out of here *now.*" These variations within variations give more meaning to Sigurd Olson's comment about an endless repertoire.

THE WAIL

Oliver L. Austin called the wail of the common loon " . . . one of the loveliest sounds in nature." Often termed the night call, the wail is probably the favorite call of contemporary loon watchers. John McPhee, a devoted follower of loon religion, believes the wail call "authenticates the northern lakes." That's quite a compliment, considering the many other options such as eagles, wild rice, lake trout, silence, and the howl of the wolf. Many people, Thoreau and Olson included, have mentioned the wail of the loon and the howl of the wolf in the same breath. In his 1939 book, *The Natural History of Birds of Eastern and Central North America*, Edward H. Forbush captured the similarity beautifully: "Often toward nightfall I have heard his storm call far out to windward against the black pall of an approaching tempest like the howl of a lone wolf coming down wind." It might work both ways. Loon calls are known to elicit the howls of wolves and coyotes. I know the wail can stop dogs in their tracks. Our two not-so-wild collies freeze and utter low growls whenever a wail call comes through our stereo speakers during playings of *Voices of the Loon*.

Watching loons give the wail, Olson noticed that the call was given with the bill almost closed, causing the throat to swell considerably. He even put the call on paper—"ahaa-ooo-oooo'oooo-ooo-ahhh." (Maybe he *can* catch brook trout with his bare hands.)

Looking at audiospectrographs of wail calls, Barklow sees a call with a structure very similar to the tremolo call. He hears in the wail the most primitive loon sounds and notes that the wail is the first call attempted by chicks. On his audiospectrographs Barklow sees, as with tremolos, three distinct call types, going from simple to complex calls. The Type 1 is a relatively unchanging tone lasting usually just a couple of seconds. Types 2 and 3 last longer and include tonal jumps. Normally wails are given in a series of five to twenty calls.

The wail conveys a general message of interaction which varies by context. However, in almost any circumstance, the wail results in a response wail and in the two calling loons coming closer together. The wail is the call of choice when a loon on the nest wants to exchange places with its mate. Many careful loon watchers observing loons on a small lake have seen one loon fly off to a nearby lake while its mate remains to incubate the eggs. Later, the sitting loon wails and its mate calls back from the other lake. Only minutes later, the absent loon flies back attesting to the power of the wail—in both distance and in meaning

Adult loons give the wail to find chicks which have become separated from their parents. Similarly, members of a mated pair often wail to each other when they become visibly separated in their territory.

According to Lauren Wentz, once an Ohio State University graduate student researching the meaning of nocturnal chorusing of loons in Michigan's Upper Peninsula, the wail is almost always the call that opens an evening of loon music.

The bottom line is that wails are the calls used to contact other loons and they work for contacting people as well, penetrating human consciousness to the deepest levels.

What would our northern lakes be without this mournful cry of the wilderness?

THE YODEL

Listening to the yodel call of the common loon is a twilight zone experience. Sigurd Olson describes it as "the weirdest and wildest of calls . . . beautiful and thrilling . . . maniacal and blood-curdling." He even spelled it for us— "a-a-whoo-queee'queee-wheoooo'queee," but drew the line at trying to interpret the endless variations of the yodel. In 1950, Olson believed that task was impossible. In the 1980s, with modern equipment, researchers are trying. Because it can be used to identify individual loons, the yodel has opened new horizons in contemporary loon research. The audiospectrographs of a given loon's yodel

Only males perform the yodel call as a warning to other loons.

calls give one-of-a-kind voice prints. After studying yodel audiospectrographs of the same loon from different years, Barklow is convinced that a loon's yodel does not change over time, which provides researchers with the acoustical equivalent of bird banding.

For a species as difficult to capture and tag as the loon, this capability represents a major breakthrough in loon research. Other birds with unique individual calls include the chickadee, the indigo bunting, the white-throated sparrow and the song sparrow. Whether loons can recognize other loons as individuals is uncertain, but such recognition could serve a potentially valuable purpose by reducing aggression between neighboring pairs.

The yodel is the only loon call claimed by a single sex; it's given only by the male. Once field researchers see a loon giving the yodel call, they then can look for subtle plumage or behavioral variations to give them some needed help in field identification of the sexes. Ed Miller, a professor from Governors State University near Chicago, has worked on loon vocalizations for many years in the Wisconsin-Michigan border country near the Sylvania recreation area, a wonderful mosaic of lakes and forests. Aided by his field experience, he can distinguish one male from another without the aid of any equipment, and like other scientists, is convinced that the yodel call is exclusive to the male.

The message of the yodel has been fairly well defined—it is the loon's territorial imperative. Barklow calls it the "attack" message which conveys an aggressive message to nearby birds. During territorial confrontations, the yodel is frequently used in what Barklow calls "counter-singing."

Loons can hear the flight calls of invaders long before seeing them.

Imagine two boys shouting across their parents' property lines and you've got the picture. When males are involved in this singing match, the female on the territory will often support her mate with wails and tremolos. Even after the battle for turf is over, the resident male will often continue to yodel for an hour or more. While the use of the yodel peaks in early June, corresponding with incubation, yodels are heard throughout the summer. The yodel is most predictable when an intruding loon approaches another loon's territory, stimulating yodels seventy-five percent of the time, according to Barklow.

Several field researchers have mentioned that one stimulus always seems to provoke a yodel—a small low-flying airplane. Doing vocalization studies in northern Wisconsin, Rob Denkhaus, a University of Stevens Point graduate student, and Jim Pierce, Coordinator of Wisconsin Project Loon Watch, were having trouble getting yodels, often waiting hours to record one. They found a solution when they went to the Ashland airport (not quite the size of O'Hare) and recorded small planes taking off. Bingo. Yodel calls, and only yodel calls, responded to each playing of the airplane tape.

The yodel has considerable variability. Middle sections of the call can be repeated reflecting the intensity of the call and the strength of the stimulus. In his audiospectrographs, Barklow sees as many as eight of the middle units repeated, creating a call as long as six seconds. By contrast, the familiar call of the chickadee lasts only a second. He believes the longest yodels, and consequently the most heated loon discussions, occur during night chorusing.

extended horizontally. Usually the confrontation ended quietly with the intruding bird casually swimming away. This territorial defense did not always extend to non-paired, single birds. Rummel and Goetzinger often watched unmated birds pass freely through territorial waters.

While the yodel is almost always given in territorial encounters, loon occasionally give it at strange times. A few scientists have heard loons give the yodel in flight and Paul Strong watched a male loon give the yodel repeatedly from the nest while sitting on eggs that were in the process of hatching.

The yodel is also used to settle non-territorial disputes during summer flocking periods. While loons are social, they have their limits; the yodel is a handy signal to tell other loons to "back-off."

THE HOOT

This one-note call sounds just like it reads if you go softly on the "t." Frequently used but not often reported because it is a quiet, intimate call, the hoot is used mainly between family members and may serve an "I'm O.K./are you O.K.?" function. Barklow terms the hoot a location call, letting the mate or chicks know the sender's whereabouts. It is often used by adults to bring the chicks in close for feeding.

The most common occasion when hoots are given is during social interactions among groups of adult loons. A flock of a dozen or so loons swimming peacefully together often produces what can best be described as a tin whistle concert of hoots of various pitches and volumes.

Other conversational sounds from loons include what Judy McIntyre calls the "mew" call. This call comes close to the soft cry of a human baby and is primarily used to communicate with chicks. McIntyre has heard adults luring the newly hatched chicks off the nest with the call. I recall first hearing the sound in 1980 during a September canoe trip. While watching an undisturbed adult and two nearly full-grown young, I heard frequent cries, like a gull but softer.

NIGHT CHORUSING

The full loon repertoire can best be appreciated during night chorusing. Early in the summer season, mid-May to mid-June in most regions, loons talk a good part of the night, using mainly the tremolo but also the wail and yodel. Of the many moments of loon magic, these are special. On the first night of a trip in May of 1970, I camped with three friends at Saganaga Lake right on the Minnesota-Canadian border. The calling began at sunset and lasted well into the night, and it will stay with me a lifetime. On an island in the middle of this sprawling border lake, we were surrounded and we surrendered. Sigurd F. Olson described in his book *The Singing Wilderness* an evening of night chorusing on Lac la Croix, a similar lake

Two other scientists have taken a close listen and look at the yodel. Lynda Rummel and Charles Goetzinger have studied common loons in Algonquin Provincial Park north of Toronto and on Press Lake in the Kenora District of Ontario. They view the yodel as a total audio-visual display in which the call is only half the show. The other half is a posture—the loon's hunching down low in the water with its neck and head horizontal to the water and the bill tipped up slightly. After giving the yodel call, loons bring their heads back to the alert position with the neck raised and head high. Rummel and Goetzinger's observations support Barklow's view of territorial connections. They often watched a defending loon begin a yodel exchange with the intruding bird. While yodeling, the defender faced the intruder directly with wings cocked and about thirty miles to the west of the site of our Saganaga symphony:

> *That night it was still, and in the moonlight the loons began as I had heard them before, first the wild, excited calling of a group of birds dashing across the water, then answers from other groups until the entire expanse of the lake was full of their music. We sat around until long after dark and listened, but instead of becoming quiet as the moon went high, the calling increased and there again was the wild harmony, the music that comes only once a year, when it is spring on Lac la Croix.*

Sigurd T. Olson, Sig's oldest son, was probably with his father that night, although there were too many similar nights to know for sure. Years later, after his formal study of loons at the University of Minnesota, Sig Jr. offered a couple of generalizations regarding loon choruses: choruses are restricted to spring and early summer and dusk to dawn, and they include most loons in the area. Olson's early observations have been supported by recent research by Lauren Wentz who identified 9:30-10:30 p.m. and 3:30-5:00 a.m. as the peak chorusing time periods. Her studies at Michigan's Sylvania recreation area indicate that chorusing occurs from ice-out until the end of June. Most likely the role of these extravagant audio-displays is linked to territoriality; Barklow has observed pairs of loons going to the middle of their territory before joining the choir, perhaps to stake out their aquatic turf and perhaps to protect their mates from the unwelcome advances of other loons.

Calling at night is natural for loons. While the rates aren't lower, the conditions are perfect for long distance communications. Judy McIntyre points out that during the day loons can use visual cues, wing flaps for instance, to communicate, but at night they have only calling to keep in touch. During a two year study of loons in the Minnesota-Ontario border country, Jim Titus heard the peak of evening chorusing occur between the third week of May and the first week of June. (An association with nesting and related territorial defense is probable.) Titus described in his doctoral thesis a typical evening chorus: the first call is usually a wail, followed quickly by tremolos and an occasional yodel with calls spreading to every nearby loon until an area for miles around was "permeated with an orchestration of loon sounds."

Titus believed loons throughout his entire sixty-four square mile study area participated in the same chorus. While no one knows for sure how far loon calls carry, Sjolander and Agren estimated that the yodel of the yellow-billed loon can be heard by people for up to five miles. But here we are concerned with the hearing ability of loons, a more complicated unknown. Whatever the listening range of evening chorusing, all loon watchers should make a late spring trip to high-density loon country, like Minnesota's Boundary Waters Canoe Area Wilderness, Ontario's Quetico or Algonquin Provincial Park. The traveler will be rewarded with music that will echo in memory for a lifetime.

A TIME TO LISTEN

It is difficult to believe that the loon's incredible range of sounds come from a simple organ, the syrinx, in the lower part of the windpipe. So much music, so much meaning. Is it all territorial instinct or could loons be calling, partly at least, to express joy? I've never counted calls during a frenzied evening chorus. Each loon must call hundreds, if not thousands, of times. Could each call have a biological function? Most scientists would answer "yes," "probably" or "we don't have adequate data."

A traditional Ojibwa, Delores Bainbridge would answer the question with a definite "no." She hasn't studied loons, but she knows loons. When an undisturbed loon, for no apparent reason, holds forth with a half-dozen beautiful wails, she knows that the loon is talking not only to other loons, but also to every other animal, including human, willing to listen. Humans in particular should listen carefully. In 1939, Edward H. Forbush suggested the loon's call seemed " . . . wailing and sad as if he were bemoaning his exile from his forest lake." Little did Forbush know that about half of a century later, loons would be missing from many of his favorite eastern haunts. It's time to listen.

The faster and louder the tremolo, the more distressed the loon.

Loons arrive on their nesting grounds as the ice melts away.

To anyone who has spent a winter in the north and known the depths to which the snow can reach, known the weeks when the mercury stays below zero, the first hint of spring is a major event. You must live in the north to understand it. You cannot just come up for it as you might go to Florida for the sunshine and the surf. To appreciate it, you must wait for it a long time, hope and dream about it, and go through considerable enduring.

—Sigurd F. Olson, 1957

Northward Bound

For people who spend their winters in the north, spring is a precious season. In March there are always days when the mercury creeps up to fifty or sixty causing the snow on the south-facing slopes to retreat in panic. But the next day often brings bitter winds, more snow, and disappointment to birds and people waiting for spring. Later, many migratory birds may be lured north by April's promise, only to freeze or starve in a misplaced blizzard. Not loons. When they come north, winter can be safely forgotten.

Loons seem to know exactly when their northern nesting lakes open. Often they arrive on the very day of ice-out. What pushes them north at precisely the right time? Is there animal ESP working here? Some telepathy between loons and year-around avian residents—owls, perhaps—telling loons the lakes are cracking and soft, calling them northward? Most scientists call this amazing timing "instinct," but that only names a fascinating mystery.

THE MYSTERIES OF MIGRATION

Most birds participate in this mystery. Of the 215 species nesting in Michigan, for example, only twenty including grouse, quail, owls and woodpeckers accept winter's full challenge. In Canada and the northern United States, about two-thirds of all species here in the summer are gone in the winter. The spectacular migratory flights of ducks, geese and other waterfowl are seasonal milestones. For most waterfowl the journey is relatively short, often a thousand miles or less. For other birds a thousand miles is just a small step in the journey. The tiny barn swallow flies from Argentina to the Yukon and the globetrotting arctic tern makes a one-way trip of 11,000 miles every spring and fall.

A comprehensive understanding of the migration of birds has stubbornly eluded even the most sophisticated and persistent efforts of scientists. In some ornithological laboratory, scientists are probably debating right now the various theories of bird migration. There is no shortage of theories.

One theory postulates a system of orientation by the sun, giving birds the equivalent of a built-in solar compass. But many birds, including loons, often fly at night. Well, then, how about the theory that birds orient themselves by the stars? In the late 1940s, German ornithologist Gustav Kramer discovered that starlings in cages properly oriented themselves on clear nights but were totally disorganized on cloudy nights. Using a planetarium as a laboratory, Kramer's colleagues later refined this navigation-by-the-stars theory.

Studying migration at night has always been tricky. For years the best a birder could do was to watch for silhouettes across the face of the moon or send a powerful beam of light into the sky. Those techniques provided limited information. After World War II, a new era in migration studies unfolded—radar ornithology. Although designed for finding enemy aircraft, radar also found birds, and uncovered a wealth of information: night migration peaks at midnight and gradually falls off until dawn; night fliers apparently fly low, around 3,000 feet, and ignore ground features such as rivers, lakes or valleys, but fly in a straight path.

Working out of Point Reyes Bird Observatory in California, Kenneth Able modified some Korean War vintage tracking radar, giving him the ability to follow individual birds over a wide flight path. On clear nights, he "watched" birds orient themselves in predictable migratory directions, but on nights with thick cloud cover he saw migrating birds fly with the wind even if it pushed them off their traditional migratory pathways. So the stars probably do play a role, but so does the wind.

The earth's magnetic field might also be involved. This theory emerged in 1855 and still claims followers. Experiments at Cornell University in the late 1960s revealed that pigeons with magnets on their backs were unable to find their home lofts and scattered at random when released. Pigeons with identical but non-magnetized bars on their backs returned directly to their lofts. This theory covers the successful migratory flights in dense fog or heavy rains where neither sun, stars nor wind could be involved.

It is safe to conclude that no single orientation system guides birds. Many cues are employed, possibly involving interplay among several orientation systems. The migratory debate will probably continue for many loon lifetimes, keeping migration a mystery beyond the reach of science.

While little is known about the "how" of migration, even less is known about the "why." If birds like it so well in South America, Mexico, or off the warm United States coastal waters, why don't they just stay there? They don't make trips of a thousand or more miles just to please northern tourists. Again, lots of theories. It is likely that the ice age pushed birds from their original northern breeding areas. When the glaciers receded some 20,000 years ago, descendants started returning to their ancestral homes. This approach, however, does not explain migration patterns in tropical areas. Competition provides one general answer to

the question of why birds don't live in the lands of perpetual sunshine. In tropical areas, bird densities are high. Birds of all description are forced to compete for the available food resource. Even in paradise only so many birds can be fed. In the broad northern temperate regions, competition is less severe. During the critical nesting and chick rearing period, birds in less crowded northern climes can find plenty of food and much more room. The availability of an abundant resource, insects in particular, in northern climes is the other general answer. For many species, the risks of two annual migrations are outweighed by the lure of unlimited food, limited competition by year round residents, and the high probability of producing young.

HEADING NORTH

For loons in particular, the trip north in spring makes a lot of sense. There are far fewer stresses and dangers on the northern nesting lakes than on the coastal waters. Disease, pollution and violent storms are not as devastating in northern Minnesota or Maine as they are off the Florida coast. In fact, loon mortality on the summer nesting range is minimal. Of Wisconsin's roughly 3,000 loons, only five or six dead loons are found each summer.

Recent studies indicate that East Coast loons start moving northward while still on Atlantic coastal waters and gradually work their way up the coast prior to overland migration to the breeding areas. While large numbers of loons winter off Florida's Atlantic Coast, these loons leave by the first of April.

While movements of loons on the West Coast are not as well studied, it appears a similar pattern of gradual migration is at work. Large numbers of loons, mainly Pacific, start leaving southern California coastal waters in March. Guy McCashie, California editor for *American Birds*, talks to birders who see "tens of thousands" of loons pass some coastal points within a given week in early spring. Between March and May of 1977, one observer at Goleta Point just north of Santa Barbara counted 22,768 Pacific loons, 4,355 red-throated loons and 3,891 common loons in just sixty-eight hours of observation. This river of loons, which probably winters in Mexican coastal waters, will not reach their probable Alaskan breeding areas until late May or early June.

Most lakes in loon country open in mid-to-late April, but in Alaska, and most of Canada, ice cover on the larger lakes is not unusual during the first week of May.

In 1950, Sigurd Olson first identified the overland, "drifting northward," migratory behavior in loons that remains well accepted today. Common loons do not take off from the Florida coast in March and fly directly to

Loons are capable of flying over 90 miles per hour.

Ontario, Michigan, Maine or any other nesting area. As ice recedes, they follow any open water, stopping to fish and rest, moving slowly northward. How else could loons hit the ice-out dates so accurately?

Olson also discovered that open lakes in central Minnesota held loons several weeks prior to the opening of the far northern lakes. In April and the first week of May, about twenty-five loons were present on Como Lake, right in the center of St. Paul. By May 6, all were gone. Centerville Lake, another early opening Minnesota lake just north of St. Paul, had about 300 loons in late April but none after May 6. Similar reports have come from other northern states. In 1977, Gary Zimmer, a University of Wisconsin-Stevens Point loon researcher, observed sixty loons in early spring on the Wisconsin River, always an early opening river. They stayed for three days before moving on.

LOON SCOUTS

Perhaps loons utilize a "scouting" system with some birds traveling to the north, checking out the conditions and reporting back. The New Hampshire Loon Preservation Committee office has received numerous reports of loon tremolos heard in early spring when local lakes are still frozen. "I believe they're flying overhead," explains former Committee director Jeff Fair, "perhaps on reconnaissance flights, checking for open water. I've seen them flying myself." While the scouting theory is speculative, it would provide loons with a mechanism for their otherwise uncanny ability to land on northern lakes often within hours of ice-out. When Sigurd Olson paddled into Knife Lake, a large wilderness lake in the Quetico-Superior Canoe Country, just two days after ice-out, he found loons waiting for him.

For loons, capable of flying over 90 mph, distance is not a major obstacle. At that speed a loon could travel from a "base camp" in the open waters of the southern Midwest to the northern nesting lakes in just a few hours. These flight speeds are impressive. Ducks and geese, by contrast, migrate at only 45 to 60 mph. Loons do hurry the spring migration. But then, they have to. Their early arrival to northern lakes is likely related to the brevity of the summer season. To secure a territory, find a nest site, lay and incubate eggs, care for chicks and get the juveniles flying before ice sets, the adults have few days to waste. The loons' arrival is probably geared to the ice conditions, not the calendar. If lakes open early, loons will usually arrive early.

That proposition holds up well in most, but not all, of loon country. It seems some of New Hampshire's loons are a bit tardy. As a former director of the New Hampshire Loon Preservation Committee, Scott Sutcliffe kept close track of spring arrivals. Loons there returned an average of nine days after the ice left New Hampshire's scenic lakes. Sutcliffe believes the short distance from New Hampshire's lakes to ice-free, oceanic wintering areas could be a factor in the late arrival.

MIGRATORY ROUTES

The migratory routes of loons do not parallel the "regular" waterfowl routes. For mid-continent loons, there is not, for example, a Mississippi or an Eastern loon flyway. Rather, according to Judy McIntyre, there are multiple land routes. She notes that some Minnesota loons arrive via the Mississippi, while others cross into the state from Wisconsin, and still others fly up the center of the state. Loons heading north of the Great Lakes migrate in a general northwesterly direction.

McIntyre does see some evidence, though, for two distinct eastern North American breeding populations, one wintering on the Atlantic and the other on the Gulf Coast. The Atlantic Coast loons would gradually move north up the eastern seaboard until April when the birds would move

Splash-down on a northern lake.

overland to northeastern states, like New Hampshire, Vermont, New York and Maine, and to Quebec and northeastern Ontario. The Gulf Coast loons would begin migrating in March and fly to Minnesota, North Dakota and possibly Wisconsin or the central Canadian provinces. While more research is required to support this hypothesis, it does offer an interesting framework for studying migration patterns. Loons wintering on the Pacific also take overland flights. During spring migration loons have been observed in Rocky Mountain states like Utah, Wyoming, and Montana.

WELCOME TO PARADISE

The eastern end of Lake Superior is an ideal place to study migrating common loons. Imagine seeing a thousand common loons in a single day. Volunteers at the Whitefish Point Bird Observatory in Michigan's Upper Peninsula don't have to: they counted 1,882 loons on May 8, 1982. In the peak hour of 8:00-9:00 a.m., volunteers recorded 740 flying loons. One hour. According to David Ewert, coordinator of the annual count, 4,838 loons were observed at the site between April 23 and June 6 with seventy percent of the total sighted during the four-day period of May 7 to 10. Whitefish Bay on the "big lake" is a natural loon funnel. Nearly all of these loons are northbound birds. Before passing Whitefish Point, these loons may leave favorable feeding and resting areas in northern Lake Michigan or Huron. Departures of loons from these areas an hour or two after sunrise would account for the heavy flow over Whitefish Point in the 6:00-10:00 a.m. time period. Research is continuing at Whitefish Point to pinpoint the migration pathways.

The work of Ewert and other volunteers has generated some valuable migration data. While most loon observers refer vaguely to loons migrating alone or in small groups, Ewert gives specific information. Of 180 random observations of passing loons, the Whitefish Point volunteers recorded 104 individual birds, thirty-seven groups of two, twenty groups of three, ten groups of four, five groups of six, and four groups of between eight and eleven loons. The mean size of migrating groups was 1.91. Counting gets tough, Ewert recalls, on those days in May when loons pass in an "almost continuous stream."

Looking at a number of possible weather variables, Ewert found no strong relationships between wind direction or speed, cloud cover, temperature or barometric pressure and loon migration patterns. In contrast to other published reports, he did see loons flying against strong headwinds. Heavy rain or fog, however, apparently puts loons down. The Whitefish Point volunteers saw little or no migration activity during periods of heavy rain or dense fog. During light rain or moderate fog, loons appeared to fly at lower heights than during clear weather conditions. Loons generally fly higher over land than water. At inland sites in New York, Paul Kerlinger located loons by radar at altitudes of 7,000 feet, their ascent presumably aided by thermal currents.

Even for permanent residents of loon country, seeing a thousand loons is probably the work and pleasure of a lifetime. Seeing a thousand loons in a single day would be the experience of a lifetime for many. Pull out your Rand McNally and find Whitefish Point. It's just a bit north of Paradise, Michigan. Check your map. Dave can use a little more help.

A loon patrolling its territory at sunrise.

Adult loons are aggressive in their territorial defense.

The remote, spruce-edged lake shown under the cold, bright moonlit spring night; a gray crust, the last remains of winter's ice, glittered along the lake's shore. Abruptly the silence was broken by loud wails, yodels, eerie cries and splashing of water. It was our first signal that the loons had arrived back from their winter sojourn in the south, ready for another season.

—David Ewert, 1983

Aquatic Turf

Announcing their arrival on the northern lakes with yodel calls, common loons waste little time in establishing their territory. Most scientists believe the male (only the male gives the yodel call) arrives first, a few days to a week before the female. In the southern part of the loon's breeding range in the northern United States, the disparity between the arrival of the pair is greatest. In the far North, particularly during years with late ice-out dates, the pair may arrive on the same day. There is great variability among years and areas. For some unknown reason, on certain lakes in Maine, Minnesota, Ontario, and Wisconsin, the pair arrives around the same time almost every year.

There is a growing body of scientific evidence to support the long-held belief that most loons return to the same territories each year. Judy McIntyre was the first to document an adult loon she had caught and banded the year before on the same lake in northwestern Minnesota's Roseau Wildlife Area. Since her discovery in the early 1970s, a number of researchers throughout Canada and the United States have observed banded loons on the same lakes year after year. Much of this work has been done in northeastern Wisconsin and Michigan's Upper Peninsula. In the mid-1980s, Jerry Belant, then a graduate student at the University of Wisconsin–Stevens Point, along with Wisconsin DNR biologists John Olson and Jeff Wilson banded several loons on the large Turtle-Flambeau Flowage. In the early 1990s, Dave Evers, a University of Minnesota graduate student, banded hundreds of loons across Wisconsin and the U.P. While their findings largely supported the territory fidelity hypothesis, they found that loons didn't always return to the same lake or territory, occasionally choosing new lakes and/or mates.

So, is it your loons that come back to your lake each spring? Perhaps, and most likely yes. The romantic notion of annual fidelity to mate and lake needs to be tempered with a bit of reality, but not so much that the magic is lost.

THE PAIR-BOND

After establishing a territory, the male waits for the arrival of a potential mate. Recent findings suggest that the nest site itself is the magnet which brings individual loons together. If the pair-bonding alone between loons were strong enough to ensure the annual spring reunion, it should also be strong enough to keep loons together on the fall migration and coastal wintering range, but it doesn't. Loons generally do not migrate as mated pairs, nor do they spend the winter together. When he was director of the New Hampshire Loon Preservation Committee, Scott Sutcliffe noticed that loon pair-bonds gradually disintegrated as the season progressed. By the time the birds congregated in fall, he noticed little typical pair behavior. These are strong arguments for the breeding-site-affinity argument. So perhaps it's not each other they love; maybe it's home sweet home.

With birds there are no firm rules about the duration of the pair-bonds. For grouse, the attachment lasts about as long as copulation—a couple of minutes. The ruby-throated hummingbird's family ties last only a few days. For the majority of perching birds, however, togetherness extends through the breeding season. Many large birds such as swans, geese and cranes mate for life. While most pair-for-life birds find another mate if the first mate dies, some are known to wait several seasons before mating again.

Two resident loons defend against three invaders.

The bonds between birds can be strong. In 1901, W. H. Hudson, an English writer and naturalist, observed a female goose with a broken wing walking in the direction she should have been flying. Another goose, presumably the mate, was flying overhead, returning often to keep in contact. Together they moved southward on a doomed but touching expedition.

There would be significant biological advantages (particularly the familiarity with a territory and its food supply) if loons did return to the same nest site each year. After all, fishermen always return to familiar waters. To test the theory, Paul Strong, when he was a loon researcher at the University of Maine in Orono, placed barricades in front of "traditional" nest sites to make access to the sites quite difficult. He discovered that some loons, when they arrived later that spring, actually nested adjacent to his barricades. While he could not be certain that these loons nested on the sites in previous years, he could conclude that they demonstrated an unusual preference for a particular site. While Strong, a careful scientist, limited his conclusions, his experiment adds strength to the argument that most loons do return to the same territory each spring.

Evidence also exists for the theory that a site which looks good to one loon will look as good to a different loon. Judy McIntyre watched two pairs of loons prove this point. After the nesting season, both members of one pair were killed. The following spring another pair of loons nested on the exact site used the year before. Lakeshore residents, unaware of the death of the previous year's pair, probably thought "their" loons had returned again. Look-alike loons can easily create confusion.

What does look good to loons? What is happening in the central nervous system of a loon coming north for the first time? Since two or three years of living on coastal waters would cloud any "memories" it might have of its natal home, the loon would know nothing about selecting nesting sites.

The flying loon is armed only with instinct—a powerful, if mysterious ally which "tells" a loon that three things are needed to make a productive territory: an adequate food resource with water clear enough for foraging; a protected nest site close to water; and a place nearby to rear chicks, preferably a shallow bay sheltered from the wind.

TERRITORY SIZE

Loon territories vary greatly in size. In northern Minnesota, Sigurd Olson identified territories ranging in size from small bays of fifteen acres to entire lakes of a hundred acres or more. On very large lakes, territories were defined by natural boundaries such as islands or long points. The first judgment call for a young male returning north and sizing up potential territories is a simple one of size—is the lake big enough? Although it's unusual, there are records of loons successfully nesting on lakes of ten acres. There is even a confirmed 1984 report of a pair successfully nesting on a northern Wisconsin lake of only 1.3 acres. So the old claim that loons need a quarter of a mile of wet runway just doesn't hold water.

Even though early loon researchers observed loons flying off their home lakes to presumably feed and socialize with loons on other lakes, it wasn't until the late 1980s that we had the first evidence of loons claiming and defending more than one lake for their home turf. Ed Miller, a professor at Governors State University in northern Illinois, had been spending his summers near Land O' Lakes, Wisconsin studying loons for several years. In 1986, he and one of his students, Timothy Dring, discovered that a male loon whose yodel they had voice-printed on a small lake, was also defending two other nearby small lakes. Later that same summer, they documented another similar event, but this time the male loon being observed defended a small lake on which he and his mate nested and a small bay which was part of a large lake just across a county road from the nesting lake. So, lake size is important, but the proximity of lakes also appears to play a role in which lakes will be occupied by loons.

Just how much water a loon pair requires depends upon many variables including the quantity of available prey. For field scientists, estimating territory size can be tricky. If there are several pairs of loons on a large lake, a researcher is tempted to simply divide the number of territorial pairs into the lake's total acreage. That number reveals the space available to each pair but does not give true territory size. For example, on New Hampshire's larger loon lakes, each territorial pair has about 475 acres to roam, while in northern Minnesota each pair has seventy-two acres. A study by K. S. Yonge indicated that each loon pair in east-central Saskatchewan has only forty-three acres of available space. The territories of New Hampshire loons are not really ten times larger than those of Saskatchewan birds. There is simply more water in between territories, empty space available for loons that just aren't there. In the high loon density areas of Minnesota and Saskatchewan, it is evident that loon territories cannot be larger than an average of seventy-two and forty-three acres respectively, assuming territories do not overlap. Also, some room has to be allowed for the unmated loons on the lake. An important variable in the territory size discussion is the lake configuration. Highly convoluted lakes can support many more loons than round lakes of the same acreage. The additional shoreline area means more food because loons feed primarily in productive, shallow-water areas. Don't ever expect loons to be as abundant as robins, which require only about one-half acre to sustain a family. By the same token we can expect to see more loons than bald eagles, which require nearly 2,000 acres of territory, or golden eagles, which need ten times that space.

WHAT KIND OF LAKE?

Just any lake is not good enough for loons. They need more than water to survive, yet pinning down the critical factors in loon habitat is difficult. Loons live on shallow lakes with emergent vegetation, on deep lakes with no vegetation, on lakes with many islands, on lakes with no islands, even on lakes with no fish at all. The popular view of loons as creatures only of cold, deep-water lakes in the heart of the wilderness just doesn't fit the facts. Defying that stereotype, loons nest right on the edge of metropolitan Minneapolis, in central Massachusetts on the Quabbin Reservoir and in southern Michigan right down to the Indiana border, all unlikely places for this symbol of wilderness.

Ironically some of the likely places—the big, deep, clear and cold lakes of the far north—have limitations. Many of these lakes have short, simple food chains; so while they often have large fish, they often do not have many fish. The productivity and diversity of many northern wilderness lakes is actually considerably less than that of the typical shallow, warm-water lakes on the southern edge of loon country. While this does not render these large lakes loon-less, it does imply that loons on these lakes will have large territories.

An ideal loon lake would have clear water and many small fish. But loons are pragmatic and often live on less than ideal lakes. Being flexible in their feeding habits, loons can utilize a broad range of lakes. Even quite shallow lakes with no game fish at all can support loons if there is an ample supply of minnows. In addition to being more productive, shallow lakes allow the loons' prey less room to roam, making escape from a fast-swimming loon a low-odds proposition. Clear water is critical for sight feeders and without it, loons are forced to feed off the bottom, which supplies a less than ideal diet. The loss of clear water, due to human settlement and the subsequent agricultural activities of the nineteenth century, may have been a major factor in this species' retreat to the northern end of its original breeding range.

IT'S MY LAKE

Territoriality is basic. Nearly all higher animals establish and defend their turf, be it wet, dry, or a piece of sky. Probably every bicyclist or runner has encountered the farm dog who owned not just the farmer's yard but also part of the public road. Walk down any rural roadway during the nesting season for blackbirds or grackles and you will start to understand the notion of territory. During July in northern Wisconsin, I've had to forfeit the right-of-way more than once to swooping blackbirds.

The defensive instincts of loons are quite evident; they don't enjoy the company of other waterfowl, especially during the nesting season. There are many reports of common loons attacking mallards that come a little too close, including one from biologist Jim Titus who on three occasions in northern Minnesota watched loons chase merganser hens with broods. In New Hampshire, Tudor Richards, a former Executive Director of the New Hampshire Audubon Society, observed an immature common loon attack four white-winged scoters. The loon "stalked" the scoters with a slow, low profile approach, then made an underwater rush. There were no injuries except perhaps to avian pride.

A dramatic account of a loon attacking another bird was reported in the ornithological journal *Auk*. According to Jones and Obbard, an arctic loon approached the nest of a Canada goose. As the gander moved out to meet the intruder, the loon savagely attacked the larger bird. After thirty seconds of "violent splashing and flapping of wings," the goose retreated toward its nest but died en route. An examination of the goose revealed that the loon's bill had penetrated full length puncturing the goose's lung.

Reports of "killer loons" roaming Squam Lake surfaced at a New Hampshire Loon Festival. Several loon watchers on the lake are convinced a group of unmated loons—"the gang of ten"—attacked and killed two loon chicks. After working so hard to protect loons from people, the volunteers on Squam Lake were perplexed by the prospects of protecting loons from other loons.

This aggressive loon behavior should be put into perspective. While it happens, it is not common. According to the New Hampshire Loon Preservation Committee officials, the gang of ten's behavior resulted from the crowding of loons, possibly caused by unusual weather patterns. A better reason is cited by biologist Paul Strong who claims such behavior is simple natural selection. The object of any species is to produce as many surviving offspring as possible. Protecting your own young is a good strategy but equally effective is reducing the young produced by others. This is common throughout the animal kingdom, especially with polar bears, lions and apes. While loons encounter countless thousands of other birds without violent attacks, they can be tricked into aggressive behavior. Rick Newton, a Wisconsin Project Loon Watch staff member, attempted to capture and band loons. To lure loons near the capture area, he placed a simple wood loon decoy near a nest site and then played recorded loon calls. It drove one resident loon over the edge. The loon swam directly to the decoy and began a fierce attack which left the soft pine decoy a little the worse for wear. No loons were banded that day but the intensity of territorial defense was dramatically demonstrated.

Physical battles between loons are rare. Studying loon territorial defense in Ontario's Algonquin Provincial Park, Lynda Rummel and Charles Goetzinger observed fifty-four confrontations between loons. Only two culminated in fighting or chasing and typically the territorial defense was only posturing or bluffing, a technique animals of the same species have been using for millions of years to avoid dangerous battles. Instead, loons will put on a good show, calling, threatening and intimidating.

This behavior is well-developed in many animals. Monkeys and wolves, for instance, have vicious sounding encounters, which usually end quietly when the individuals or groups retreat.

While loons do not rival the howling monkey in intensity of display, they employ a similar behavioral system—protection of territory without direct, physical contact. The loon's ritual defensive behavior is the yodel/crouch, a combination of sound and sight designed to drive away trespassers. When confronted, a loon will raise its head, thrust its body forward, cock its wings and give the yodel call, the basic hostile message. Rummel and Goetzinger have compared this posture to the threat stance of the vulture, an unlikely comparison given our human perceptions of bird beauty, but nevertheless a descriptive one.

Although the vulture position of the common loon is used primarily for territorial defense of the nest area, it has also been observed during the mid-to-late summer social flockings. In these post-breeding flocks, loons apparently still like some privacy and use this display as a signal to "back off." A behavior usually seen only on large lakes, this flocking occurs in a neutral zone between established territories. In these buffer areas large groups of loons often mingle peacefully with only occasional defensive posturing. On Knife Lake in northern Minnesota, Sigurd Olson identified a social area about the size of the three adjacent loon territories, where unpaired loons could wander at will. The territory of a nesting pair, though, is rarely left unguarded. In twenty-nine visits to established territories, Olson found loons on the territory twenty-three times.

Generally the intensity and frequency of the territorial defense increases toward the end of the incubation period and climaxes with the hatching of the chicks. Additional variables are the number and size of other territories on the lake. Studying loons in northern Minnesota, Jim Titus observed territorial defense far more often on large lakes which had many pairs of loons. On small lakes he often heard resident loons use yodel and tremolo calls to warn potential intruders flying overhead that "this lake is taken."

Titus did see evidence of nesting loons tolerating an intruding single loon, especially if the entry were some distance from the nest site. If these intruders were young, non-breeding loons, as he speculated, they would pose no threat to the nesting pair's territory. However, a mated pair of intruders is a different story, and a potential problem arises when recreational disturbance pushes loons into the hostile territory of nesting loons. While defending their nest site, disturbed loons cannot give adequate attention to incubating their eggs or brooding their chicks.

In his spectacular study area around Millinocket Lake in northern Maine, Paul Strong watched loons of a different stripe. The traditional view of territorial defense just doesn't fit these Maine loons. Several thousand hours of observations by Strong produced few sightings of territorial defense displays. Even during incubation and chick rearing periods, Strong often watched several loons casually wander into another loon's territory. Instead of chasing away the intruders, the resident birds just socialized. Strong's problem was often not knowing who was who—the resident and intruding loons behaved in exactly the same fashion. He also saw flocking behavior very early in the season; flocks which sometimes included one or both members of a nearby nesting pair. These observations over several seasons underscore the danger of stereotyping loon or other wildlife behavior.

Ray Anderson, a wildlife biologist from the University of Wisconsin–Stevens Point, observed similar non-aggressive

The classic "penguin dance" posture.

behavior while conducting telemetry studies. He was watching a resident pair (one had a radio transmitter attached to its back, so later identification was definite) with two chicks when a group of four adults swam into the area. The resident loons "stashed" the chicks by escorting them to the shoreline but then proceeded to quietly socialize with the intruders. No defensive displays were given. In fact, there was no behavior to indicate nervousness or stress. Could these loons have been related, even adult offspring of the pair with the chicks? Impossible to say at this point. There is a possibility that something cues loons to defend sometimes but not other times.

COURTSHIP

Like the territorial defense display, the courtship behavior of loons is ritualized. In most animals, specific behaviors of the opposite sex are needed to move things along; the system's signs and signals must be exactly right to prevent breeding attempts between different species. With loons, however, all the evidence isn't in yet. While most scientists are convinced that the wild, frantic displays reported by many canoeists and fishermen are not courtship behaviors, they often disagree on just what is and what isn't courtship behavior.

Even though descriptions of courtship and copulation are rare, scientific literature does provide some insight. Writing in the ornithological journal *Auk,* Jean and James Tate from Cornell University described the courtship of a pair of loons on French Farm Lake in Michigan. They saw no dramatic displays, no over-water chasing, no aerial displays and heard no vocalizations. What they did see they termed "ritualized preening," with the loons often showing their throat patches. They observed bill dipping, head rubbing, tossing up of the head, and simultaneous dives. At times the pair, to the Tates, appeared to dive in perfect synchronization. Copulation occurred on land. The Tates summarized the courtship process as "secretive behavior and unobtrusive displays."

In her doctoral dissertation, Judy McIntyre describes common loon courtship as "simple, aquatic and diurnal." Like the Tates, she reports no over-water chases or aerial displays. In her view, the running and flight displays signal aggression, which could not strengthen the pair bond, and are probably territorial.

McIntyre believes the courtship process involves a combination of displays, including short dives, bill dipping, bill flicking (an abbreviated bill dip), tucking the head low and facing away (an appeasement gesture). She contends that both sexes use the same display while quietly swimming near the shoreline, often giving the soft "mew" vocalization. She believes diving plays a major role in courtship. Both a short, quiet dive and the splash dive were used in most of the courtship sequences she observed.

McIntyre observed copulation on terra firma only, twelve times, involving four different pairs. Her observations divided about evenly into two separate procedures—male on shore first and female on shore first. When the

male was on shore first, he attracted the female with the soft "mew" call, keeping his head low. If the female then approached, he slid off the site and waited until the female arrived on shore. With the female on land, he returned to the site and mounted her. Usually, after copulation, the female stayed on the site, sometimes beginning the first phases of nest building. If the female went to shore first, the process was speeded up. The male followed and mounted immediately. In this sequence nest building activities followed. Post-copulatory displays were not observed.

Sverre Sjolander and Greta Agren observed similar courtship behaviors between yellow-billed loons. They saw shoreline search-swimming but no elaborate courtship and twice they watched the female go ashore with the male following quickly. Copulation required only ten seconds after which the male returned immediately to the water. The female stayed on shore for about three minutes. In the Crex Meadows area of northwestern Wisconsin, at least one pair of common loons did create a little fuss. William Southern observed two loons skimming over the water at varying speeds, striking the surface with their wings, one bird pursuing the other. Southern watched the pursuer overtake and mount the other loon, submerge for about forty seconds and resurface still coupled.

It is very likely that this observation was related to aggression not courtship. The wing-rowing behavior is frequently seen and the apparent copulatory mount was probably an attempt by the pursuer to drown the other loon. It most likely hung-on by grasping the other bird's neck with its bill. As with many other aspects of loon study, however,

it's dangerous to say "always." While some animals do exhibit rigid, stimulus-response patterns, loons quite simply do not. After years of relative obscurity, loon behaviors are today being observed by thousands of interested people. Someone is bound to see something "new." No one should be disappointed.

A loon rotates the eggs before incubating them.

In breeding season loons love the solitude of northern lakes where shores are shaded by fir and spruce and where the still pure water seldom mirrors a human face.

—*Edward H. Forbush, 1939*

Calling It Home

Loons are homebodies. It's one of the things people like best about loons: they can count on seeing their loon in their bay. While loons summer within a restricted territory of perhaps a hundred acres or less, they have for about six weeks in early summer an even sharper focus—the nest site. Except for occasional fishing trips by the non-incubating member of the pair, life during the nesting season revolves around a very small piece of ground and water.

THE NEST SITE

It's not difficult to find loon nests if one starts looking on islands. Of fifty-four nests in one Minnesota study area, fifty were on islands. Similar island preference has been documented in both New Hampshire and Alaska, where seventy percent of all loon nests were found on islands. Loon islands are usually small and have low-lying vegetation and generally loons select the side of the island protected from the prevailing winds.

While islands are the clearly preferred sites on many lakes, loons sometimes choose mainland sites even when apparently suitable islands are available. In a study of five large, wild lakes in northern Maine, Paul Strong noticed loon pairs building nests on the edges of small, slow-moving inlet and outlet streams called deadwaters. One of the nests was more than a quarter of a mile from the main body of the lake. The rate of successful hatching was actually greater for the deadwater nests than for those on islands. Strong speculated that nests removed from the main body of the lake were disturbed less frequently than those on other parts of the mainland or on islands.

The common denominator in nest site selection is proximity to water. Nearly all loon nests are right on the shore's edge. In New Hampshire, Scott Sutcliffe estimated the average distance from nest to lake at sixteen inches. Exactly how far the nest is from water varies, unfortunately, with the lake's water level. A loon pair might start the incubation period with their nest a convenient six inches from water but find their site landlocked if the lake level drops, or flooded if the level rises. One New Hampshire loon pair found their nest eighty-eight feet from water after the lake level dropped. Traveling that distance over land or mud is no small task for birds so poorly adapted for locomotion on land. This loon pair successfully hatched two eggs but, according to a local observer, lost both chicks to a hawk on the long journey from the nest to water. Typically, loons will abandon their nest when dropping lake levels create such conditions, especially if the vertical distance up to the nest has changed dramatically. While loons can push themselves across mud flats, they have great difficulty climbing over obstacles such as exposed rocks or large logs. Problems associated with lake levels are particularly acute on reservoirs where hydroelectric dams raise and lower water levels to meet electric generation demands.

The Nest

Because nests are just small heaps of readily available vegetation, a common loon would never win a prize for either design or construction technique. After one nesting season, Sigurd Olson dissected a few loon nests and could not find a single material common to all the nests. Popular nest materials in his Minnesota wilderness study area were sweet gale, sedges and cedar boughs. Most likely, loons first select a site and then utilize whatever material is handy.

Loons are open-minded in their selection of the exact spot for their nest. Olson observed loons nesting on everything from sedge mats and floating muskeg to gravel bars and bare rock ledges. Often loons will plunk down right out in the open, making no attempt to camouflage their nest. Perhaps being large and aggressive compensates for such indiscreet behavior. However, many loons do build nests in heavy cover and attempt to keep their presence quiet, and such loons probably have greater nesting success.

The loon nest is primitive, indicative perhaps of the loon's ancient heritage. There is no careful interlacing of materials or delicate placement of vegetation. Observing loons construct a nest, Judy McIntyre thought the placement of materials to be careless, a "lucky throw" when something landed in the right place. The loons she watched did not travel for any supplies; they simply pulled materials from within reach. Such an approach limits the physical dimensions of the nest. The largest nest McIntyre found weighed about forty pounds. Not much compared to an eagle's nest which crashed to the ground in Ohio years ago—it weighed over 4,000 pounds. Of course, that nest housed eagle families for about forty years, with each family, no doubt, doing a little custom remodeling work.

Common loons are not as tenacious to old nest sites as bald eagles, but annual nest reuse is the norm. Paul Strong and Jeff Fair compiled data for nest locations of loons on seven large lakes in Maine and New Hampshire over the late 1970s and 1980s. They found that just over half of the pairs used the same nest year after year. Approximately 80-90 percent of the pairs used either the same nest or a site so close by that it could be considered the same nesting area. This held as true for loons on wild lakes in northern Maine as it did on the more heavily developed lakes in New Hampshire.

The nests of the yellow-billed and Pacific loons are used more than one season and are far more substantial. Living on tundra lakes with little relief, yellow-billed and Pacific loons may need larger and consequently higher nests to provide a vantage point in the endlessly flat tundra country.

The nest building of the common loon does not consume a great deal of time. Judy McIntyre watched a pair of loons construct a nest over a four-day period. Recording the time the loons actually worked on the nest, McIntyre clocked the building project at three minutes shy of six hours. The male provided slightly more than half of the avian labor.

Eggs and Incubation

If the nest is neither high and dry nor flooded, loons have a good chance of hatching their eggs. Within a couple of days from the start of nesting, the female will lay her first egg. Observing a common loon lay her egg, McIntyre watched the loon's body rise up and down nineteen times before the egg appeared. Six minutes of what appeared to be voluntary expelling activity was required. After laying the egg, the loon panted and repeatedly opened and closed her eyes during a twenty-minute recovery period. Probably the degree of effort relates to the size of the egg. Loon eggs are quite large. Thirty loon eggs measured by Olson had an average length of 3-3/4 inches and an average diameter of 2-1/4 inches, about the size of the eggs of the white pelican, a larger bird. While their color varies tremendously, even within the same clutch, loon eggs are generally olive-brown with dark brown or black splotches.

Typically, there is a one-day delay before a second egg is laid. Usually loons lay two eggs, but it's difficult to be definitive: a one-egg nest might well be the leftover from a nest which had an unwanted visitor, such as a gull, raven or raccoon. Looking at nests in northern Minnesota, Jim Titus counted seventy-three two-egg nests and fifty-six one-egg nests, roughly the sixty percent/forty percent split suggested by several other biologists. While a few three-egg nests have been documented, they are rare.

The egg or eggs must be incubated for about a month. While most bird books list the loon's incubation period at twenty-nine days, actual incubation time varies greatly.

Common loons usually lay two eggs per clutch.

Scott Sutcliffe observed the incubation of several New Hampshire loons, finding an average incubation period of twenty-eight days with a range from twenty-five to thirty-three days. Recording the incubation periods of four Minnesota loons, Judy McIntyre found an average of twenty-seven days with a range of twenty-six to thirty-one days. (Knowing just when incubation begins is often a judgment call by the observer—it's rare for anyone to actually watch a loon lay an egg.)

While incubating, loons keep their eggs quite warm, around 95° F. While some birds like the penguin have a featherless brood patch, loons have a feathered area of their breast where blood vessels in the skin increase in size during incubation, better transferring the bird's body heat to the eggs. Like nest building, incubation is shared by the pair, a behavior common in birds. A loon pair shares nesting duties about equally. With stopwatch in hand, McIntyre estimated the average incubation bouts for common loons at just over two hours for the males and just under two hours for the females, who typically covered the late evening and early morning shifts. The length of each incubating session does not seem to follow a rigid pattern. Owen Gromme, a wildlife artist, recalls a pair of common loons which changed positions every half-hour; and others have recorded incubation duty shifts at random intervals.

One yellow-billed loon demonstrated an extreme devotion to nesting duty. Sverre Sjolander and Greta Agren watched a yellow-billed loon incubate a clutch for fourteen consecutive hours. They never heard this or any other yellow-billed loon call while on the nest, but common loons often prompt incubation duty changes with vocalizations. Olson remembers one loon that regularly revealed its fatigue or frustration by repeatedly broadcasting a long and mournful wail. After entering the nest, loons usually rearrange things slightly before settling in. On the nest they sit quietly, almost always face open water, and watch alertly with the head and neck extended.

Incubation doesn't appear to be stressful work. All loons need to do is turn their eggs occasionally. With awkward-looking but surprisingly efficient movements, loons turn the eggs at irregular intervals with partly open mandibles. Yellow-billed loons carry this irregularity to its extreme. Sverre Sjolander and Greta Agren recorded egg turnings at intervals ranging from twelve seconds to six hours. The typical turning interval for common loons is about an hour.

When loons are not turning eggs, they are just sitting; as yet, no one has reported a loon napping on the nest. Loons are faithful incubators. In 1919, naturalist Arthur Cleveland Bent commented that incubation " . . . is practically continuous; the eggs are never allowed to cool." Judy McIntyre quantified "continuous" at ninety-nine percent. For each hour of incubation, loons in her studies were off the nest for only thirty seconds. Even in stressful circum-

stances, loons stick to the nest. In her doctoral dissertation on the common loon, McIntyre described a loon, "whose head could be seen crawling with blackflies," patiently sitting on the nest for over nine hours without relief. Trying to keep hordes of blackflies at bay, the loon shook its head an average of once every ten seconds.

The need for such stoic devotion to duty has been questioned by some biologists, citing evidence that loons have successfully hatched their eggs without a continuous incubation effort. During the 1984 nesting season, the common loons on Massachusetts' Quabbin Reservoir were carefully monitored. Between July 1 and August 5, two nesting loons were watched on six occasions with the total observation time exceeding sixteen hours. A loon stayed on the nest for the full observation period on only one of the

If the chicks cannot swallow the crayfish, the parent gladly will.

six visits. On July 29, a day of heavy boat traffic, a loon was on the nest just seventeen minutes during a three-hour watch. Over the entire observation time, the loons were incubating only fifty-five percent of the time, yet the pair hatched two eggs and successfully raised two chicks.

Wisconsin photographer Woody Hagge also watched a pair of common loons break the incubation rules. On an unusually warm day in May a loon pair, though undisturbed, left the nest for several hours. Hagge presumes the departure was prompted by the discomfort of sitting on the nest in the blazing noonday sun. While loons are able to dissipate some excess heat by panting, sitting in direct sunlight could possibly overload a bird's cooling systems. Could it be these loons, with a wisdom acquired over millions of years, knew the eggs were okay? With the air temperature at

80° F, it is possible that the eggs were being incubated adequately by a substitute parent—the sun itself. Of course, the eggs were exposed to potential predation and the same loon wisdom should have encouraged the birds to at least stay near the nest. These loon eggs, by the way, did turn into loon chicks. Many eggs do not.

PREDATION

Predation takes a bite out of loon productivity. In most areas this is a natural part of the loon's life cycle. In some locales, however, predation has been the limiting factor in loon reproduction. On Lake Winnipesaukee up to eighty percent of the lake's egg production has been destroyed by raccoons. In 1975, this seventy-square-mile lake produced just one loon chick, and on nearby Squam Lake, raccoons had about the same success rate. On both lakes, most of the destroyed nests were located within a few hundred yards of homes or other centers of human activity.

People and raccoons go together. Wherever there are people, garbage is not far behind, and behind the trail of garbage will be the friendly masked bandit, whose populations explode when their natural food supply is supplemented by human leftovers. In many resort areas the feeding of raccoons is encouraged because tourists love raccoons. Loons don't. Studying the effects of predation on loon productivity in Minnesota's Itasca State Park, Judy McIntyre found evidence of predation in over seventy percent of the unsuccessful loon nesting attempts. As in New Hampshire, the raccoon was loon enemy number one. Inspecting the nests destroyed by predators, McIntyre could implicate raccoons in seventy percent of the predation cases.

Raccoons, however, are not the only predators. The list of potential egg robbers is long, and includes crows, ravens, gulls, skunks, mink, otter, and possibly muskrat and beaver. Since some of these critters can destroy loon nests without leaving any tell-tale evidence, Judy McIntyre decided to experimentally identify potential predators. She built clever "track traps" by constructing a flat, smooth circle of sand and clay around former or simulated loon nests. In those nests she presented her bait—turkey eggs dyed to match the color of loon eggs. Raccoons loved this Easter egg party, showing up first eighty percent of the time. While this experiment does not prove that raccoons destroy eighty percent of all predated loon nests, it does provide strong circumstantial evidence that raccoons and loons, at least from a loon protector's perspective, don't mix.

Where raccoon numbers are low, as in remote wilderness areas, predation on eggs is not as serious a problem. A 1978 study by the Maine Audubon Society implicated predation in only three of eighteen nest failures. In northern Minnesota's wilderness lakes, Olson found evidence of predation in about half of all loon nests, but he carefully qualified his findings by suggesting that abandonment of the nest might have preceded the predation. If loons leave their eggs, predation at some point is almost inevitable. For a researcher covering a large study area, judging which came first is often speculative.

A quarter of a century after Olson's work, Jim Titus studied loons in the same area. For two years, Titus monitored every loon nest in the study area. Predation interfered with only twenty percent of the nesting attempts. Much lower than predation estimates from New Hampshire, this estimate reflects the relative scarcity of raccoons in the Minnesota wilderness, and explains Titus' data showing no difference in predation rates between island and mainland sites. In raccoon infested areas, islands are relatively safe nesting sites. While raccoons can swim, they rarely bother loons on small islands.

AVIAN PREDATION

Islands do not offer protection from avian predators. Titus believed crows and ravens were the major predators in Minnesota's wilderness areas. He found many loon eggs with puncture marks and even caught one crow red-handed in a loon nest. Believing ravens could actually fly off with a loon egg, Titus and a cooperative raven researcher working a nearby study area devised an experiment. They placed the largest chicken eggs they could find (turkey eggs were apparently hard to come by in northern Minnesota) in simulated loon nests. Then they watched ravens land, pick up a whole egg, and easily fly off. They presumed that ravens could also carry off slightly larger loon eggs. An investigation of raven nests in the area did turn up a positive identification of loon egg fragments. For Titus it explained why he rarely found successful loon nests near raven nests.

Where loons and gulls overlap nesting areas, loons often lose the battle for prime nesting sites. Titus frequently watched gulls harassing loons. In an attempt to protect its own territory, one gull set up house within three feet of an active loon nest; the loons quickly moved out. This could be a sign of the times. In recent years the increased levels of human activity in wilderness areas have provided more food for gulls. During twenty years of canoeing the Boundary Waters Wilderness Area of northern Minnesota and the adjacent Quetico Provincial Park, I have watched gull populations boom. It's not hard to figure out why. Quetico Provincial Park officials have been instructing fishermen to place fish remains on rocks near the shore. While this practice keeps campsites clean, it also creates fast-food stands for gulls. An expanding population is the price for their excellent scavenging services.

The common loon's predation problems are mild compared to those of the Pacific loon. In a two-year study of the nesting success of Pacific loons, Margaret Peterson estimated the nest failure rate at ninety-five percent one year and sixty-eight percent the next. Two avian predators, the long-tailed jaeger and the parasitic jaeger, were responsible.

STICKERS OR FLUSHERS

Loons do not defend against humans. When people approach, loons will quietly slip off the nest and dive to a safe position. Typically, human intrusion does not provoke any displays unless the loon is caught completely by surprise. Some loons sit passively on the nest despite a close approach.

This tendency to sit tight varies greatly among bird species and individuals. The term *flushing distance* is used by biologists to describe a bird's tendency to flee. Trumpeter swans are quite touchy, flushing often at a hundred yards. Great blue herons are idiosyncratic, flushing at distances from fifteen to one hundred yards. Loons are more like great blue herons.

Some loons abandon the nest at the first sign of a person while others refuse to budge even if some biologist is standing over them. Do loons realize their odds of hatching eggs increase if they ignore those funny-looking two-legged animals with long black protruding eyes? That's doubtful. Some loons just have more stick.

Scott Sutcliffe met one loon who was either very tolerant or very stubborn. This bird would not move even as he approached within a couple feet. Maggie McGook is such a loon. Named by Dr. Glenn Irwin, retired physician and loon photographer extraordinaire, Maggie is a classic sticker. Glenn can approach to within two or three feet without disturbing Maggie. While there is no tag on Maggie, Glenn is convinced that she (he knows Maggie is a she) returns to his lake every year.

UNPREDICTABLE BUT PERSISTENT

It's always dangerous to generalize about loons, but after quantifying approaches to hundreds of loons, Jim Titus was able to catalog a few predictable behaviors, including a tendency of loons to flush more quickly if approached within their direct line of vision or if the movements of the person approaching are exaggerated or erratic. He also noticed that in the later stages of incubation loons sit tighter than loons just starting incubation. The most predictable response he uncovered was even more interesting: loons are not predictable at all, demonstrating a wide range of individual differences.

As an eagle passes, the loon flattens down.

Loon eggs are not predictable either. Sometimes, despite adequate incubating, they simply do not hatch. Like many other birds, loons will try again. There are birds, termed indeterminate layers, which will keep laying eggs until some hatch. As an experiment, Arthur Cleveland Bent kept robbing eggs from the nest of a flicker. In forty-nine days, the poor bird laid thirty-seven eggs.

Loons are not that persistent. While they can lay up to four clutches, one re-nest is usually their best effort. And they will re-nest only if the egg or eggs are lost during the incubation period. Once an egg hatches the re-nesting instinct dies.

Loons often move their nest site when they re-nest, especially if predators were involved in the first nest loss. Jim Titus found re-nesting attempts to be less successful than first nests. He believes first attempts are aided by greater nest attachment than later attempts. Titus rarely observed second re-nestings. Only three pairs out of a group of 112 pairs attempted a third nest. Even though the percentage of success is low, re-nesting is important for overall loon productivity. In Olson's study, thirty percent of all chicks hatched came from re-nests. Persistence pays.

Hatching the eggs is not the end of parental duties for loons. Loons take the tasks of caring for and feeding their offspring very seriously. With a month of incubation behind them, loons now look forward to about two months of family-raising responsibilities. A loon's work is never done . . .

A TALE OF TWO NESTS

Loons can hatch some memorable experiences. Ask Bruce Lutz, owner of the Newmann Lake Lodge in Price County, Wisconsin. A pair of Newmann Lake loons put Bruce in a difficult situation. For four years a pair of loons (he presumed the same pair) had nested on a small island. During the spring of 1984, high water levels forced the loons to build a nest about ten yards from their traditional spot. The nest was a good one and an egg was laid. But then the lake level dropped and the loons moved back to their "old" nest site, but naturally were unable to bring their egg along. A second egg was laid in the old, new nest. Two eggs, two nests, but one pair of loons.

The math didn't work too well and apparently the loons were not pleased with their decision. Lutz called Jim Pierce, Wisconsin Project Loon Watch coordinator, to report that the loons were spending a lot of time swimming between the two nests, calling almost continuously. The loons were upset. Lutz was upset.

Jim advised Lutz to wait until the loons settled upon one of the nests before attempting an egg rescue. The loons finally chose their old nest, abandoning the first egg. Then Bruce swung into action. He carefully picked up the abandoned egg, carrying it in a sheet of Saran Wrap, and brought it to the other nest. The loons were very suspicious. For about eight hours they would come near the nest, inspect it but quickly leave. Finally, early in the evening, one of the adults climbed onto the eggs and stayed put. Twenty-eight days later two chicks were hatched. Both survived their first summer. Lutz still enjoys watching loons but hopes his pair has learned to make up their minds about which nest is home. For his sake, as well as theirs.

A fourteen-day-old chick stretches its wings.

Raising a Family

The hatching of loon chicks is a cause for great joy—at least among humans. In New Hampshire, a tradition of celebrating hatchings with birth announcements has caught on, all apparently part of a "loon religion." That's a human response. What loons think, feel, or sense about the end of their incubation period will never be known. Anyway, that's a question for philosophers, not scientists.

The scientific community has, however, answered a lot of questions relating to the hatching and rearing of chicks. Scientists know that loon eggs, usually two, hatch about a day apart. Although it varies greatly by region, hatching dates typically occur during the last half of June. Scientists also know that loon chicks are precocial, being sufficiently developed at hatching to leave the nest quickly. Most ground-nesting birds like geese, ducks, grouse or cranes have precocial chicks, while tree-nesting birds like robins, bluebirds, owls or hawks have altricial or less developed chicks. For tree-nesters there is plenty of time to develop in the safety of a lofty nest. Not so on the ground, where chicks need to move out quickly before some predator stumbles onto the nest.

THE FIRST DAYS

For loon chicks the nest is home for only a very short time. After a half day of drying, chicks are capable of swimming. The first chick hatched will be called into the water with a soft call. After the second chick is hatched and dried, both chicks are lured to the water. Then the nest is abandoned. Usually neither the chicks nor the adults return to the nest, but there are exceptions. In 1984, a seasoned New Hampshire loon watcher observed an adult and a week-old chick climb up onto a nest to spend about ten minutes looking over the place the adult probably knew all too well.

Not all chicks make it out of the nest. During his 1984 field season in Maine, Paul Strong encountered three different nests where the dead chicks were still in their shells. Strong speculates that the pressure to remove the first hatched chick might be strong enough to pull the adults off the nest early, thus abandoning the second chick. Any disturbance after the hatching of the first egg, including natural events such as a heavy rainstorm, could force the adults to abandon the nest and leave the second egg unhatched and fair game for crows, gulls or raccoons. Most loon researchers believe that the productivity of loons is reduced more by the failure of eggs to hatch than by the mortality of hatched chicks. Once hatched, most chicks survive. Scott Sutcliffe monitored the survival rate of New Hampshire loon chicks over a four-year period and found that eighty-four percent of all chicks hatched made it through the summer.

With sooty black down, except for the throat and upper breast which tends to be mouse-gray, a loon chick is a photographer's dream. The best description of young chicks dates back to 1906 when William Beebe, Curator of Ornithology at the New York Zoological Society, received an unusual gift of a one-day-old loon chick and a companion egg which was almost ready to hatch. Beebe was delighted with the opportunity to study birds which had never seen their parents or their natural environment. According to Beebe, the day-old chick pecked at everything and made low peeps much like a barnyard chick. When placed in water, the chick swam without hesitation and pushed its head completely underwater to look around at this new wet world. The chick did not appear to recognize live minnows swimming below, but did eat when fed small pieces of fish held by forceps.

A day after the first chick hatched, the other egg hatched revealing a loon chick sheathed, in Beebe's words, within a fine "hair-like wrapping of tissue" which required about three hours to split off. The chick helped by rolling on its back and scrambling around. At two days, the chicks were eating whole live minnows and each weighed about a quarter-pound. At three days they were preening and using the oil gland at the base of the tail. The only sound in the zoo environment which registered with the chicks was the call of the giant kingfisher. It threw them into fits of excitement, prompting Beebe to speculate that the similarity between the rolling call of the kingfisher and an adult loon's tremolo call stimulated the response. At one week of age the young loons finally captured two dying minnows. A day later the chicks pursued and caught live minnows. In the ninth day of this fascinating experiment, a sudden temperature drop on a chilly New York evening caused the death of both chicks.

Watching loon chicks in the wild is a pure delight. Their early attempts at diving are quite comical. I recall watching three-day-old chicks with their parents on Day Lake in northern Wisconsin. It was like watching diving ping-pong balls. The chicks tried to dive but their buoyancy made them pop right back to the surface. The deepest dive by two day old chicks is about a foot, but within a few days chicks can dive to depths of ten feet.

Once chicks are hatched, adult loons take them to a special part of their territory termed "nursery areas" by researchers. Judy McIntyre first described these in a 1983 article in the *Journal of Field Ornithology*. On her Saskatchewan study lake, she watched adult loons swim a zig-zag pattern from the nest to shallow coves and bays protected from prevailing winds. Judy believes the zig-zag swim imprints the parents on the chicks and has never observed adult loons giving their chicks back rides during this initial movement from the nest. The nurseries McIntyre identified comprised roughly fifteen percent of the loon territories. The bottom, under an average of about four feet of water, tended to be soft and mucky unlike the bottom at the nest site which is usually sand, gravel or rock. McIntyre feels nurseries play a critical role in chick rearing. Artificial nest islands, she suggests, should be placed near a potential nursery area.

According to research conducted in Maine by Paul Strong, nurseries are very identifiable on large lakes with multiple pairs of loons. Similar to McIntyre's results, he found nurseries in shallow coves protected from wind. The nurseries were reused each year during his three-year study suggesting that loons choose these areas carefully. On small lakes, the entire lake may be used as a nursery although near shore areas are used more than deep water areas. Jerry Belant found larger nurseries on northern Wisconsin's Turtle-Flambeau Flowage than Strong or McIntyre did in Maine and Saskatchewan but thought that the loons on that large water body may have been using less than optimal habitat.

Nurseries usually harbor abundant populations of minnows which the adults catch easily and feed to the young chicks. Later, the chicks are able to catch some on their own. Chicks are kept in the nursery areas for two or three weeks. After that, they begin to expand their use of the rest of the territory.

Like just about everything else about loons, use of nurseries varies. Disturbance by people or groups of floater loons or a severe weather event may cause loons to move very young chicks over a mile across a territory.

While most chicks survive, they are vulnerable to the predation of northern pike, muskellunge or snapping turtles from below and hawks or eagles from above. In Wisconsin, nine years of volunteer population surveys have produced numerous reports of eagles attacking, but rarely taking, loon chicks. Woody Hagge, Wisconsin photographer, has a dependable system for spotting eagles: loons tell him when an eagle passes over his lake by giving wild tremolo calls, even if it is well beyond the loons' nesting season.

Parents devote their full attention to newborn chicks.

Loon lover, Joe Anderlik, sitting on the deck of his Flambeau Lake home near Lac du Flambeau, Wisconsin, watched a dramatic encounter between a mature bald eagle and two adult loons. The eagle divebombed repeatedly at the loons who had to escape the eagle's talons by quickly submerging. It is obvious that loons and eagles are not birds of a feather.

THE CARE AND PROTECTION OF CHICKS

Because chicks are quite vulnerable to exposure and fatigue, chilling is a more serious problem than predation. According to McIntyre, body temperatures of chicks are about 7° F lower than the 102° F temperature of adults. This may be an important reason for the lengthy free rides adults give their chicks. Back-riding is a priceless sight seen only in the first few weeks of a chick's life. During the first week, the adults carry the chicks about sixty-five percent of the time. It saves the chick's energy and provides warmth. The free ride also offers the chicks protection from predators and allows the adults freedom of movement. To get on board, chicks often wait for the adult to partially submerge and lift its wings out of the way. To unload the chicks, the adult may dive quickly or rear back, leaving the chicks afloat and maybe a bit surprised. Some observers have watched chicks climb aboard without any help from the adults. Back-riding is not common with most other waterbirds, though grebes do carry their entire brood of three or four chicks at once.

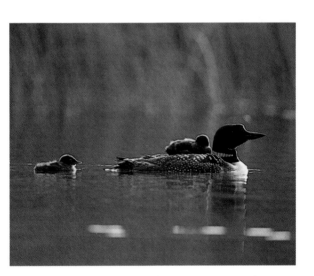
Parents and newborn chicks are never separated.

The care and feeding of loon chicks is a full time vocation for the adults. In a doctoral dissertation on loons, Jack Barr estimated the energy requirements of chicks at eight times those of the adults. While studying yellow-billed loons, Sjolander and Agren watched the adults feed their chicks as frequently as seventy-three times during a single day. About fifteen percent of those feedings involved plant material. During the first twelve days of a chick's life, the two University of Stockholm researchers never saw them farther than six feet from the adults.

Although chicks start looking for fish early, they do not catch many until they are about a week old. Even at three weeks of age, chicks have a capture efficiency rate of only three percent, according to McIntyre. She has observed adults "teaching" fishing techniques to their chicks by dropping an injured fish or minnow in front of the chick.

The feeding of chicks peaks at about two weeks and gradually drops off until the chicks at about eight weeks old can be considered independent.

In 1838, John James Audubon reported loons regurgitating food to feed their chicks. Unless loon behavior has changed since then, Audubon was mistaken. Chicks are fed small, live minnows between a half-ounce to one ounce in size after begging for food by pecking at the base of the adult's bill. Adults often dip the food in the water and splash it sideways before offering it to their young. With captive chicks, Olson discovered that food had to be presented in a similar fashion or the chicks refused to eat. While most food items are presented whole, there are enough observations of young loons being fed fish or invertebrates ripped apart by their parents to make the argument that it isn't all one way.

The early days for loon chicks appear to be easy ones, with time for feeding, riding on the adults' backs loafing, preening and cruising—all with no apparent regularity. Olson once even observed a chick being fed by one adult while freeloading on the back of the other parent. What a life!

The level of parental care is impressive. When Olson captured chicks to mark them for his Minnesota study, the adults would perform spectacular displays, rushing up to within ten to twenty feet of the canoe while giving high-pitched tremolo calls. These protective efforts would last up to three minutes and would be repeated with decreasing intensity over a longer period. When the chicks were released, some parents immediately rejoined them while others offered "wary acceptance," but no chicks were rejected. Olson summed up loon parental behavior as "striking."

Loons are also known to accept orphan chicks. In June of 1980, Wisconsin Department of Natural Resources wildlife biologist Ron Eckstein took a ten-day-old abandoned chick to a pair of loons with one chick. When the chick spotted the other loons, it immediately swam toward the new family. The adults escorted the chick to a nearby shoreline and within one minute the chick climbed on an adult's back, fully accepted. A month later, Eckstein observed the adult loons feeding two healthy chicks of about equal size. This foster parenting role might explain reports of three-chick broods such as the one spotted on Second Connecticut Lake in New Hampshire.

The protection of chicks continues for at least one month and in some cases up to three months. Adults with slow-moving chicks, one week to three weeks old, often employ a distraction display when threatened. If disturbed, the adults will act as decoys, diving to open water and remaining conspicuous while the young lie flat on the water to lower their profile.

This behavior is similar to the broken-wing act of the blue-winged teal. While trout fishing on the Sioux River, a Lake Superior tributary, I encountered a teal flapping her wings and moving upstream just ahead of me. Entranced by her performance, I nearly missed seeing the brood of fuzzy chicks which were swimming quietly downstream tight against the bank, given away only by their "peeps." When I was about fifty yards upstream from our first point of encounter, I watched the teal recover miraculously and fly downstream to rejoin her brood. Female killdeer and ruffed grouse are famous for their performance of similar tricks.

Growing Up

Loon chicks are cute but they aren't always gentle. Loon chicks quickly establish a dominance hierarchy with one chick dominating over the other. During the time Gary Dulin was a graduate student at Central Michigan University studying loons on lakes on Beaver Island in northern Lake Michigan, he carefully documented the establishment of the dominance hierarchy and the eventual effects later in the summer. During the first few days off the nest, loon chicks fight fiercely with pecks to the head and back. The parents will watch calmly from nearby. The chick losing the battle assumes a submissive posture with its head down in the water. This stops the attack, but the submissive chick will often later resume the fighting.

The fighting among the chicks doesn't typically result in any injuries. However, once in a while the fighting goes a bit too far. Lorraine Hunsicker of Wausau, Wisconsin saw two chicks fighting on Virgin Lake in Oneida County. One chick was so aggressive that it drove the other all the way to the opposite side of the lake. Instead of leaving it alone, it came back repeatedly and pecked at it, eventually opening a wound over one eye. Finally, the submissive chick swam into a marshy area and eventually died.

Why all this fighting? It may be related to food. In lean years, the dominant chick gets first choice of food items and ensures its survival. Without the dominance hierarchy, both chicks might be fed equally and neither may survive. It's important to note that the adults do not choose whom to feed. They simply give food to whichever chick comes to them first.

Dulin followed the fate of pairs of loon chicks as well as watching their feeding patterns. The dominant chick was first to an adult approaching with food. Almost always, it took the fish. However, occasionally, it would refuse a large minnow that might be difficult to swallow. The fish would

then be offered to the submissive chick. So, not only do the submissive chicks get less food, but they get the least preferred food items!

The effects of the dominance hierarchy don't usually show up until five or six weeks after hatching. At that time on the study area, several pairs of loons lost one of their chicks. Dulin suspected that the rapid growth of loon chicks at five weeks and the replacement of downy feathers with adult-like contour feathers at the same time created an energy "bottle." Dominant chicks were fed enough to get through this period, but some submissive chicks, perhaps already weakened by their inferior status, perished.

As summer wears on, the chicks require progressively less attention and can catch most of their own food. Not depending any longer on shoreline cover, by August the chicks will roam the entire territory. At ten weeks they are considered juveniles and their downy plumage has been entirely replaced with the drab-colored feathers of typical immature loons.

As with many other aspects of loon behavior, the adult/juvenile bond appears to be variable. As late as September, some juveniles remain with adults. While some juveniles may receive parental attention at this stage, the young loons can care for themselves. A turning point in the relationship between adults and juveniles is the development of flight feathers, which occurs at about eleven weeks of age. At this age, some immature loons leave their natal lake. Although McIntyre saw no young all summer on Lake Itasca in north central Minnesota, eleven juveniles were present by mid-September. She believes immature loons establish "autumn" territories on large lakes, retain distinct feeding areas, and often migrate together in pairs or small groups.

Some Notes on Productivity

Everyone wants "their" loons to hatch a pair of chicks, raise them successfully and go on to do it all over again every summer for the next twenty or thirty years. One biologist/mathematician determined that robins producing their typical two broods of four young each year would be responsible, counting the work of their offspring, for nineteen million robins over a ten-year period. That's a lot of robins.

Using the same concept, but plugging in a different formula because loons only produce two young per year and the offspring don't breed for at least three years, a loon mathematician, assuming reproductive maximums, can project a total of 1,180 new loons over fifteen years. That total assumes several things: the first pair and all their offspring produce two chicks per year, every year; all young mature and reproduce at three years of age (their fourth summer); and none of the loons die.

While there are many factors that prevent populations from expanding in such geometric proportions, the most significant limitation in loon productivity is delayed breeding. Most birds and small mammals will breed within their first year and even large mammals like the white-tailed deer will breed in their second fall. Although the breeding age of loons is not known with absolute certainty, most biologists believe loons are sexually mature in their fourth summer; six years must pass before the first grandloons appear. Many biologists contend this delayed breeding period allows immature loons time to develop the fishing skills necessary to provide proper parental care later, but it certainly affects productivity. To continue their species, loons have to survive three winters in coastal waters where severe stress, disease and pollution cause significant mortality.

The delayed breeding in loons is not uncommon. Albatrosses do not breed until they are five years old and lay only one egg. Many seabirds follow the same principles. It could well be that the low productivity of loons is an evolutionary protection of the loons' food supply.

In addition, the significant number of loons that return north in breeding plumage but don't breed must be considered. There are quite a few territorial pairs that do not attempt nesting and a larger number of unpaired single birds, possibly very young or very old loons. Surveying Wisconsin's loons, Gary Zimmer classified twenty-eight percent of the entire population as non-breeding birds. Studies by Scott Sutcliffe in New Hampshire suggest that loons occupying the same territories each year will attempt nesting only three years in four, but will defend the territory in the off-year. Data from other studies support this theory. Studies in Minnesota and Alberta estimated that about twenty percent of the territorial loon pairs did not nest. Since the original calculation assumed that all three-year-old loons would reproduce, subtraction of at least twenty percent is in order.

Then there are egg loss and chick mortality; eggs and chicks face many dangers from predators. Another ten to twenty percent should be subtracted from the theoretical productivity.

Loons live in a real world, not a mathematical one. The annual productivity of loons is measured as the number of surviving chicks per territorial pair. Obviously that number is not 2.0 with each pair contributing their fullest to the preservation of the species, but is typically within a range of 0.30 to 0.50, or thirty to fifty chicks per 100 pairs of adults. Considering historical data, one may expect 100 pairs of loons in the Boundary Waters Wilderness Area of Minnesota to produce forty-seven chicks; 100 loon pairs in New Hampshire to produce fifty-one loons and 100 pairs in Wisconsin to produce forty-eight chicks. For some areas the productivity is extremely low. In her 1978 study in north central Minnesota, Judy McIntyre found a productivity rate of 0.27, or twenty-seven chicks per 100 pairs.

When all the data on nesting success is reviewed, areas of special interest stand out. If loons are nesting in raccoon country, island locations are clearly more successful. In wilderness areas, however, location is not a factor. Titus found that smaller lakes produced relatively more young than larger lakes. He believed that the effort required to defend larger territories typical of large lakes might help explain the lower success rate. Smaller lakes in his Minnesota study area also had a considerably better ratio of loons to surface area of water: an average of one loon per forty-nine acres in small lakes, compared with one loon per 121 acres in large lakes.

According to Titus' data, the lucky loons are those in two-egg clutches. In his northern Minnesota study, eggs from one-egg nests had a mean of 0.21 chicks surviving per egg while eggs from two-egg clutches had a 0.40 mean

An older chick begs its parent for some fish.

rate of survival. So an egg has double the chance of producing a loon if it happens to have another egg next to it.
While common sense might suggest loons could provide
better incubation and care for a single egg and chick,
common sense doesn't work well on this point. Olson's
results were even more dramatic. Of nineteen one-egg
nests only one succeeded, while fifteen of twenty-two of
his two-egg nests produced chicks. He speculated that
there might be less attachment, and therefore, less care for
one egg than two.

While different studies show slightly different loon
nesting success percentages, the nesting success average is
about forty percent, which isn't bad when compared to
other birds. In a 1979 study, Margaret M. Nice estimated a
forty-nine percent success rate for all birds with open nests
and a sixty-six percent success rate for cavity nesting birds.
Common loons have a system that works. They have main-
tained viable populations for thousands of years. Given a
little room, they will probably continue their survival game
for thousands more.

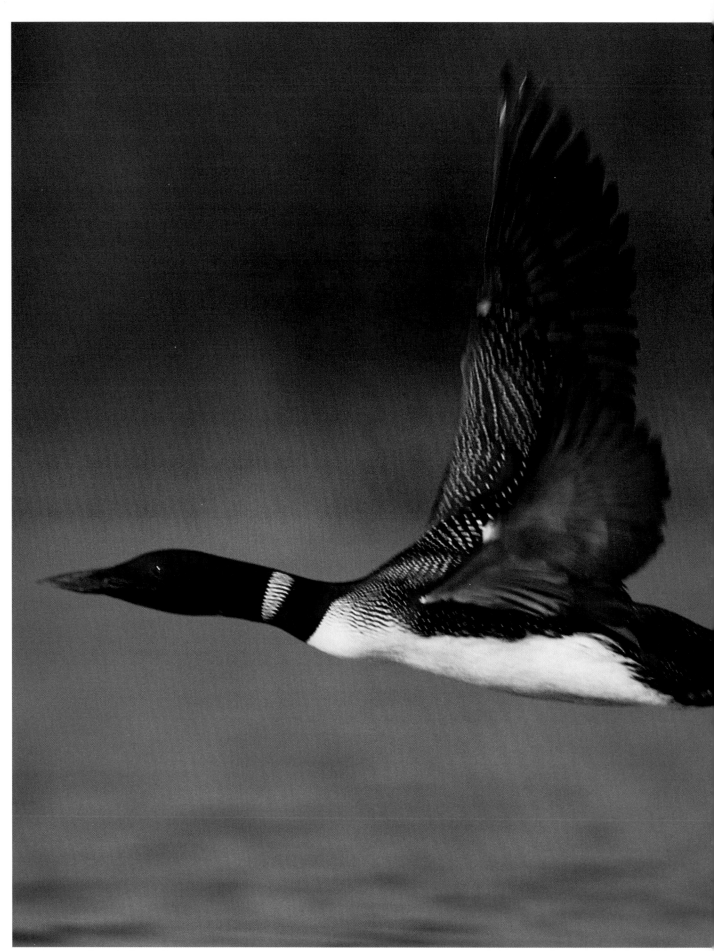

Loons are powerful and efficient fliers.

*The woodland lakes would be soli-
tudes, indeed, did they lack the finishing
touch to make the picture complete, the
tinge of wilderness which adds color to
the scene, the weird and mournful cry
of the loon, as he calls to his mate or
greets some new arrival. Who has ever
paddled a canoe, or cast a fly or
pitched a tent in the north woods and
has not stopped to listen to this wail of
wilderness? And what would the
wilderness be without it?*

— Arthur Cleveland Bent, 1919

Looking South

The fall migration of loons is not a "here one day and gone the next" phenomenon. It's quite difficult to pin down a departure schedule because the migration process may begin as early as late July or early August when loons, at least to human eyes, begin to get restless. As summer wears on, the birds start a gradual movement from smaller to larger lakes, perhaps to find better fishing or to join other loons in pre-migratory flocks.

BIRDS OF A FEATHER

On large northern lakes, it's tough to separate the early summer social flocking, often evident as early as mid-July, from the later pre-migratory flocking. In some areas, the two behaviors blend into each other. The early-season flocking usually occurs on large lakes where groups of a dozen or more loons assemble for afternoon sessions of cruising, preening and loafing. The early summer concentration sites often are used year after year. Of course, you have to be in high-density loon areas to find this behavior.

In July of 1976, Joe Anderlik found himself in very high-density loon country. He was fishing on 265 square-mile Molson Lake in northern Manitoba. He recalls that the weather had been lousy for several days but finally cleared, and days of ninety-degree heat followed. On the fourth day of the heat wave, the Cree guide motored the fishing party a considerable distance from their base camp. The lake was perfectly calm. Dozing off occasionally in the bow, Joe sat up quickly when he noticed a large congregation of birds. Instructing the guide to head toward the group of about 600 birds, Anderlik quickly realized he was watching his favorite bird, the common loon. Loons in the huge flock quietly preened as the boat passed. In over forty years of watching loons Anderlik had never seen anything like that assemblage. Few people have ever witnessed such a loon gathering, even once.

Loons gather on lakes known as "stopping areas" in autumn.

Ontario biologist Peter Croskery has observed summer flocking of loons in northwestern Ontario for many years. He has noted flocks of fifteen to seventy loons that stay together throughout the summer. Flocking seems to be more common on larger lakes with open water basins.

In the northwoods of Maine, researcher Paul Strong saw flocks of loons nearly all season long. Groups of fifteen to twenty were evident in his wilderness study area north of Baxter State Park as early as June. On small lakes the same flocking phenomenon occurs but with smaller numbers, usually four or five individuals. These groups are probably non-breeders or unsuccessful breeding pairs. They often stay together well into September when the early migrants decide to test their wings.

In his northern Minnesota wilderness study area, Sigurd Olson kept track of the total number of adult loons throughout the season and found a surprisingly steady decline. In June, he was seeing 109 to 114 adult loons. In late July, he counted 128 to 143 adults—the increase likely due to single loons and unsuccessful pairs moving in from other areas. In early September, however, he observed only eighty birds. By late September, he saw forty birds in the area and by early October he could find only twenty loons. Just a few hardy loons stayed around until the late November ice closed the lakes. The juveniles followed a fairly similar pattern with twenty-one young on the scene in early September, fourteen in late September and ten in early October. Olson recalls the canoe country becoming strangely quiet as the hardwoods dropped their color. While coastal arrivals of loons have been observed in August on the Atlantic and late September off

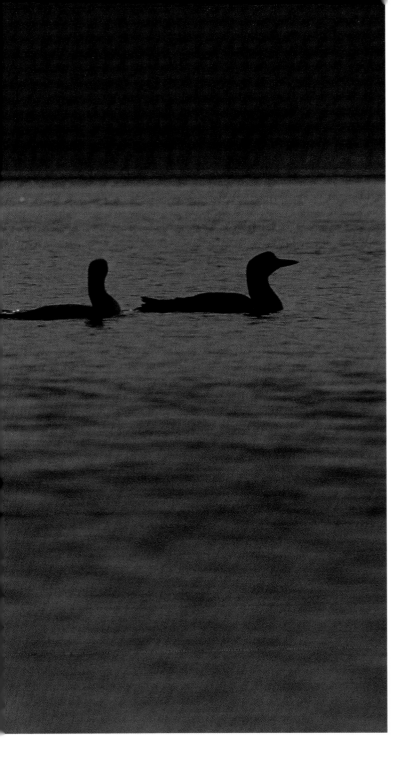

where large numbers of common loons gather for fairly short loon conventions. In Maine, October loon gatherings are quite predictable on some of the state's large lakes, like Pushaw near Bangor, Flagstaff Lake in western Maine, and Great Pond near Belgrade, where groups of a hundred or more loons visit annually. A lake with only one or two nesting pairs, Trout Lake in northern Wisconsin hosts around fifty loons each fall, and New Hampshire's Squam Lake may accommodate fifty or more "guest" loons each fall, while nearby Lake Winnipesaukee provides for up to 100 extras. The Great Lakes provide several major gathering points like Kettle Point on Lake Huron, where every fall concentrations of hundreds or even thousands of loons can be viewed.

One of the more unusual fall migration stopover spots is in the desert of western Nevada. There, on deep Walker Lake, Larry Neel, a nongame wildlife biologist with the State of Nevada, conducts fall surveys of waterbirds. In 1989, he and his crew counted 1,090 common loons and a few Pacific and red-throated loons. These thousand-plus birds are more than the known breeding populations of northwestern states and may represent all of the breeding birds in Montana, Wyoming, Idaho, and Washington as well as some from parts of southern Canada.

The best studied of the stopover lakes is Minnesota's Mille Lacs Lake, a shallow lake of 133,000 acres. In 1975, Judy McIntyre monitored loon movements during September, October, and November. While over the summer Mille Lacs had just a few resident loons, during October there was considerable loon movement. By the third week of October, around 100 loons were present. During the final week of October, the population peaked at between 600 and 750 birds. By the end of the first week in November, nearly all the loons were gone. Residents of the area felt the build-up was normal, suggesting loons had always used the lake in this fashion.

Like the loons on the Maine and Wisconsin lakes, these were not local birds. If the numbers seem large, keep in mind the tremendous Canadian loon population. The large fall concentrations on the U.S. lakes could be loons coming from distant Canadian lakes to rest and refuel after their travels, adding a little fat by fishing on well supplied lakes. Mille Lacs, for example, is an extremely productive lake, and the Great Lakes stopping places could provide an abundance of alewives and smelt. From McIntyre's research on Mille Lacs Lake, it is evident that loons spend a lot of time feeding on these fall gathering lakes, termed "staging lakes" by scientists. From noon to about five o'clock, the loons spend most of their time feeding.

Once loons leave their staging areas they probably move quickly to the coast and then turn south, picking up their pace. During spring migration loons fly at a maximum speed of 93 mph, but reach flight speeds of 108 mph during the fall migration. Apparently winter's approach is a good motivator for loons. The final stimulus for the flight

Florida's Gulf Coast, most loons wait until late October or early November to head south.

For loon watchers, fall can be a time of mixed emotions. Are "your" loons just heading out for a feeding visit to another lake? Or are they leaving for the year and consequently leaving a big hole in your lake? It's hard to say good-bye to friends, even if you know they're going to warm, coastal waters. Unlike geese, which fly in large flocks, loons migrate singly or in small groups. Few people notice migrating loons. Given the typical early morning flights and the lack of calling, it is not surprising.

THE FIRST LEG

Many migrating loons may not be going far, at least at first. There are a number of traditional fall stopping places from the staging areas might well be weather. Most birds take maximum advantage of the wind, leaving when a wind from the northwest will give them a little help heading south. Some research doors concerning the migration of loons have yet to be unlocked, leaving the study of the roles of photoperiod, temperature and behavioral cues from other migrating birds as unexplored avenues for future study.

Not all loons make the big trip south. At least a few find the cold but open waters of the Great Lakes appealing enough to spend the winter. It's difficult, of course, to separate wintering loons from late migrants, but a U.S. Fish and Wildlife Service researcher did uncover some interesting evidence pointing to a Great Lakes wintering population. In October of 1983, Christopher Brand, a scientist at the National Wildlife Health Laboratory, was studying loon botulism mortality on Lake Michigan. Brand inspected forty of the nearly 600 loons estimated to have died during the outbreak. Of those forty loons only two had black and white breeding plumage. While the other thirty-eight birds fell into two distinct plumage types, examination of sex organs indicated that none of the thirty-eight loons were young-of-the-year. Most likely Brand was looking at immature loons which had spent their second or third fall on Lake Michigan.

PROBLEMS EN ROUTE

Some loons try heading south but have a hard time. Loons seem to have a fatal fascination for wet highways, and reports of loons attempting to land on rain-slick roads are common. In 1982, sixteen immature loons tried to land on highways near Rhinelander, Wisconsin. It was a windy and snowy November evening. Between 7:00 and 8:00 p.m., the loons started dropping on blacktop roads. Apparently the glare from car headlights gave the roads the appearance of rivers; no loons were found along the many miles of gravel roads in the area. Of the sixteen birds, thirteen were successfully treated by the Northwoods Wildlife Center in nearby Minocqua and returned to open water.

While not all loons are given such a second chance, another loon traveling through Wisconsin had luck on its side. On New Year's Eve of 1982, an immature loon crash-landed next to a farmer's barn near Antigo in northeast Wisconsin. The Northwoods Wildlife Center again did some minor repairs and sent the loon south early in the new year.

Some loons flying down the East Coast have had similar problems. In early December of 1984, nine loons decided to land in some unusual places in suburban Maryland. One landed in the parking lot of a shopping center, another in a swimming pool in Bethesda and one dropped down on the runway of an airport. All nine loons were rescued and treated at The Chesapeake Bird and Wildlife Sanctuary in Bowie, Maryland. Some had bleeding feet but all were released to the waters of Chesapeake Bay.

The problem is not limited to common loons. Red-throated loons have crash-landed, including one in July of

1985 which tried to land at Pearson airport in Toronto. It landed safely and was rescued.

A few loons wait a little too long before starting their flight south. In November of 1979, on Tiger Cat Flowage near Hayward, Wisconsin, another immature loon became trapped when ice started closing in on it. Since loons cannot run on ice to take off, this bird was doomed. Two Wisconsin Project Loon Watch staff members arrived at the lake with a canoe, paddles, an ax, a flashlight and a landing net. Three hours later they captured the reluctant loon, needing every piece of equipment and some luck to get the loon out of the rapidly freezing water of the lake. After spending a comfortable evening in a bathtub at Northland College in Ashland, the loon was tagged and released to the open waters of Lake Superior.

Not all the loon-trapped-in-the-ice stories have such happy endings. An immature yellow-billed loon near Prudhoe Bay in northern Alaska did not pick up on Nature's cues. The freezing lake closed in on the loon, but the ice was not solid enough to allow an attempted rescue by a nervous lakeside family. For about a week a pair of adult yellow-billed loons flew over the stranded bird daily, but did not land in the small patch of water. The adult birds, presumably the parents, attempted through vocalizations to get the young loon off the lake, but it was too late. Finally the adults left and natural selection played out its ancient role.

EMPTY LAKES

After the last loon has left a northern lake the silence is complete, almost painful. There is still life on most lakes, a few bluebills passing through perhaps or a lingering kingfisher, but it's not the same. Bent had it right in 1919: the woodland lakes would be "empty solitudes" without the cry of the loon. The North's loss is the South's gain. While loons are not as attractive in their gray winter plumage, they do add to the diversity of bird life on coastal waters. The exact overland routes from the upper midwest are not known for certain. For most northeastern loons the trip south follows the Atlantic Coast. Loons in Alaska and the Canadian northwest take a general southwest flight path to the Pacific Coast wintering areas.

Someday a radio telemetry study of loon migration will provide exact information on the routes loons take. Such a study might even provide clues regarding the relationships between weather and fall migration, or food supply and fall migration. But telemetry will never offer a single clue to help mortals understand why it hurts a little to see loons head south for a long winter.

Parents abandon chicks to migrate on their own.

Young loons migrate to salt water coastal areas, where they remain for several years.

The loon's natural environment is northern. When they're out of their natural environment, they're just another bird.

—Joe Anderlik, 1984

Winter Vacation

Loons and winter? It's not quite like love and marriage, or Friday and fish fries. Interest in wintering loons is somewhat like Christmas sales of air conditioners in Bangor—a little restrained. It's no surprise. The striking summer bird of the north with the beautiful voice becomes a drab, shy coastal resident. The two things Northerners love about loons—the dramatic plumage and the haunting calls—are not enjoyed by southerners. After the late fall molt, the northern postcard loons just aren't the same.

I recall sitting on a Key West boardwalk watching an immature loon feed and loaf in the warm, shallow waters. Several tourists stopped to politely ask what I found so interesting. I offered the spotting scope. Two of them responded with a statement something like, "What a funny looking duck, is it rare?" These "ducks" are typically very quiet on the wintering grounds. While a two-week exploration of the Keys produced many loon sightings, not a single loon was heard calling. Many northern loon lovers who spend each winter in Florida wait patiently for the calling they love so deeply up north. Few are rewarded. Loons do vocalize in some areas of their wintering range, but it's not as predictable or as sustained as in their summer environment.

Loon religion has not invaded the Deep South. Even bird groups there don't give the loon much more than a passing interest. In 1982, Jim Pierce of Wisconsin Project Loon Watch and Jeff Fair of the New Hampshire Loon Preservation Committee tried to organize bird groups in southern coastal areas to provide loon population data. The response was as lukewarm as Florida tidal pools. Another effort to organize professional and amateur ornithologists in 1984 met with similar disinterest. Of 850 birders asked to provide information on wintering loons, only fifty-five responded. And just try to find loon postcards, tee-shirts, ties or whiskey glasses in Florida, Texas or the Carolinas! While the highest concentrations of wintering common loons on the East Coast are found off the North Carolina, Virginia and Maryland coasts, loons can be found in almost all coastal waters from Maine to Texas. T. A. Imhof, a University of Alabama researcher, estimated the wintering population at over 10,000 in an area from the mouth of the Mississippi to St. Mark's, Florida.

On the West Coast, where the loon populations from Alaska and western Canada winter, the estimates are much higher. Approximately 12,000 loons of three species (common, red-throated and Pacific loons) spend the winter off the Washington coast, according to Kelly McAllister of Washington's Non-Game Office. Bill Haight, an Oregon Non-Game official, termed loons "abundant" in the coastal estuaries of that state. Loons of all four species winter along California's 800-mile coast and John Gustafson of the California Non-Game Department receives reports of common loons wintering on inland lakes and reservoirs of the state.

A survey completed in the spring of 1984 added considerably to our knowledge of winter loon movements. Coordinated by Judy McIntyre, the survey indicated a northward movement of loons along the Atlantic Coast during the winter. In January and February, the greatest concentrations of loons were found off the coast of South Carolina. In March, the largest groups were observed off the New Jersey coast. In April, the concentrations moved up to the Massachusetts and New Hampshire shores. Both north-south and inshore-offshore movements were noted along the west coast of Florida, normally an area of substantial loon numbers. On the Texas coast, loons were seen in modest numbers in January and February but by March a pre-migration buildup had occurred.

We still do not know exactly where loons nesting in Michigan, Maine, and Manitoba spend their winters. Despite the increase in numbers of banded loons in recent years, the specific wintering grounds for each breeding population remains a mystery. However, limited band returns suggest that mid-continental nesters winter in the Gulf of Mexico, northeastern breeders along the Atlantic Coast, and northwestern birds along the Pacific Coast. Beyond this intuitive general pattern, little is known. Loons spread themselves out from the Aleutian Islands to Baja California and from Newfoundland to northeastern Mexico. In doing so, they have thus far stymied the efforts of researchers looking for ties between summer and winter grounds.

It is impossible to know at this time if all loons from a given nesting region travel to a specific wintering site. There would be an adaptive survival value for loons from geographically distinct populations to spread out all over the coast. The potential for a single catastrophe involving disease, pollution or a violent storm to affect an entire population would be reduced. We do know that winter is a time of great stress for the loons and it is on the coastal waters that natural selection does its work. McIntyre terms winter mortality "considerable." Of nine loons she banded between 1970 and 1973, three died during their first coastal winter.

Malcolm Simons, Coordinator of the Atlantic Beached Bird Survey which monitors bird mortality along the U.S. coasts from northern Massachusetts to Texas, has termed loon mortality in winter "out of proportion to its population throughout its coastal ranges." Started in 1975, the Beached Bird Survey utilized volunteers to walk stretches of coast tallying the dead seabirds they encountered. During the first four years of the survey, loon mortality was low but, according to Simons, it increased steadily until the major loon die-off in 1983 when loons accounted for over seventy percent of all the birds found. While Simons cites severe weather as the greatest cause of seabird mortality, he does not ignore pollution, especially oil spills. Looking at all the survey records, he estimates that about seven percent of all loons found were oiled. The 1983 sinking of the *Marine Electric* off the Florida coast resulted in thirty-two loon deaths and an additional 134 oiled loons required assistance.

Pollution in winter habitats is not easy on loons, and adjusting to salt water may be an added stress. Like many other birds utilizing the marine environment, loons are able to cope with salt water by secreting excess salt through a nasal gland. Not found in songbirds, the "salt gland" is used by cormorants, grebes, herons, gulls, terns and loons to limit the salt concentration in the blood to about one percent, approximately one-third of the salt concentration of sea water. This marine bird adaptation was first identified in 1957. Although some avian physiology textbooks do not list the loon among the thirteen orders of birds possessing a functional salt gland, researchers at the Fish and Wildlife Service's National Wildlife Health Laboratory in Madison, Wisconsin have located the gland in common loons.

The most detailed single study of wintering loons was conducted by Judy McIntyre in 1978 near Assateague Island, Virginia. With highly productive waters supplying an abundance of fish and shellfish, the Assateague Island study area provided a nearly ideal habitat for wintering loons. McIntyre found that as in summer, loons in winter will mix with other loons but rarely with other species. By carefully watching for individuals with distinctive markings, such as one loon with a bent bill, McIntyre determined that loons utilize distinct feeding territories. Each loon, not each pair as in summer, has its own area and defends it with displays and occasional vocalizations.

Wintering loons spend just over half of their daylight hours feeding. Preening and other maintenance activities take up another quarter of their day, with the balance spent drifting and sleeping. Apparently the tides are important for feeding loons, bringing in new, unsuspecting prey twice a day. All of the loons McIntyre observed fed in the early morning and midafternoon with a final surge in late afternoon. The feeding activity usually includes at least some bottom feeding since shellfish were brought to the surface on several occasions.

The call of the loon is seldom heard in wintering areas.

Loons take off into the wind for lift.

There are reports in British bird journals of wintering loons feeding heavily on crabs. North American loons, especially when stormy weather creates turbid water conditions, will also feed on crabs. During McIntyre's study, she never observed flock feeding: spaced about 150 yards apart, the birds always fished as individuals. In winter, feeding dives averaged just under forty seconds, only three seconds shorter than average summer dives timed by McIntyre. With ample prey available, the loons typically stayed in a protected area all day and kept fairly regular habits.

Those habits included flocking at sunset when a raft of about 100 loons would form about twenty minutes after sunset. While the exact location varied, the raft could be seen in the same general area—the deepest part of the cove—each evening throughout the winter. Given the extensive evidence that loons are sight feeders, it is doubtful that loons feed at night either in winter or summer. A spurt of feeding at low tide is probably stimulated by the concentration of potential prey as the water recedes. This abundance of prey probably accounts for the relatively small winter feeding territories of ten to twenty acres in winter, as contrasted with the summer territories of five to ten times that size.

Loons on their wintering grounds face a larger population of competitors and predators. While attacks on loons anywhere in their range are uncommon, they are even less so in winter on the ocean where few people closely watch these drab tourists. However, sea otters off California's coast are now known to kill and eat loons. One otter was seen eating a common loon in Monterrey harbor and two loon carcasses were found stripped of flesh in kelp beds in a fashion similar to other birds known to be eaten by otters. Large fish are likely more dangerous to loons than otters, but we can only speculate as to what kinds of fish and how often it happens.

Something that probably occurs fairly frequently is the attempt to steal food by gulls. While studying wintering loons on the Atlantic Coast, Betsy Daub saw herring gulls steal fish from loons twice and suggested that underwater consumption of fish may have evolved as an adaptive behavior to limit stealing, or kleptoparasitism as it is known, by gulls and other competitors.

The function of evening rafting is anyone's guess. It is unlikely that safety in numbers is the answer. On coastal waters loons have few enemies, except possibly the thresher shark. McIntyre suggests the rafting could simply be a behavior which keeps the birds offshore and prevents possible strandings on the beaches in storms. Another possibility she suggests is more subtle. If the loons stay together the probability of roughly synchronous spring departure and subsequent arrival on the breeding grounds increases. This would force all birds to play by the same rules and give none an advantage of early nesting site selection. But since the actual arrival on northern lakes is usually preceded (at least for midwestern and Canadian loons) by a series of stagings on any available open water, the necessity to leave together is questionable.

Even when defending their winter feeding territories, loons seldom call. During her research at Assateague, McIntyre heard the yodel occasionally and the tremolo only twice. The melancholy wail apparently is reserved for the solitude of the summer lakes.

Other researchers have noted that loons can be found well offshore. Observing from merchant ships several miles offshore, Chris Haney, a University of Georgia researcher, noted that loons and other seabirds were most abundant near upwellings where two currents meet to provide abundant food.

The population of wintering birds reaches all the way to Nova Scotia and Newfoundland. Along the Maine coast winter survey is conducted annually by the Maine Audubon Society. About 300 loons are sighted annually. Since some areas of the coast were not covered, the total coastal population is probably in the range of 500 birds. The majority of Maine's approximately 3,000 summering loons decide, like many other Maine residents, to spend the winter in a slightly warmer clime. According to Maine Audubon's Jane Arbuckle, Maine's wintering loons do spend the entire season off the Maine coast braving the famous, bitter nor'easters. Paul Strong, one of the cooperators in the winter census, reports that the Maine winter population is composed primarily of single birds and small groups of from two to six loons. He also reports that, at least in Maine, the wintering loons are silent. Over several years of monthly coastal observations, he has yet to hear a loon calling. It may well be that the calling reported by McIntyre occurs only where large concentrations of loons are present. Or it could be that Maine loons are like the stereotypical Maine residents—strong and silent.

Clearly, loon numbers on the wintering grounds are not what they were in 1907 when Frank Chapman, author of *Handbook of Birds in Eastern North America*, noted in his journal: "They winter in large numbers some distance off the coast. I have seen several thousand in a day east of Hatteras when sailing from New York to Florida." Loons on their wintering waters will get plenty of attention in the future. Winter studies are a high priority for the North American Loon Fund's research grant program. Winter studies are important in determining the mysterious link between summer and winter populations as well as identifying action that may have to be taken to protect loons in winter, the most stressful and hazardous season for loons.

Chicks enter the water soon after hatching and never return to the nest site.

probably very low. Some bird species, like the turkey vulture whose appetite for carrion is well-known, can resist 100,000 times as much Type C botulism as a pigeon. Although loons haven't been tested, they would, no doubt, be closer to pigeons in their resistance to botulism.

A study of a 1983 botulism outbreak, conducted by the U.S. Fish and Wildlife's National Wildlife Health Laboratory in Madison, Wisconsin, concluded that between October 10 and 31 at least 582 loons died of botulism Type E in the Lake Michigan waters off the Garden Peninsula. Because of probable removal by scavengers and winds which kept many dead birds offshore, the mortality estimate is conservative. As many as twenty-two dead birds per mile washed up on the beach.

Laboratory tests confirmed the presence of botulism E, but could not pinpoint the source. The possibility of contamination from large numbers of dead pink salmon was considered, but since loons are not scavengers this theory was rejected. Five species of baitfish found on the beach were collected and analyzed; three species—burbot, alewife and smelt—tested positive for botulism E. Both smelt and alewife are common loon prey. While there is a possibility that the botulism toxins formed after the baitfish died, there is a stronger possibility that moribund prey, with botulism E, were eaten by loons.

National Wildlife Health Lab researcher Christopher Brand commented in an interview that no feasible control or prevention methods yet exist to protect loons from botulism. The bacteria will always be present and loons, most likely migrants from Canadian nesting areas, will likely return to their traditional stopping places en route to the Atlantic or Gulf coasts. Since it would be impossible to keep loons off thousands of square miles of Lake Michigan, botulism E may continue to be an unavoidable and substantial source of natural loon mortality.

THE FLORIDA DIE-OFF

According to a March 1984 *Audubon* magazine article by Frank Graham Jr., the first victim of the "Florida die-off" washed ashore on January 4, 1983 at Dog Island, a 1,800-acre barrier island on the northern Gulf coast of Florida. Many more followed. By early February, ten to twenty dead or dying loons came to Dog Island's beaches. All along the Gulf Coast the story was repeated, hundreds of times a day. While the U.S. Fish and Wildlife estimate of the total mortality was 2,500, some observers in Florida believed the total mortality was much higher, perhaps as high as 10,000. Smaller numbers of loons died along the Virginia and North Carolina coasts.

Most of the dead loons were in an extremely emaciated condition—some had a body weight of under three pounds, about a third of a loon's normal weight. A Dog Island regular and field researcher for The Nature Conservancy, Laurence Alexander saw many loons in that

condition. Watching a Fish and Wildlife scientist perform a field necropsy, Alexander was startled to see birds which, in his words, "lacked the very stuff of life. You cut them open, and you didn't find the basic things a bird needs to survive: muscles, blood and food."

Even after years of study, the die-off perplexes scientists. They know more about what it wasn't than what it was: it was not caused by botulism, an oil spill, nor any clearly defined pollutant. As in any good mystery, though, there are a few clues.

One of the clues found by Bob Lange, a U.S. Fish and Wildlife scientist working on the case, was the presence of mercury and selenium in the tissues of dead loons. Of sixteen loon livers analyzed, nine had mercury concentrations of greater than 20 ppm, considered a "danger zone" by mercury in some areas enters aquatic systems as effluent from industrial plants. Most insidiously, mercury also enters aquatic systems through airborne deposition.

A study of mercury contamination in loons was conducted in northern Minnesota by the Minnesota Pollution Control Agency and the Minnesota Department of Natural Resources. Feather samples were taken from adults and chicks and analyzed for mercury content. Mercury is known to concentrate in the feathers of other waterfowl and this is an excellent method of evaluating mercury contamination without sacrificing the animals. The levels of mercury found in the feathers of juvenile and adult loons were very high. In addition to the feather samples, twenty-seven loon carcasses were recovered. Of the twenty-seven at least three may have died from mercury poisoning based on the levels of mercury found in the livers.

Loon feeding habits may offer some protection from DDT and other toxic chemicals. Because toxic chemicals can work their way up through the food chain by a process of bio-accumulation, chemicals in lake water may be present at a relatively harmless level of parts per trillion, but when microscopic zooplankton absorb the chemicals, the contaminants can be concentrated to parts per billion. And when small minnows and fish eat the zooplankton, the concentrations can reach parts per million. When predator fish eat small prey, they store this cumulative contamination in their fat tissues; so, an eagle feeding on the carcass of a large fish can get a heavy dose of chemicals. Since loons usually feed in a safer area of the food chain, they do not pick up nearly the contamination absorbed by eagles or ospreys feeding on large prey.

The 1980s and 1990s have brought the specter of chemical poisoning of loons clearly into focus. What was once thought to be a rather localized and minor problem for loons is now recognized as perhaps the most dangerous threat to loons. Mercury is showing up in loons all across their range from the Atlantic to the Pacific coasts and into Canada. Amazingly high percentages of adult and young loons have some measurable amounts of mercury in their bodies and many have levels high enough to impair reproductive success. Areas with lakes susceptible to acidification because of low buffering capacity or high inputs of acid precipitation seem to be the worst. In Minnesota, despite the abundance of lakes and loons, mercury seems to threaten the statewide population. In Wisconsin, Mike Meyer with the Wisconsin DNR has been sampling loons throughout the northern part of the state. Far too many have high levels of mercury to make any scientist or loon lover comfortable.

Mercury is not the only heavy metal contaminating loons' bodies. Lead poisoning is a frequent diagnosis of death in loons that are turned into wildlife authorities. The most common form is from ingestion of lead sinkers used for fishing. For some unknown reason, loons seem attracted to these smooth "stones" and swallow them for use in their gizzard in grinding up fish bones, scales, and fins. Lead poisoning occurs all over, but has been reported most frequently in New England.

Despite bodies full of lead and mercury and chemicals, many loons are still able to reproduce and bring off young. So far, no population-wide decrease in reproduction has been found. However, scientific studies have demonstrated impaired reproduction as a result of high levels of mercury and it only seems a matter of time before lower numbers of loon chicks leads to lower adult populations. Already, in a few localized areas, scientists and wildlife managers speculate that mercury is leading to small population declines. The fact that loons continue to reproduce despite their body burden of chemicals and metals is no cause for joy; it might just buy them a little more time.

BOTULISM

A little more time is something disease rarely gives its victims. Probably more loons have died from disease than all other causes. In the 1960s alone, Type E botulism killed at least 10,000 common loons. A silent and efficient killer, botulism has been a major cause of waterfowl deaths, killing in 1952 five million ducks in the western United States. Botulism is a disease caused by the ingestion of food contaminated by toxin from the bacterium *Clostridium botulinum*.

In its spore stage, this microorganism is not a problem, but under the proper conditions—suitable nutrients, favorable temperature and the absence of oxygen—a very powerful toxin is produced. If loons pick up this pre-formed toxin by eating contaminated baitfish, they can be killed by the toxin. There are six types (A through F) of botulism: Type E is no friend of loons.

Major epidemics (termed *epizootics* by wildlife scientists) of Type E have visited Lake Michigan repeatedly, destroying thousands of loons; eight major autumn outbreaks have occurred between 1959 and 1983 and the outbreaks of 1963 and 1964 alone killed an estimated 6,870 loons. The diagnosis of botulism E was definite. When laboratory mice were injected with blood serum from dead loons, the mice died. When the mice were first given Type E anti-toxin, they lived. While gulls and other waterbirds were affected in these fall die-offs, common loons were most severely affected. Why loons? Fall is the time for the annual pre-migratory flocking and Lake Michigan has several traditional staging areas where hundreds or even thousands of loons congregate.

Just how the disease is transmitted is perplexing. Normally loons eat only live fish, and botulism toxin is rarely present in samples of live, healthy fish. Possibly, loons eat sick baitfish in which the levels of the botulism toxin are present but low. Since botulism is not a significant problem in most of the loon's range (Lake Michigan has had the only major occurrences), the resistance of loons to botulism is

DDT use and indirectly launched the environmental movement. By the mid-60s, the spectacular peregrine falcon had disappeared from much of its range, a victim of DDT. The osprey, once a familiar East Coast raptor, declined rapidly, as did the bald eagle. In 1972, the Environmental Protection Agency banned DDT in the United States, but DDT is still being used in other parts of the world. While the worldwide situation is improving, many birds now pick up DDT in their wintering habitats. Of the 650 species of birds breeding in the United States, 332 species spend the winter in tropical areas of Mexico, the West Indies, Central and South America—all areas where DDT is still used. In the northern half of the Midwest, decreases in the eggshell thickness of many birds, including eagles, have been documented. Studies by University of Wisconsin researchers Joseph Hickey and Raymond Faber indicated eggshell thickness decreases in nine of thirteen fish-eating species when shells from 1970 were compared with museum samples collected before 1946. In great blue herons, the eggshell thickness decrease was twenty-five percent. Black terns, double-crested cormorants, herring gulls and red-breasted mergansers had shell thickness decreases of thirteen to twenty-three percent.

Fortunately, loons have not as yet been as seriously affected. In a *Wilson Bulletin* article, Scott Sutcliffe reported an eleven percent decrease in loon eggshell thickness when comparing 1978 eggs from Squam Lake and Lake Winnipesaukee in New Hampshire with museum samples. The level of DDT present correlated with the thickness of the shell—the higher the level of DDT, the thinner the shell—but the differences were slight. The average thickness of the fourteen 1978 eggs was 0.59 mm while the museum samples, all dating to a pre-DDT era, had an average thickness of 0.65 mm. According to Sutcliffe, the eggshell thinning problem had little or no effect on loon productivity in New Hampshire.

Canadian research has also demonstrated the presence of chemicals in loons. Eggs collected in 1970 were significantly thinner than thirty-nine eggs from The Royal Ontario Museum which were collected before 1947. More importantly perhaps, the more recent loon eggs contained traces of DDT, Mirex, PCB, dieldrin and mercury. Mercury levels in eggs from the Algonquin Park area were quite high, 1.11 parts per million (ppm) in one case.

Contaminants were found in loons, too. As reported in

Loons succumb easily to toxins and pollutants.

the *Journal of Environmental Contamination and Toxicology*, one group of investigators analyzed 204 loon carcasses found between 1969 and 1979. Except for a few that were shot or died from swallowed fishhooks, these loons drowned in commercial fishing nets. Of the 204 loons, thirty were found in an emaciated condition. Of these thirty, seven loons had lethal levels of mercury and one a very high level of lead. All of the loons had evidence of at least some DDT, PCB, dieldrin and mercury contamination, but the levels in the emaciated loons were significantly higher than in the 174 non-emaciated loons. The levels of mercury in the livers of healthy, juvenile loons, for example, averaged 1.92 ppm while the average in emaciated juveniles was 26.4 ppm. For adults, the equivalent numbers were 6.35 ppm in healthy loons and 16.3 ppm in emaciated birds.

Jack Barr, a well-known Canadian loon researcher, has documented mercury problems for loons in northwestern Ontario. Studying loons on lakes on the Wabigoon-English River system, Barr found mercury contamination in fish and loons and noted reductions in egg-laying, and in nest and territorial fidelity. The source of mercury in many lakes was the chloralkali plant at Dryden. Loons farther downstream from the plant had less mercury and were able to reproduce better than loons occupying lakes closer to the Dryden plant.

Barr also noted that some lakes had naturally occurring mercury associated with greenstone deposits. Acidification of these lakes will probably elevate mercury levels and cause further problems for loons and other aquatic birds.

Barr found that there was enough mercury in some prey species to inhibit reproductive activities of some loons. In one part of his study area loons either failed to produce eggs, laid eggs that did not hatch, or hatched chicks that died soon after. Additionally, he suggested that mercury may have caused some aberrant behavior by loons that resulted in nest and territory abandonment.

Although Barr's study was not conclusive, the results strongly implicate mercury as a factor negatively affecting reproductive success for common loons. Unfortunately for the loons and the humans who enjoy them, there is little that can be done to rectify the problem. The sources of the mercury are not well known for most areas. While mercury occurs naturally at high levels in some parts of the Canadian Shield, particularly areas associated with greenstone deposits,

The plight of the loon takes many forms, often human-induced: artificial water level fluctuations that flood or strand vulnerable nests; predation; loss of nesting habitat to development; disturbance during the nesting season. The most insidious threat of all is acid rain, which has already killed hundreds of lakes, and will destroy all life in many more unless its sources are controlled.

—Jeff Fair, 1983

Hanging On

It's a tough world for loons. They have battled diseases, competition from other species, high and low water levels, predation and other natural threats for millions of years—and survived them all. During the past few decades, however, *Homo sapiens* haven't made the loon's lot any easier. While the sport shooting of loons is thankfully a sad memory, a frightening list of new and more insidious problems is facing the bird: toxic chemicals, acid rain, destruction of nesting habitat, nest flooding, increased predation caused by the exploding populations of some predators, commercial fishing operations which net loons in addition to fish, and harassment by people. None of these problems faced loons when Native Americans developed their versions of loon religion. Some are serious enough to threaten the very existence of the species; others are just nagging problems in restricted geographic locales. But all must be dealt with if the cry of the loon is to be heard in the twenty-first century and beyond.

CHEMICAL CONTAMINATION

The story of chemicals and birds has always been disturbing. While most of the more than 60,000 manmade chemicals in our environment do not cause problems, at least a few are potentially dangerous. The role of dichlorodiphenyl-trichlorethane (DDT) in the population declines of the eagle, osprey and peregrine falcon is well documented. At high levels, DDT prevents the eggshells of these and other birds from reaching normal thickness, and when a nesting bird sits on its thin-shelled eggs, the eggs are crushed. Synthesized in 1874 but used widely only during and after World War II, DDT was called a modern miracle.

For a time it controlled mosquitoes and other pests, but the miracle was short-lived. Pests developed resistance, even immunity, to the toxin. By the 1960s, a few people saw the tip of the DDT iceberg. In 1962, Rachel Carson's *Silent Spring* alerted the public to the dangers of indiscriminate

A chick injured by a rogue loon.

scientists. Mercury has long been known to be bad medicine for wildlife.

These loons apparently did not die of mercury poisoning per se. In an unpublished report on the die-off, Fish and Wildlife Service scientists concluded: "We do not believe a diagnosis of mercury poisoning can be substantiated as a general diagnosis for loon deaths over such a wide area." They termed mercury "contributory" to the emaciated condition of the birds.

Also termed contributory were the large numbers of *microphallidae* (internal parasites) found in the loons. These parasites, according to Lange, were found in incredibly high numbers. Normally present in loons at levels measured in hundreds, the parasites were found in the dead Florida loons at levels of up to 80,000. Such parasite burdens could

have easily killed the loons. But the story doesn't end there. Healthy loons have no business feeding on the grass shrimp or mole crabs (not blue crabs as previously reported) which probably are the hosts to this parasite.

If the loons were in a weakened condition, however, they might have stopped feeding on fish, swam to shallow water and started feeding on the grass shrimp or mole crabs. Enter mercury. While this is only a theory, it is possible, even likely, that the loons suffered from central nervous system damage due to the mercury in their systems. Bob Lange recalls that many of the loons he observed during the die-off acted blind and demonstrated behaviors which to him were not consistent with simple weakness due to the parasite problems.

Mercury is widespread in the environment, and over

the past thirty years, mercury in eggshells has greatly increased; it is now found in the shells of most fish-eating birds, including the shells of loons. In twenty-one New Hampshire loon eggs, the mercury content averaged 0.54 ppm, a level above the 0.5 ppm "concern level" for ring-necked pheasants and near the 1.0 ppm concern level for most waterfowl. Some loon eggs from the New Hampshire sample did have over 1.0 ppm of mercury. Unlike many other contaminants such as DDT or PCBs, mercury levels in loon eggs have not decreased in recent years.

But unlike mysteries which tie-up nicely with a confession in the last chapter, this story is complicated by Dr. Donald Forrester from the University of Florida's College of Veterinary Medicine. He had the vision to look at healthy loons a year after the die-off. In 1984, a few loons were collected and analyzed for mercury. These loons had levels of mercury similar to the loons which died the year before. But no loons died on the Florida beaches in 1984. Like everyone else who has looked at the issue, Forrester is confused by the findings. In 1983, some other factors—inadequate prey populations or weather conditions possibly—must have worked with the mercury to start the chain of events ending in the destruction of thousands of loons.

So there is not enough information yet to write the final chapter in the Florida die-off/mercury story. While the connections between mercury levels and acid rain have yet to be clearly demonstrated, circumstantial evidence suggests an interplay. It is known that under the effect of strongly acidic rain, mercury commonly present in soil and rock can be released. When the acidity of rainfall is strong enough to break the chemical bonds holding the metal, mercury can be percolated into a lake or river making it available for fish and wildlife to absorb. This has happened in Scandinavian countries where several heavy metals including mercury have been implicated in serious fish and wildlife problems. If acid rain is increasing the levels of mercury in the northern breeding range, the Florida die-off becomes a bit less mysterious but far more ominous. Alone, mercury probably does not kill loons, but combined with the stress of migration, storms and parasites, it could be a silent killer.

Laurence Alexander continued to study the winter ecology of common loons in northeastern Florida until his untimely death in 1989. During the winter of 1986-87, Alexander observed many loons displaying symptoms of mercury poisoning. The birds appeared disoriented and severely underweight. Mercury may have been affecting their neural system making it difficult to find and capture fish.

ACID RAIN

Of all the threats facing the loon, acid rain is one of the most serious. Jeff Fair, formerly of the New Hampshire Loon Preservation Committee calls it the "most insidious" threat to loons. Rawson Wood, Chairman of the North American Loon Fund, terms it the "most urgent issue for loons." Nearly all scientists, even electric company scientists, admit that there is an acid rain problem, but there is considerable debate regarding the specific solutions, timing and costs of control measures. While most coal and utility representatives argue for more research and no action, environmental groups point out that every nation in the western world, except the United States, is committed to at least a thirty percent reduction of acid-causing pollutants (SO2 and NOx gases). Indeed, several United States scientific organizations, including the National Academy of Sciences, recommend an immediate control program.

One could debate the relative threat to loons of acid rain versus mercury poisoning or the debate of how to deal with lake acidification. Both debates are critical for loons. It requires little scientific sophistication to realize that fishless lakes will become loon-less lakes. Because they mainly feed on rough fish and minnows which are less sensitive to acid rain than most game fish, loons might stay around after a lake's walleye and trout populations have disappeared. Unfortunately, the maps of acid-sensitive lakes and the maps of the common loon's breeding range overlap all too well. Both cover the Laurentian Shield like a blanket of acidic snow.

Likewise, it matters very little whether loon populations decline from acid rain or from mercury contamination. However, it is crucial that both problems be addressed for acid neutral lakes full of fish are of little use to loons who carry so much mercury in their bodies that they are like the Mad Hatter in Alice in Wonderland who suffered nerve damage from applying a mercury-based fungicide on hatbands. Fortunately, in a somewhat twisted way, there is a connection between the two problems that scientists have begun to unravel.

Two studies conducted in the 1980s have provided several important pieces to the loon/acid rain puzzle. Scientists expected to find poorer breeding success for loons on lakes with higher acidity. However, Karl Parker, then a graduate student at Syracuse University in New York, found that loons on heavily acidified lakes in the Adirondack Mountains produced chicks at comparable rates to those on well-buffered lakes. The loons on the acidic lakes seemed to be able to cope by spending more time procuring food items for their chicks and by switching from small fish (the typical food for chicks) to larger fish or crayfish, prey items less sensitive to acidity. Parker even observed adult loons flying to the lake with fish in their bills.

Robert Alvo, then a graduate student at Trent University in Peterborough, Ontario, studied loons on acidic lakes in the Sudbury, Ontario region from 1982 to 1984. Alvo predicted that loons living on highly acidic lakes in the Sudbury area (one of the areas most severely

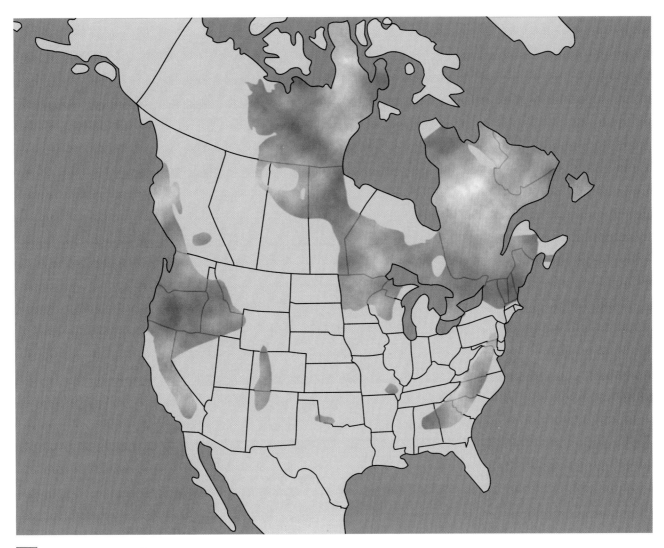

affected by acidification in North America) would have low reproductive success. Unlike Parker, Alvo found that common loon breeding success was significantly lower on low alkalinity (poorly buffered) lakes. This was not due to avoidance of these lakes by loons, fewer eggs laid, or poor hatching success for eggs, but to the effects of acidification.

Like Parker, Alvo observed loons feeding their young unusually high amounts of non-fish items like algae and aquatic invertebrates. However, on these highly acidic lakes there did not seem to be enough food to keep the chicks alive through the eleven week period before flight. Unfortunately, the adult loons apparently did not recognize that there was insufficient food for the young on these lakes. Their strong sense of year-to-year fidelity to nesting lakes kept the adults coming back to poor quality lakes.

The acidification of lakes does not seem to affect adult loons. The failure of fish to reproduce, however, means that there are few or no small fish for the chicks. The adults eat larger fish which can withstand moderate amounts of acidification. Even when there are few or no larger fish, the adults can still cope by flying to other lakes to feed. This, of course,

means that the adults end up spending less time on their nesting lakes tending the nest and defending the territory from intruders. The flights are also energy-expensive for loons which typically don't have to fly often during the summer. These factors in an indirect way may also be adding to the problems with brood survival.

Why were the effects of acid rain on loon reproduction evident in Ontario but not New York? No one knows for sure, but it is likely the result of more acidic input over a longer period of time for the Ontario lakes. The picture in Ontario may very well be the state of affairs in upstate New York if lake acidification continues.

Studies of acidified lakes have also revealed the startling fact that mercury in its dangerous organic form, methylmercury, is often present in much higher concentrations in lakes undergoing acidification. Apparently, as lakes acidify, they become more hospitable to a bacteria that is able to convert inorganic forms of mercury often found in lake sediments into its organic form. Methylmercury works its way up through the aquatic food web from algae and small invertebrates to fish and the birds and mammals that eat them.

Chicks quickly learn to mimic their parents' behaviors.

It accumulates along the way so that it may be present in unacceptably high concentrations in animals like loons, terns, herons, pelicans, eagles, ospreys, mink, and otters.

Acid rain is an issue vital to North American wildlife. Not just loons but many species of ducks, especially black ducks, game fish and perhaps even our forests are threatened by the continuing emissions of coal-fired power plants. Based mainly in the Ohio River Valley, these outdated facilities will have to be replaced or modified to keep the cry of the loon a common sound on northern lakes. There is time to act, but precious little time to waste.

COMMERCIAL FISHING

Nets set for trout or other game fish often catch more than fish. Deep-diving loons entangle themselves in nets

with all too frequent regularity. In 1960 and 1961, a combined total of about 5,000 common loons died in nets on Great Slave Lake in the Northwest Territories. While losses on the Great Lakes do not reach that level, John Lerg of the Michigan Department of Natural Resources reported at a 1981 loon conference in Minneapolis that a "substantial" number of loons are killed in Michigan waters of Lakes Superior and Michigan through commercial fishing operations. As many as 450 loons per year have been estimated to be drowned in Michigan waters, not all of them Michigan breeders. In fact, many may be migrants heading for the wilds of northern Canada.

Bill Robinson, a professor of wildlife at Northern Michigan University has been coordinating loon surveys for many years. Despite the recovery of loon populations in

holes and escape. Several commercial fishermen tried the nets and found they didn't suffer lower catches of fish and no loons were caught. Not enough fishermen are using them and not enough time has passed to draw conclusions about the nets, but like those used to help sea turtles escape shrimp nets in the Gulf of Mexico, they are promising.

An unknown, but probably large number of loons are netted and die in oceanic waters. Japanese fishermen have followed loons wintering off their coast to lead them to large schools of lance which they net. If loons are caught in their nets alive, they are removed carefully and released. If a loon is caught dead, the fishermen hide it in their boats so as not to disturb the other loons. Apparently, loons are revered in coastal Japanese villages and throughout Japan as loons were authorized as Japanese National Monuments in 1931.

HYDRO POWER WATER LEVELS

Loons require relatively stable water levels for successful nesting. Fluctuating water levels caused by hydro-electric dams can be detrimental to loon populations. The problem is particularly acute in the Northeast where hydro developments control the levels of many important loon lakes. New Hampshire's Lake Umbagog is a case in point. According to a longtime lake resident Armand Riendeau, Lake Umbagog's wildlife, especially ducks and loons, has suffered in some years from the policies of the company owning the water rights on the river systems feeding the sprawling wilderness lake. Riendeau claims up to ninety percent of the nesting ducks have been lost in some years to nest flooding. Despite the presence of eleven common loon nests on Umbagog in 1978, chick production was zero. This prompted the New Hampshire Loon Preservation Committee to contact the power company and negotiate an informal agreement to maintain water levels during the loon nesting season at a fairly constant level. It worked. Umbagog is now in the top three New Hampshire loon lakes for chick production.

Maine, too, has experienced problems with water fluctuations on some of its reservoirs, but according to Jane Arbuckle of the Maine Audubon Society, Maine utility officials have been cooperative by attempting to hold levels stable during the spring nesting season. Jeff Fair has been working with power companies in Maine and New Hampshire for years to develop lake management plans that allow the power companies to create electricity, but at the same time minimize the effects on nesting loons and other waterfowl.

Almost by accident, a discovery was made that has helped to mitigate the problems fluctuating water levels create for loons. In 1969, John Mathisen, the wildlife biologist on the Chippewa National Forest in northern Minnesota, home to over 3,000 common loons, discovered loons nesting on log rafts he had made for resting areas for ducks. His discovery led Judy McIntyre to try these artificial nest islands during her doctoral research on loons in the same area.

states like Wisconsin, Michigan loons continue to stay at low numbers. Bill and others believe that loons nesting within short flying distance of the Great Lakes may suffer higher mortality because of the probability of netting. The small loon population within the Seney National Wildlife Refuge in the eastern Upper Peninsula has years of population data which supports Bill's hypothesis as does a small isolated population of loons living on the lakes on Beaver Island in northern Lake Michigan.

Corinne Carey developed modified trap nets used by commercial fishermen on the Great Lakes in an attempt to find a partial solution to the netting mortality. The nets had holes in them large enough and in places where loons might find them and swim out. She tested the nets on captive loons and found that eighty percent could find the

Their successes gave confidence to the New Hampshire Loon Preservation Committee and other loon preservation groups who began using these "rafts" to partially mitigate loss of nesting habitat and fluctuating lake levels. The rafts have been a big success in some areas where chronic nest loss is occurring. However, biologists warn that they are not a panacea for loon problems. Unlike the popular nest box programs for wood ducks and bluebirds which are successful because quality nests are the limiting factor, the use of loon rafts should be limited to necessary circumstances.

Hydro power hasn't been all bad for loons. New loon habitat has been created by the damming of rivers and the creation of flowages such as the Stillwater reservoir in upstate New York where Judy McIntyre has been monitoring a growing and successful loon population. Similarly, in northern Wisconsin, the Turtle-Flambeau and Chippewa Flowages provide some of the largest water bodies in the state and their convoluted shorelines create plenty of potential natural loon territories. However, creation of new loon habitat must be balanced against other environmental problems that often result from damming river systems including the disruption of the hydrological system that is the very lifeblood of rivers, barriers to the movement of fish that must swim upstream to spawn, and the accumulation of mercury which has occurred in reservoirs in Quebec.

HARVEST OF LOONS

In some parts of North America, loons are still used as a food source. Native Americans in Quebec kill an average of 4,500 loons each spring. Quebec fish and game officials estimate that the harvest is roughly twenty percent of the region's common loons, but add that it has not threatened the stability of the population. It is a small component of the Indian's diet, less than one-tenth of one percent according to a Quebec government report.

In the far northwest, the Cree and Inuit have traditionally hunted loons, but the harvest now is thought to be slight.

While loons are not in a class with grain fed mallards, they should not be considered inedible. The early scientific literature has several references to the table quality of loons. One naturalist in the late 1800s termed loons "quite good," but few today are hungry enough to try one.

PREDATORS

Faced with normal numbers of predators, loons do just fine, but the populations of some predators, especially gulls and raccoons, have exploded in recent years, putting extra pressure on loon productivity. In Maine, gulls are a definite problem for loons. They take chicks, as well as eggs, often harass nesting loons, and sometimes take over prime nesting spots. Gulls are pretty, but they are also nasty. Niko Tinbergen, a Dutch naturalist, called gulleries "cities of thieves and murderers." To survive, gulls need to be aggressive. They will take whatever they can find, including loon eggs and chicks.

The damage raccoons can inflict on the loon population is well known. In New Hampshire they have been a particular nuisance. Like gulls, raccoons seem to be increasing in number throughout loon country. The feeding of raccoons by resort owners and tourists, coupled with the availability of garbage at land fills and waysides, has helped fuel the raccoon population expansion.

A SILVER LINING

While this chapter presents a litany of problems, it does not translate into an epitaph for the loon. Though often costly, there are solutions to all of these challenges.

Sometimes a story is more appealing than its plot. The loon's story is part of a larger effort to put the world back together.

Adults will refuse backrides to chicks when they become too large.

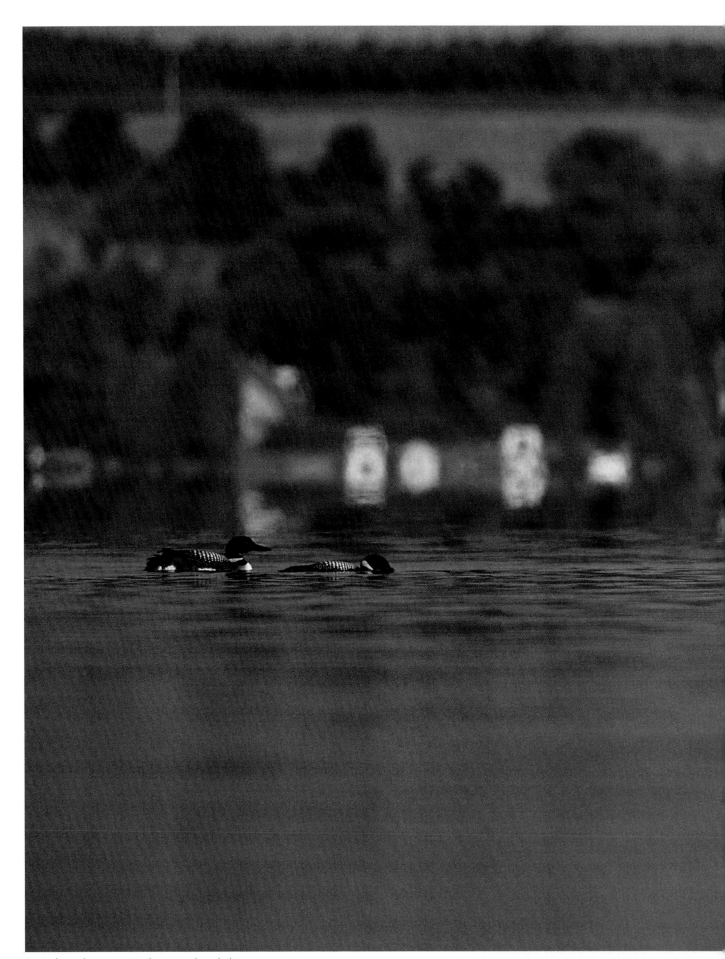

Spreading urbanization is destroying loon habitats.

If lake residents are committed to preserving the primitive, pristine aspects of their lakes by protecting optimal nesting habitats for loons, then a comeback in loon populations can occur, and their presence will, in turn, enhance the lake's wild qualities.

—Scott Sutcliffe, 1980

People Problems

Most loon problems are really people problems. Some, like chemical contamination, or excessive gull and raccoon populations, are camouflaged and removed by a layer or two from the core of loon problems—human ignorance and apathy. Other loon problems are all too visible: a loon with gunshot wounds, a loon with a hook deeply embedded in its gullet because a "sportsman" left a minnow unattended for hours, a loon entangled and immobilized by a plastic six-pack holder, a loon found dead from internal bleeding, the result of a let's-run-down-the-loon joyride. While all of these problems are real, they are fortunately rare. Aggressive public education efforts in most states have eliminated or at least reduced these excesses, but the quiet problems remain, like the nature photographer who must get a nesting loon shot and needs twelve attempts before getting the focus perfect.

RECREATIONAL DISTURBANCE

The role of disturbance—intentional or unintentional—has been given considerable attention in loon management circles and has been frequently identified as the number-one threat to loon population stability. In nearly every state with a loon population, public education efforts have been mounted to prevent the disturbance of loons, especially during the nesting season. In Wisconsin, the line "Leave the Loons Alone" became the battle cry of loon protectionists with posters at boat landings, radio public service announcements, newspaper articles and campground slide programs all echoing the message. In New Hampshire, the issue was carried to its logical extreme. To protect loons from people, ropes with floats were strung across the mouths of bays or inlets to prevent boats from coming near a nest site. The rationale for this separation of loons and people was simple: boaters approaching the nest site dislodge the nesting bird and leave the eggs vulnerable to chilling or predation.

Some loons are more tolerant to the proximity of humans.

Recent loon research, however, questions the conventional wisdom. While it's certainly true that high levels of recreational activity near nest sites can affect hatching and chick rearing success, long-term recreational pressure is usually just one of many variables affecting productivity. The issue of recreational disturbance deserves a close review.

While loon researchers sounded the recreational alarm earlier, few people in wildlife management listened until non-game wildlife attracted the public's attention in the 1970s. A grass roots movement to stop harassment of loons began in New Hampshire in 1974 and quickly spread west.

DISTURBING RESEARCH

Beginning in 1976 Jim Titus, who was completing his requirements for a Ph.D. at the State University of New York in Syracuse, conducted a detailed study of the impacts of recreation on loon productivity. Staking out the same study area that Sigurd Olson had used in 1950, Titus spent two full summers in the Boundary Waters Wilderness Area. With its loons, eagles, wolves, moose, northern lights, inspiring granite outcroppings, towering pines and over 1,000 lakes, the Boundary Waters is a magical place.

Titus claimed that the Boundary Waters Wilderness Area has "perhaps the largest and most concentrated contiguous breeding population of the common loon still remaining in any portion of the forty-eight adjoining states." When you add the million-plus acres and hundreds of lakes of Ontario's adjacent Quetico Provincial Park to the north, the many hundred lakes of the Superior National Forest to the south and the large loon lakes of Voyageurs lakes. When he compared lakes where no motors were permitted, he found a similar difference; on paddle-only lakes the survival rate of juveniles per breeding pair was 0.71 compared to 0.50 on motor lakes. He reports in his dissertation that "pairs on non-motor lakes were consistently and significantly more successful in hatching young and raising broods."

The reason for these differences, Titus contended, is the loon pairs' attentiveness to nesting duties. When loons are defending their territory or hiding from human presence, they are obviously not on their nests and they expend considerable energy just avoiding people. (Judy McIntyre estimates that chicks facing heavy recreational pressures will expend up to eight times more energy than normal movements require.) When leaving a nest in a hurry, loons are not particularly careful. In his two-year study, Titus found eight intact loon eggs in the water near nests and suggested the hurried departure of disturbed birds was involved. Titus feels motors are a particular problem: "We had little doubt that the average party with motors on their craft affected the loons more than the average non-motor party." Forest Service biologist Catherine Ream also believed nest disturbance by canoeists was the primary limiting factor for loon reproduction in the Boundary Waters Wilderness Area.

By stepping back from the Titus and Ream studies and reviewing population trends for the area over a thirty-year period, a different perspective comes into focus. There is no question about the increase in recreational use of the Boundary Waters Wilderness Area: it was nearly ten times greater in 1984 than in 1950, when Sigurd T. Olson established a baseline estimate for loon population. Assuming that recreationists do disturb nesting birds, which in turn reduces productivity, a consistent decline in loon numbers would be expected. Such a decline has not occurred. With a survey completed in the summer of 1984, a thirty-four-year span of population estimates indicates that there were more loons and chicks in 1984 than in 1950, despite the tremendous increase in recreational use. Even though some loon nests in the Boundary Waters have been passed by 15,000 people per summer, loons have continued to successfully reproduce, although some territories have moved away from high use areas.

Learning to Cope?

This speaks well of the loon's tenacity and flexibility. It is quite possible, even likely, that loons have learned to tolerate human presence. Barrett Christenson, a graduate student from the University of Maine, concluded that "loons in Maine are habituating to disturbance by humans." He studied one group in a remote area of northern Maine and another in a heavily used area of southern Maine. While the birds in the remote areas quickly flushed when their nest was approached, the loons in southern Maine tended

National Park to the west, a picture of nearly perfect loon habitat emerges.

Studying all aspects of the disturbance question, Titus concluded that " . . . increased recreational use patterns had a negative effect on the productivity of the common loon." He found that the heavy use of islands by campers offset the normal advantages of island nesting; that loons on small, remote lakes had a better hatching rate than those on large lakes in heavy recreation areas; that paddle-only (no motors allowed) lakes had better hatching and brooding success; and that where loons had fewer human contacts they produced more surviving young.

Comparing fifty nests in low-use areas with fifty nests in high-use areas, Titus found 0.61 juveniles per breeding pair surviving on low-use lakes and 0.43 surviving on high-use to sit tight when a boat came near. One particularly touchy pair of birds on Scraggly Lake in the northern study area flushed on thirty-seven of fifty approaches, even though the boat never came within a half-mile. A similar phenomenon was observed by Elizabeth Smith, a graduate student from Colorado State University, who studied common loons in Alaska. Working in the Kenai National Wildlife Refuge, she measured the average flushing distance on remote refuge lakes at about 350 feet. However, loons nesting along a heavily used refuge canoe route (2,500 canoes per summer) flushed at an average of just under thirty feet. Both these researchers concluded that loons simply get used to people.

Some loons carry this tolerance to an extreme. Titus discovered seven loons in his flock, all on high-use lakes, which refused to budge from their nests. Calling these birds "stickers," he found that even with approaches as close as three feet the birds never moved. In New Hampshire there are at least two loons whose mental glue to the nest was nothing short of bizarre. Scott Sutcliffe found two nesting loons, apparently in good health, so persistent in incubating that they had to be lifted off the nest to allow an egg count. Both birds were on busy lakes with heavy motorboat traffic. Another New Hampshire pair nested adjacent to a boathouse and actually swam through the boathouse to enter and leave the nest. Are these the last symbols of the wilderness we keep hearing about, or just smart loons?

There is a surprising twist to the disturbance story. In all studies, the birds on heavy-use lakes produced more chicks. The "stickers" on busy lakes produced far more chicks than loons on remote lakes. Two-chick broods were the norm for these tight-sitting birds. In a study of nesting success, Judy McIntyre found twenty-one of thirty-one loons (sixty-eight percent) nesting on high-use lakes were successful, while only thirteen of twenty-two loons (fifty-nine percent) nesting on low-use lakes were successful. Christenson's study in Maine demonstrated little difference in reproductive success. In the busy southern lakes twenty-one pair fledged fourteen young (0.67 per pair) while on the isolated northern lakes, fifteen pair fledged seven young (0.47 per pair). Christenson concluded that the "presence of people, cabins and human activity does not by itself appear to influence loon reproduction," but he did note that disturbances which keep birds off the nest for more than one hour are likely to cause nest abandonment.

So it's not just people—it's what they do and how long they do it. And it's not always a brash, insensitive fisherman who refuses to leave a nesting area. It can just as easily be the local naturalist in a cedar-strip Old Town with a Nikon who "needs" the ultimate loon photograph. People pressure does bother loons. The overlap of loon incubation and the prime fishing season may be a negative factor in loon productivity for some areas, and shore-to-shore boat traffic on Memorial Day or Independence Day certainly does not help. The success story of New Hampshire's loon protection effort clearly demonstrates the loon's need for separation from heavy recreational activity.

Certainly some human behaviors bother loons. I recall hearing loons on Trout Lake in northern Wisconsin start to call wildly on summer Sunday afternoons as soon as the weekly trapshoot began. Trout Lake resort owner Dan Cardinal told me the loons always react to the shooting. But the loons stay. They can tolerate disturbance and people, up to a point. Exactly where that point is will be the subject of discussion and debate for years—and maybe if we're lucky, forever.

A nervous loon can be driven from its nest at the slightest disturbance.

Floating platforms can be the answer to fluctuating water levels near nest sites.

Though the loon's breeding territory has shrunk dramatically, there is no reason that humans and loons can not share the same remaining northern waters, provided appropriate care is taken. It is the belief of The North American Loon Fund and the dedicated people who operate its programs that loons can not only survive in the modern world, but can thrive.

—Rawson Wood, 1982

Recovery Efforts

For loons, the present is better than the past, and the future will be better than the present. The first half of that summary judgment on loons requires little supporting evidence. In the late nineteenth and early twentieth centuries, loon populations dwindled. At best, loons were considered a silly bird. At worse, they were seen as fishermen's competitors. Countless thousands were shot to protect fishermen's table fare. In the first quarter of the twentieth century, Edward H. Forbush documented an annual rite of spring when hundreds of loons were shot off Buzzards Bay in Massachusetts. In Maine, on postcard-perfect Lake Umbagog, tourists shot loons for sport from cruise steamers. As late as the 1950s, loons served as targets on some Minnesota lakes.

CHANGING ATTITUDES

Carroll Henderson, the Minnesota DNR's NonGame Coordinator, recalled at a Minneapolis loon conference that "sportsmen" in the late 1950s considered it their special responsibility to shoot all cormorants and loons on one western Minnesota lake. Henderson quickly noted that in a relatively short time people have come a long way; there are no more organized shoots for non-game waterbirds in Minnesota. Believing education programs about non-game wildlife are working, Henderson points to the recent re-establishment of white pelicans in Minnesota. Because their take of fish averages four pounds a day and their fishing technique is showy, even boisterous, fishermen despised the white pelican. By the late nineteenth century, these beautiful birds disappeared from Minnesota lakes—victims in a battle over fishing rights. The white pelican again nests on many Minnesota lakes and produces over a thousand young per summer. People are learning to live with predators, both feathered and furred. After years of expatriation, timber wolves have returned to northern Wisconsin's forests. And ospreys and bald eagles are expanding their range throughout the north. These are signs of the times. Positive signs.

Today, loons are riding a high tide of good will. In New Hampshire, Rawson Wood has watched interest in loons grow tremendously over the past two decades. He senses a deep emotional attachment between loons and New Hampshire's lake country residents and states the case quite graphically: "The Old Man of the Mountain is a beautiful part of New Hampshire. Anyone who destroyed it would probably be shot. Loons are a beautiful part of New Hampshire also. People feel strongly about loons. I don't think that will change."

Wood knows how deeply people in the East treasure the feeling of wilderness. He recalls the often quoted line from Edward Forbush's 1939 book, *The Natural History of Birds of Eastern and Central North America*: "Of all the wild creatures that persist in this region today, the loon seems best to typify the stark wilderness of primeval nature." Forbush was speaking of the Northeast in the early twentieth century.

His sentiment is echoed by many in the Northeast today. In New Hampshire and other areas of the East and Midwest, the loon is the only remaining symbol of wilderness. Rawson Wood estimates that few people in New Hampshire have ever seen an eagle, and ospreys are still rare. That makes loons all the more precious. In Wood's view, the future for loons depends upon how rapidly lakes are damaged by development, and how effectively people concerned with loons rally to protect them. With many other observers, he believes loons and people can live together, citing as proof recent productivity gains on New Hampshire lakes where heavy recreational pressure has been neutralized by aggressive public involvement and loon protection measures. He has watched with some pride the numbers of loons in New Hampshire have nearly doubled from 254 in 1978. The return of loons to Massachusetts is also encouraging to Wood and other North American Loon Fund officials. The first loon pair in years was spotted on the Quabbin Reservoir in 1975. By 1977 there were three pairs, and by 1984 there were five. In 1994, eleven pairs of loon staked out claims to Massachusetts lakes. Small numbers but in the right direction. Management programs have made these gains possible.

For centuries people have needed loons, but now, at least in some areas, loons need people, too. The *right* people. In New Hampshire, The Loon Preservation Committee considers public education and public involvement, their primary management tools, more important even than artificial nesting islands. A Squam Lake resident for many years, Rawson Wood knows how important people are in the loon's future: "Loons can't possibly survive in New Hampshire without complete protection; the loon nests singly, in scattered locations, and can only be protected by the people who live on or visit its breeding lakes." In New Hampshire and in nearly every area where loons nest, loons are being well protected. Once common, harassment of loons by boaters is going the way of spring loon shoots. People are getting the message.

THE NON-GAME MOVEMENT

There is another reason for optimism: the nongame concept has spawned effective management programs in many states. As a result, the quality and quantity of loon research is increasing, and protection of shoreline breeding habitat in many areas is finally improving. Voluntary taxpayer contributions for nongame wildlife programs are helping loons in many states.

In addition to education efforts, many state conservation agencies and private loon groups are protecting the loon's future prospects by placing artificial nesting islands in certain loon territories. Constructed of cedar logs, these islands are helping loon populations recover. In New Hampshire, over twenty percent of loon productivity is a direct result of their use. In the Chippewa National Forest in Minnesota, the use of artificial nest islands increased the nesting success rate on two lakes from twenty percent to seventy-one percent. By reducing the threat of predation (raccoons rarely swim to get eggs) and the possibilities of nest flooding or dry-docking (these islands float, adjusting to any lake level), artificial nesting islands work well. But they must be properly constructed and placed. Scott Sutcliffe offers a few tips: islands should be put in within two weeks of ice-out and be placed adjacent to previously used but unsuccessful sites where human disturbance will be minimal; islands should be protected from prevailing winds and located within 200 feet off shore in water ten to thirty feet deep; and the island should have a base of duff, twigs and roots with planted indigenous, low-lying vegetation.

THE BIG PICTURE

The major issues which threaten the loon's survival unfortunately cannot be solved with rafts, loon alert signs or loon bumper stickers. Even thousands of fanatics can not, by themselves, stop acid rain, toxic contamination, or oil spills. Solutions in these areas await major legislative efforts which, in turn, await basic changes in societal values and priorities. But society continues to move in the direction of responsible environmental stewardship.

While political winds frequently change direction, creating setbacks, the progress in environmental protection over the past twenty years has been nothing short of remarkable.

Due in large part to the post-Earth Day surge of environmental legislation (especially The National Environmental Policy Act, The Clean Water Act, The Clean Air Act and The Endangered Species Act), environmental concerns in the United States have been institutionalized at nearly all levels of government. While the din of 1970s "rah-rah" environmentalism *is* faded, commitment to clean air and water, at personal and most governmental levels, has never been stronger. Aided by new pollution-control technologies and strong public support, emissions of acid-creating pollutants should decline by the turn of the twentieth century, in time to save the northern loon breeding lakes from acidification.

That's a prediction based partly on knowledge and partly on faith. Its accuracy will depend, in part, on how effectively the conservation community addresses the economic questions related to acid rain control measures.

The challenges of cleaning up toxic contaminants and heavy metals such as lead, mercury and aluminum will probably be more demanding. The sources of these contaminants are usually diffuse: an insecticide sprayed on southern agricultural lands can be carried in the atmosphere to loon lakes in Wisconsin or Maine. While DDT or PCBs do not appear to be a present threat to loons, other potentially harmful chemicals could be patiently waiting in the food chain.

Information specific to the effects of various contaminants on loons is slim, although it appears loons cope fairly well with some contaminants. One does not have to be a scientist to see some of the effects of chemical contamination in waterbirds. High levels of toxicants in Lake Michigan's Green Bay, for example, have affected cormorants and four other bird species by causing gross bill deformities. Unable to feed efficiently, such birds are doomed, the victims most likely of dioxin.

At a public hearing in Green Bay, Wisconsin on former Senator Robert Kasten's "Save the Lakes" bill, a pair of these cormorants were on display. Looking at these birds elicited simultaneous feelings of revulsion and fascination.

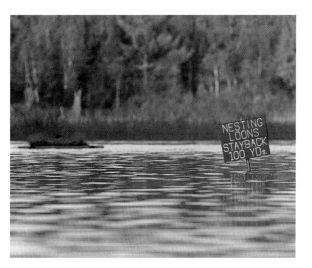

Loon platforms provide greater nesting success.

Were they just a cruel joke of nature, or an apocalyptic symbol of an unwanted future? The toxic contamination issue represents a serious challenge for the research community, government agencies, environmental groups and concerned citizens. Those cormorants do not have to represent the future of wildlife. With the proper blend of research, new technology, persuasion and patience, the toxic issue can be satisfactorily resolved.

THE ADAPTABLE LOON

Patience is something loons probably know a lot about. Over hundreds of thousands of years, loons have adjusted to a broad range of environmental change. Unlike people, loons and all other wildlife species don't worry about change; they simply adapt to it or perish. Succeeding in a variety of habitats and adjusting nesting habits to minimize human interference, loon behavior is quite elastic. Most likely, loons will not replay the sad story of the ivory-billed woodpecker. This large woodpecker was widely distributed in the virgin forests of southern North America until the logging of mature forests destroyed its preferred habitat. Today the existence of the ivory-billed is limited to rumors and hoaxes.

The loon's path will probably be closer to the one followed by the pileated woodpecker, which shared the ivory-billed's habitat and food supply. For reasons not well understood, the pileated woodpecker could adapt to changing environmental conditions; it survived and thrived in younger growth woodlands. While not as common as crows, pileated woodpeckers are turning up all over. Their flexible feeding habits gave pileated woodpeckers a second chance; the rigid patterns of the ivory-billed gave that bird a one-way ticket to oblivion.

Loons seem to be anything but rigid: they nest on a wide variety of lakes from one acre to thousands of acres in size; they construct their nests out of any available material; they eat almost anything aquatic; and in winter they disperse over an enormous coastal range. It seems like an open-ended ticket. Even if acid rain were to wipe out the trout or smallmouth bass of a given region, loons would simply feed more heavily on perch or suckers, more resistant prey species.

While there still are serious problems in the current reproductive success of loons, especially in the Northeast, these problems can probably be solved through protection and management efforts. Dominated by enormous numbers of loons breeding in Canada, the total North American population appears adequate to feed a recovery effort as suitable loon habitat becomes available. In Wisconsin, after generations of inching northward, the range of breeding loons is starting to reverse directions and move to the south. Improved water quality, resulting from a decade of tough enforcement of the Clean Water Act, and a reduction of harassment are part of that change.

There is hope that loons in Wisconsin and elsewhere can reoccupy parts of their traditional breeding range. To some, that may seem unrealistic, even miraculous. But look at some other modern environmental miracles: Lake Erie, returned from the "dead," producing some of the best walleye fishing in the world; the Connecticut River again producing Atlantic salmon; peregrine falcons now expanding their endangered population; and the whooping crane, once a lonely group of eighteen birds and written off by many biologists, is slowly moving back from the brink of extinction. We're not about to write off the common loon.

HOPE

I often receive notes from some of Wisconsin Project Loon Watch's volunteer cooperators citing the failure of a loon pair to successfully hatch a chick. Sometimes these cooperators assume personal responsibility for a loon's failure and they always use the occasion to lament about the future of loons on their lake. I usually return a note of appreciation for their concern, but remind them that loons are long-lived birds, that adult mortality of loons is relatively low and that it takes only two surviving chicks over the pair's entire life span to continue the species.

Despite the insults of water pollution, harassment and habitat loss, the population of the common loon has declined only slightly over the past thirty years, and in some parts of its range breeding populations have actually started to climb slightly. Research is expanding in a variety of areas critical for improved loon management, and new tools for research such as the audiospectrograph and radio-tracking equipment are becoming available. In July of 1984, a bald eagle was tracked by an orbiting satellite, opening a new era in telemetry research. In the twenty-first century, loons fitted with transmitters will probably be routinely followed by satellite from their northern summer homes to warm coastal waters.

All loons ask for is a place to live, clean water, some fish to eat and a little privacy. For what loons give to people, that seems a small price to pay.

Chicks flatten themselves against the water when their parents are elsewhere.

A pair of loons will not nest within visible sight of another pair.

Fifty Questions

THE TOP TEN: FOR ALL LOON LOVERS

1. *Do loons mate for life?*
    The heart says "yes," but science says "not always." Recent research on banded loons indicates that mate-switching is not all that uncommon, especially after nest failure. Scientists are trying to determine if loons living on highly acidic lakes and those with high levels of mercury in their systems might be more apt to exhibit this behavior.

2. *Why is the eye red?*
    Some scientists believe that the red eye improves fishing abilities either by improved underwater vision or by its camouflage effect (the red eye appears gray at depths of fifteen feet or more). Others feel the red eye is part of the breeding season plumage.

3. *How can you tell the difference between males and females?*
    It's not easy. You can wait for one to lay an egg (that's a female), watch a pair copulate (the male is on top) or notice which bird gives the distinctive yodel call (only males give this call). There are no apparent differences in plumage and only slight differences in size, although the male is almost always larger than the female in a mated pair.

4. *How long do loons live?*
    Most scientists believe the average life expectancy to be fifteen to thirty years, but until we get a lot more band returns, we won't know for sure. Around the year 2020, we ought to have enough information to make a scientifically sound estimate.

5. *Just how ancient is the loon?*
It is no accident that loons are listed first in bird books. They are one of the oldest species of modern birds with an ancestry dating back fifty to eighty million years. The oldest loon fossils date back twenty million years.

6. *How did the loon get its common name?*
This is a multiple choice question. Most reference books relate the common loon to the English word lumme or the Scandinavian word lom, both meaning awkward or lame. Since the loon is very clumsy on land, these references do make sense. The *Oxford Book of British Bird Names*, suggests the word loon was a seventeenth century corruption of the Old Norse word *lomr* which referred to the red-throated loon. The basic meaning of the Norse word is moaning, an allusion to the loud, wailing calls of the loon.

7. *Do loons use their wings while diving?*
Not usually. The wings are used to help execute sharp turns while chasing prey, but they are not used for propulsion except when a loon is frightened. The large webbed feet supply the power. Wings are typically held tight to the body during dives.

8. *How deep do loons dive?*
There are reports of dives in excess of 200 feet, but no scientific evidence exists for dives to those depths. It's safe to say loons dive to depths over 100 feet which is amazing enough anyway. Generally loons fish in shallow water and stay submerged less than one minute.

9. *Are loons endangered?*
Officially the answer is no. Common loons are not on the U.S. Fish and Wildlife's List of Endangered or Threatened Species. In some parts of their range, however, the common loon is in trouble. Many states list the loon as endangered, rare or threatened.

10. *How fast do loons fly?*
Loons have been clocked at speeds over 100 mph. Having wing beats of around 250 per minute, the common loon is an extremely rapid flyer considering its adaptations (solid bones for example) which favor aquatic over aerial freedom.

THE NEXT TEN: FOR SERIOUS LOON WATCHERS

11. *What's the wild calling at night all about?*
The extravagant calling at night is probably part of territorial defense. Loons like to keep track of each other. In daylight they can see each other, but at night they have only calling. Termed night chorusing, this calling peaks in early spring and has to be considered as one of Nature's most exciting audio events.

12. *How large are loon territories?*
Territory size will depend upon the quality of habitat and the density of loons in the region, but twenty to 200 acres covers the range in most places. In prime northern Minnesota loon country, the average territory on large lakes is about seventy acres.

13. *How many species of loons are there?*
A very small family, there are only five species of loons— the common, the red-throated, the arctic, the Pacific and the yellow-billed. There are no recognized subspecies despite variations in size.

14. *How large are loons?*
Common loons average around ten pounds. There is a size gradient. Loons from the northeast are larger (averaging about twelve pounds) than loons from the upper midwest (averaging about nine pounds). The typical loon is about thirty inches in length with a wingspread of fifty inches.

15. *What's the ideal nest site?*
Imagine a spot right next to the water on the protected side of a small island with plenty of low vegetation. Have the water drop off quickly to a depth of around five feet. Now you have a picture of a perfect loon nest site. If your lake has only one small island, odds are high that your loons will be nesting there. Don't be surprised to find a loon nest in a spot that appears to be less than ideal, however. Only loons know why they nest where they do.

16. *What does courtship activity look like?*
There will never be an X-rated loon movie. Loon courtship is rather mild: combinations of short dives, bill dipping and bill flicking while quietly swimming near the shoreline.

17. *Who builds the nest?*
Loons have been liberated for millions of years. Males and females divide about equally the nest building duties. Loons are not careful builders. They simply throw whatever vegetation is handy on the nest.

18. *About the eggs, how many and how big?*
Loons aren't like ducks which lay clutches of a dozen or more eggs. Generally, loons lay two eggs, sometimes only one and very rarely three. Of course if ducks laid eggs which averaged 3-3/8inches in length and 2-1/4 inches in diameter, they would not lay a dozen either. Loons

incubate their eggs an average of twenty-eight days, but successful incubation can be as short as twenty-five or as long as thirty-three days. The eggs are turned (very carefully) with the loon's open mandibles at irregular intervals.

19. *What predators go after loon eggs?*

The masked bandit (raccoon) we all know and love is presently loon enemy #1. Primarily nocturnal, raccoons are aggressive enough and large enough to barge into a mainland loon nest, chase away the adult and feast on loon eggs. Before New Hampshire's loon rangers started using artificial nest islands (raccoons can, of course, swim but they rarely bother loons on islands), raccoons destroyed up to eighty percent of all loon eggs on some New Hampshire lakes. Raccoons, though, tend to be a problem only where people with their garbage have inflated raccoon populations. Herring gulls can be a problem where they are abundant, but loons seem to coexist nicely with smaller gull species. In wilderness areas, avian predators such as ravens or crows probably take more eggs than mammals.

20. *Are loon eggshells getting thin?*

Pesticides, especially DDT, have created problems for many birds. While eagles, ospreys and peregrines have suffered from eggshell thinning, though, loons have continued to successfully reproduce. Loon eggshells are about ten percent thinner than eggshells from the pre-DDT era.

TEN MORE: CASUAL READERS BEWARE

21. *If the egg hatches, what are the odds the chick will survive?*

Very good. Since the parental care of chicks is excellent (by human standards, obsessive), adult loons usually see their chick(s) through to fall migration. One New Hampshire study determined that eighty-four percent of all hatched chicks survived, but the intensive protection efforts there may have increased the rate. Around fifty percent is a good estimate.

22. *What time of year gives loons the most trouble?*

It's certainly not summer when loons enjoy a season of easy fishing and slight stress. Very few dead adult loons are found on northern lakes. Disease often affects loons in the fall when large numbers congregate: thousands of loons have succumbed to botulism on Lake Michigan. But winter is the loon's worst season. The stress of coping with salt water, violent winter storms, marine pollution and parasites make life on the coast tough for loons. Off the coasts of the Carolinas, Florida or Texas, natural selection does its best work.

23. *How often do loons come ashore?*

Usually only to nest. A loon is a total waterbird. It is not inconceivable that a loon (if it did not mate) could live out its entire life without placing a foot on terra firma.

24. *Can loons walk?*

Not really. Loons sort of push themselves along on land but cannot stand erect and walk like a duck or goose. The legs are simply too far back on the body. Ninety-nine percent of all the mounted specimens are lies, showing loons standing up straight on their two huge feet.

25. *What do loons eat?*

Mainly fish. If a loon lives on a lake with an abundant fish population, the loon will probably eat fish ninety-nine percent of the time. Favored prey are perch, suckers, bullheads, sunfish, smelt and minnows. Non-fish items on the menu include frogs, salamanders, crayfish and leeches. Keep in mind that loons are very flexible feeders: they eat what they find.

26. *Do loons eat game fish?*

Sure. They love trout if they can find them. Small northern pike, bass or walleye all look the same to a hungry loon. Unlike people, loons don't distinguish between game fish and rough fish—a meal is a meal.

27. *What about salt water diets?*

Fewer studies of salt water feeding habits have been done but it's safe to say loons use the same opportunistic fishing strategies there. Herring, sea trout, rock cod, flounder would certainly be on the menu.

28. *How big a fish can a loon handle?*

Since loons have a rather elastic esophagus, they can swallow fairly large prey including trout up to eighteen inches. Spiny prey like sunfish or walleye may present a problem. Loons have been found dead with two-pound walleyes stuck in their gullets. Such large prey, however, are the exception: the average loon prey can be weighed in ounces rather than pounds.

29. *What is the "penguin dance"?*

Well named, the loon's penguin dance is the bird's most dramatic territorial display. Loons literally stand on the water by violently kicking their feet while holding their head down with their bill tight against their breast. While this defensive display might drive away some natural enemies, it does not work well with people. Some uninformed fishermen or boaters think it's entertainment and stimulate the display. It requires a lot of energy to perform (try it next time you're swimming). Anyone accidentally stimulating the dance should retreat immediately.

THE THIRTIES: FANATICS ONLY

30. *Why do chicks climb on their parent's back?*
The back-riding of chicks is primarily to protect against heat loss but also serves as protection from underwater (snapping turtles or pike) or over-water (eagles) predators.

31. *How high can loons fly?*
According to information from radar, at least 7,000 feet. Most flights in summer are at altitudes of only several hundred feet.

32. *Can loons lay more than one set of eggs a season?*
Yes, if their eggs are lost to predators, loons will some-times lay another clutch of eggs. Occasionally, loons will even nest a third or fourth time if the replacement batch of eggs is lost. However, loons have never been known to renest if the eggs hatch, but the chicks die.

33. *Do loons have a "brood patch?"*
While loons do not have a featherless brood patch (an incubation hot spot), they do have an area of their breast where blood vessels in the skin increase in size during the roughly one-month incubation period. This physiological change better transfers the bird's body heat to the eggs.

34. *What does the "wing flap" signify?*
The "wing flap" is done by many waterbirds. It probably has no social significance and is simply a way to shake water out of feathers.

35. *Why don't loons nest every year?*
Being a long-lived bird with the potential to raise dozens of young, loons don't need to attempt a nest each year. If the conditions aren't quite right, they often forego nesting. Typically, loons nest three of every four years.

36. *Do loons have accents?*
No. Loons from Minnesota sound just like loons from Maine or New Hampshire.

37. *What is a "rogue loon"?*
The term has been given to non-territorial birds or unsuccessful parents that wander around lakes in late summer. Occasionally, they kill other loons' chicks. This is not unusual behavior in the animal kingdom. Young, unattended birds and mammals are often killed by nonparent adults.

38. *Will loon eggs die if the nest is left uncovered?*
Loon eggs are susceptible to cooling. If left uncovered for long periods, the embryo could die. However, on hot days an egg might survive six or eight hours without incubation.

Typically large eggs hold heat better than small eggs so loon eggs are better protected than the eggs of most birds.

39. *Why do some loons tolerate people better than others?*
It appears that loons habituate to people over time. Apparently each loon has individual characteristics regarding tolerance of disturbance.

THE FINAL TEN: BEYOND FANATICISM

40. *Do some loons have green heads?*
Looks are deceiving. A loon's head sometimes looks green but it's really jet-black. When the feathers on the head are slightly raised (a display loons use in social gather-ings) sunlight refracting through the feathers creates the green, iridescent effect. In an argument, bet on black.

41. *Do loons nest on the ocean?*
No. There has been a report only one confirmed report of a loon nesting on the coast of Maine. Loons do nest in protected areas of Lakes Superior, Michigan and Huron—almost oceans.

42. *Okay, what is this foot waggle business?*
All serious loon watchers know about the foot waggle. Every ten to twenty minutes loons will extend a foot and wave it. It could be that the foot is being used as a crude solar collector to pick up heat. The waggle certainly con-serves heat since the blood vessels in the foot would release heat to the water. Supporting this notion is the fact that after the waggle, the foot is usually tucked up under the wing—a place to keep it warm. Or it could be that the foot waggle is part of a stretching exercise, loon yoga perhaps.

43. *Are small lakes better habitat for loons than large lakes?*
Small lakes are probably better habitat for loons, espe-cially if one pair is able to claim the entire lake as its ter-ritory. This reduces competition for food and other resources and allows the loons to focus all of their atten-tion on raising their young. Chicks may actually develop more rapidly on small ponds than on large lakes.

44. *When does the molt begin?*
The fall molt seems to vary by region—earlier in the west and later in the east. The first noticeable loss of feathers is usually mid-to-late September. New breeding plumage is donned in March and April. Loons lose their wing feathers only once—in late winter, usually February.

A parent and chick "footwaggle" in unison.

45. *In summer, do loons travel much?*
Recent research indicates loons travel a lot in summer, especially late summer after nesting duties are completed. One Wisconsin loon, tracked with a radio transmitter, flew twelve miles from its home lake to feed in another lake.

46. *How many loons have been banded?*
Fewer than a thousand, but that number increases every year as Dave Evers and other researchers use colored leg bands to help unlock the mysteries of loon life.

47. *How old are loons before they return to the northern lakes?*
Unlike ducks or geese, loons hang around their coastal homes for a full two or even three years before reaching sexual maturity and flying north for the first time. These immature loons do not have the black and white plumage. This delayed breeding might give loons the time they need to learn the fishing and general survival skills necessary to successfully raise young.

48. *Will loons reject a chick touched by humans?*
No. Many chicks have been handled for banding and have been safely returned to their parents. Other chicks, which were abandoned, have been rescued by people and subsequently adopted by adult loons.

49. *How long after copulation will the eggs be laid?*
That's a rather personal question and no biologist seems to have the answer. It is a short period of time though, measured in days rather than weeks.

50. *Where do I find out even more about loons?*
You are an over-the-edge loon fanatic. But if you want information on loons in your region, contact the North American Loon Fund affiliate closest to you.

Loon Protection Organizations

The North American Loon Fund (NALF) exists to support and coordinate its affiliate groups (listed below) with financial resources, technical data and educational materials. Its offices are located in Gilford, New Hampshire.

North American Loon Fund
6 Lily Pond Road
Gilford, NH 03246
603/528-4711 or 1-800-625-2555

AFFILIATED LOON GROUPS

Alaska Loon Watch
Alaska Department of Fish and Game
333 Raspberry RoadAnchorage, AK 99518

Audubon Society of New York
Hollyhock Hollow Sanctuary
46 Rarick Road
Selkirk, NY 12158

Canadian Lakes Loon Survey
Long Point Bird Observatory
P.O. Box 160
Port Rowan, Ontario
Canada NOE lM0

Common Loon Protection Project
Maine Audubon Society
P. O. Box 6009
Falmouth, ME 04105

Loons expend a great deal of energy in take-off.

Gatineau Fish and Game Club, Inc.
(Quebec)
Box 550
Maniwaki, Quebec
Canada J9E 3K6

Loon Lake Loon Association
(Washington)
P O. Box 75
Loon Lake, WA 99148

Loon Preservation Committee
P.O. Box 604, Lee's Mills Road
Moultonborough, NH 03254

Loon Survey Project
Vermont Institute of Natural Science
Woodstock, VT 05091

Loon Watch
(Minnesota and Wisconsin)
Sigurd Olson Environmental Institute
Northland College
Ashland, WI 54806

Massachusetts Division of
Fish and Wildlife
One Rabbit Hill Road
Westboro, MA 01581

Michigan Loon
   Preservation Association
6011 West St. Joseph Highway, Suite 403
P.O. Box 80527
Lansing, MI 48908

Montana Loon Society
6525 Rocky Point Road
Polson, MT 59860

Oikos Research Foundation
Utica College of Syracuse University
Utica, NY 13502

A common loon in summer breeding plumage.

Common Loon Summary

Age (Individuals)—15 to 30 years.

Age (Species)—Oldest and most primitive living bird, at least 20 million years old.

Autumn Migration—October and November. Pre-migratory flocking occurs on staging lakes. Flight groups usually small.

Chicks—12-24 Hours: leave nest with adult. First Day: make shallow dives. First Week: begin diving for food. First Month: dependent on adults for food. 6 Weeks: reach adult size. 6-8 Weeks: attain self-sufficiency. 11 Weeks: initial flight, possible dispersion.

Copulation—Normally occurs on land near nest site.

Courtship—Gentle, ritualized bill-dipping, shallow dives and head rubbing.

Diet—Mainly fish but also frogs, salamanders, crayfish, leeches, and aquatic greens. Loons feed by sight, grasp prey with their bills (they do not spear prey), and swallow most prey underwater.

Dives—Depth, perhaps to 200 feet. Duration, up to 5 minutes but generally under 1 minute. Loons are quick and mobile underwater.

Eggs—Loons typically lay two large eggs one day apart, olive green-brown with dark brown spots, 3 3/8 inches long, 2-1/4 inches in diameter.

Flight—Runway, 1/8 mile or less. Air Speed, 75-100 mph.

Incubation—Shared by both males and females for 27 to 31 days (average 28 days).

Molting—Flight feathers: once each year during late winter. Breast and back feathers: twice each year, October-December and again during March-April.

Nest Construction—Pile of mud and available vegetation with shallow depression in middle. Additional construction and repairs made during incubation.

Nest Sites—Island locations preferred near water's edge and protected from prevailing winds. Some well camouflaged, others exposed.

Physical Description—Male and female identically colored. Summer plumage: glossy black head, black neck with white and black necklace around throat, checkered black and white back and wings, white underparts. Winter Plumage: dark gray-brown head, neck and back, white throat and underparts. Bill: straight and black. Eyes: deep red.

Predators (chicks)—Large fish, snapping turtles and eagles.

Predators (eggs)—Raccoons, gulls, crows, ravens, skunks, minks and otters.

Range—Summer Nesting Grounds: Canada, Alaska, Iceland, Greenland, and northern United States (ME, NH, VT, NY, MI, WI, MN). Wintering Grounds: Atlantic Coast from Maine to Florida Keys, Gulf of Mexico from Florida to Texas, Pacific Coast from California Baja to southern Alaska.

Scientific Name—*Gavia immer.*

Sexual Maturity—3 years for loons to reach maturity.

Size—Length: 28 to 35 inches. Weight: 8 to 12 pounds. Wingspan: up to 58 inches. Males slightly larger than females.

Spring Migration—April and May. Males arrive within a few days of ice out. Females arrive a few days or a week after the male's arrival.

Loons have an ancestry dating back 50 to 90 million years.

Loons prefer lakes that offer a variety of food for their young.

A Day in the Life of a Loon

Slowly, the total blackness of a night with no moonlight begins to recede and the faintest hints of light are seen in the east. After floating in the cove all night, a loon, still with its head tucked back under its wing, watches the lake become visible in the early morning light.

Greeting the new day, the loon raises its head and looks around. Only fifty feet away, its mate sits motionless on the nest, covering the eggs, insulating them from the early morning chill. The loon on the water hoots softly and his mate returns the gentle call. Turning to face the open water of the lake, the loon suddenly rears up with its neck outstretched, bill pointing to the sky, and flaps his wings vigorously. Settling back on the water, he begins to swim slowly along the shoreline, occasionally peering beneath the water's surface.

As he swims, he stops to preen his feathers. Obtaining oil from a gland beneath his tail, he draws his wing feathers through his bill one at a time, reconnecting the web of hooks and shafts and covering the feathers with natural waterproofing. He preens meticulously making sure no feather is missed. At one point, he stretches back and rubs his head against his back feathers to waterproof one of the few places on his body he can't reach with his bill.

A fish darting in the shallows catches his attention, but he doesn't chase it. Instead, he continues to patrol the boundaries of the part of the lake he and his mate have claimed as their territory for the summer. Stopping over a submerged reef, the loon peers intently into the depths. Upon spotting a small fish, he dives quickly and pursues it, but it escapes into a weed bed. The loon resurfaces and shakes the water from his head. Several more forays along the reef fail to produce a fish.

While Minnesota, Wisconsin and Canada offer strongholds for loons, they are threatened in many regions.

Then, without warning, the loon begins to run across the calm lake surface. After 100 yards it is airborne and it circles the lake gaining altitude slowly. The female on the nest wails and the flying loon gives a flight tremolo several times in reply. The loon flies over the forest surrounding the lake to a nearby large lake almost two miles away. As the lake comes into view, he gives the flight tremolo again. On the lake below him there are many loons. One protests his arrival by giving the yodel call while a group of four loons becomes alert and watches him land.

The loon swims to the group of four and they begin some ritualistic behavior reminiscent of a dance. Slowly and deliberately, they swim in a circle and then a figure eight, heads held high. Then, they dive in synchrony and resurface one at a time. After several minutes of this, the loon breaks away from the group and swims nearly 150 yards underwater to a shallow, weedy cove. There he begins to swim slowly along the outer edge of the emergent vegetation, head held underwater, eyes fixed on the bottom. A slow-moving crayfish becomes his first meal of the day. He brings it to the surface and manipulates it in his bill before swallowing it whole. He catches several small fish in the next half hour and eats them underwater.

A distant wail turns his attention from feeding and he wails in response. Another wail is heard and he gives a wail back again. Laboring a bit with a full crop, the loon runs across the water and flies off the lake. Within three minutes, he lands on his home lake. His mate on the nest wails again and he replies. He swims toward the nest. When he is within thirty feet, the female clambers off the nest and

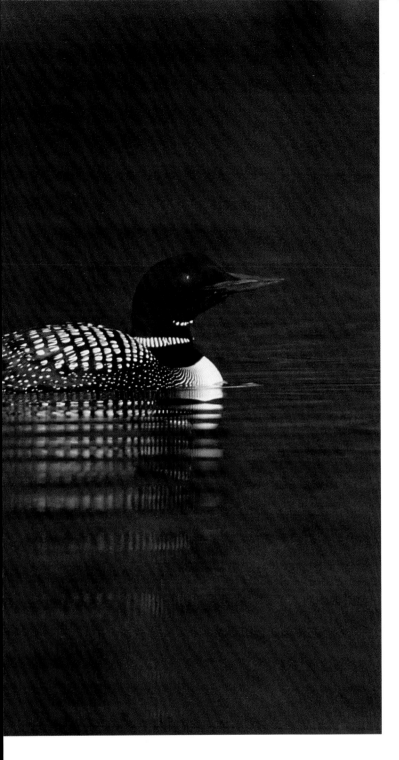

droning hum, the loon closes one eye and then the other.

An excited tremolo call from his mate startles him awake. Some children in a canoe have entered their cove and are heading right for the nest. His mate attempts to distract the canoeists by diving from one side of the canoe to the other. The children are unaware of the loon nest nearby and try to catch the female loon. They paddle furiously, shouting and laughing, but the loon escapes easily by diving underwater. The children respond as if its a game of hide and seek trying to guess where the loon will come up next. Purposely, she leads them to the open water part of the lake away from the nest. Then, she dives and swims all the way back to the nest underwater, leaving the children wondering where she could be.

Hooting softly, the loons trade places. For an hour, the male sits motionless in the shadowed shallow water near the nest, watching the lake, preening occasionally. Later, the loon swims out onto the lake toward the loon territory on the other side of a peninsula. He swims much of the way underwater surfacing only for a breath of air. He stops near an area that serves as the boundary between the two territories where he sees another adult loon nearby feeding in the shallows. He swims toward the loon. They interact nonaggressively for several minutes before a third loon approaches from behind an island. All three swim in a circle and dive several times before one of the loons lays his head low over the water and gives a yodel while the other bird watches from nearby. Feeling a bit uncomfortable away from his own territory, the loon swims away and heads back toward the nest. As he leaves, the other loon yodels two more times.

A large boat speeding across the water causes him to dive although it doesn't get closer than fifty yards. He swims to a shallow area in the cove and feeds and preens for nearly an hour.

He then swims back to the nest where he finds his mate snapping at mosquitoes and black flies buzzing around her head. Upon seeing her mate nearby, she slips into the water for a cooling dip and relief from the flies. The loons leave the eggs uncovered for a half hour as they lazily feed, preen, and loaf. They perform some subtle, pair-bonding rituals that consist of synchronized head movements and shallow dives before the female returns to the nest.

For the rest of the afternoon, the male loon swims in his territory, occasionally preening and peering below the surface. Several times, he stops and lifts one leg out of the water, shakes it, and tucks it up under one wing. Leaving one foot in the water as a rudder, he drifts with the wind, sometimes closing one or both eyes.

With the sun now low over the treetops, the loon swims back to the nest and relieves his mate of incubation duties. He turns the eggs again and picks at some vegetation with his bill, adding a few sticks and blades of grass to the shallow nest bowl.

heads for the open lake. The male climbs awkwardly onto the nest and turns the eggs several times with his bill before settling down on them.

From the nest, he watches his mate feed and preen. He also watches the first activity of the humans in the camps on the opposite side of the lake. A slamming screen door and the sight of a dog running down the shoreline cause him to lay flat on the nest, his head held over the edge and his bill almost touching the water. Some fisherman climb into a boat and start to motor along the shoreline. As they round the corner of the lake and head into the cove, he stays in the "hangover" posture. The boat passes the nest about 100 yards from shore, but the loon does not leave the nest. As the human activity increases and the sounds of human voices and outboard motors become a

His mate is off feeding as he watches the activity on the lake. A stick breaking behind him in the forest causes him to become motionless and to lay low on the nest. More sounds and the approach of an animal make him slip off the nest silently and he swims several yards from the shore. A white-tailed deer walks out of the forest and comes to the water's edge to drink. It walks along the shore in the shallow water directly in front of the loon's nest. After it leaves, the loon returns to the nest.

Just before nightfall, the loon on the nest hears the flight tremolo of an approaching loon and sees it land on the lake near his mate. The female and the visitor swim together for fifteen minutes before the visitor swims off toward the other loon territory. The female returns to the nest and they switch places again. This time the male swims out to the middle of the territory where he preens and swims around with no apparent destination.

Several hours after the sky has become dark, some people go out in a boat with bright lights and a noisy motor. The loon gives a tremolo call four times and the loons in the other territory call also. From nearby lakes more tremolos are heard. Then the lake becomes quiet.

Sitting out on the lake away from the nest, the male loon gives a wail call several times. His wails echo off the water and trees and he calls again. He hears wails, tremolos, and yodels from the other loons on the lake and from loons on other lakes. He continues to call, chorusing with the other loons. At one point, he stretches his neck over the water and gives the yodel call several times.

Later, he swims back into the cove and gives a couple of hoot calls. His mate hoots back softly and they change places once again. He sits quietly on the nest for several hours listening intently to the night sounds. Nearby, his mate sleeps on the water. Then, he sees the first light of dawn.

Common loon pairs return to the same lake year after year.

Selected Bibliography

NESTING AND CHICK REARING

Beebe, C. W. "Notes on the Early Life of Loon Chicks." *Auk* 24 (1907): 34-41.

Belant, J. L. and R. K. Anderson. "Common Loon, *Gavia immer*, Brood Habitat Use on a Northern Wisconsin Impoundment." *Canadian Field-Naturalist* 105 (1991): 372-375.

Dulin, G. S. "Pre-fledging Feeding Behavior and Sibling Rivalry in Common Loons." Master's Thesis. Central Michigan University, 1988.

Johnson, R. A. and H. S. Johnson. "A Study of the Nesting and Family Life of the Red-throated Loon." *Wilson Bulletin* 47 (1935): 97-103.

McIntyre, J. W. and J. Mathisen. "Artificial Islands as Nest Sites for Common Loons." *Journal of Wildlife Management* 41, no. 2 (1977): 317-319.

McIntyre, J. W. "Nurseries: A Consideration of Habitat Requirements During the Early Chick-Rearing Period in Common Loons." *Journal of Field Ornithology* 54 (1983): 247-253.

———."Biology and Behavior of the Common Loon (*Gavia immer*) With Reference to Its Adaptability in a Man-Altered Environment." Ph.D. Thesis. University of Minnesota, 1975.

Olson, Sigurd T. "A Study of the Common Loon in the Superior National Forest of Northern Minnesota." Master's Thesis. University of Minnesota, 1951.

Peterson, Margaret R. "Nesting Ecology of Arctic Loons." *Wilson Bulletin* 91 (1979): 608-617.

Sjolander, S. and G. Agren. "Reproductive Behavior of the Common Loon." *Wilson Bulletin* 84 (1972): 296-308.

———."Reproductive Behavior of the Yellow-billed Loon, *Gavia adamsii.*" *The Condor* 78 (1976): 454-463.

Southern, W. E. "Copulatory Behavior of the Common Loon." *Wilson Bulletin* 73 (1961): 280.

Strong, P. I. V. and J. A. Bissonette. "Feeding and Chick-rearing Areas of Common Loons." *Journal of Wildlife Management* 53 (1989): 72-76.

Strong, P. I. V., J. A. Bissonette and J. S. Fair. "Reuse of Nesting and Nursery Areas by Common Loons." *Journal of Wildlife Management* 51 (1987): 123-127.

Sutcliffe, S. A. "Aspects of the Nesting Ecology of the Common Loon in New Hampshire." Master's Thesis. University of New Hampshire, 1980.

Tate, D. J. and J. Tate. "Mating Behavior of the Common Loon." *Auk* 87 (1970): 125-130.

Vermeer, K. "Some Aspects of the Nesting Requirement of Common Loons in Alberta." *Wilson Bulletin* 85 (1973): 429-435.

POPULATION AND DISTRIBUTION

Bergeron, D. C. Jones, D. L. Genter and D. Sullivan. "Skaar's Montana Bird Distribution, 4th Edition." *Special Publication No. 2.* Montana Natural Heritage Program, 1992.

Campbell, R. W. N. K. Dawe, I. McTaggart-Cowan, J. M. Cooper, G. W. Kaiser and M. C. E. McNall. *The Birds of British Columbia. Volume 1.* Parts 1 and 2. Victoria, British Columbia: Royal British Columbia Museum, 1989.

Desgranges, J. *Preliminary Consideration of the Status of Loons in Quebec.* Quebec Region: Canadian Wildlife Service, 1979.

Dunn, T. D. "Status of the Common Loon in Wisconsin." *Passenger Pigeon* 54 (1992): 19-29.

Erskine, A. J. *Atlas of Breeding Birds of the Maritime Provinces.* Halifax, Nova Scotia: Nimbus Publications, Ltd. and Nova Scotia Museum, 1992.

Godfrey, W. E. "Birds of Canada." *Bulletin* 203. Ottawa: National Museum of Canada, 1966.

Oakleaf, B., B. Luce, S. Ritter and A. Cervoski. "Wyoming Bird and Animal Atlas." Wyoming Game and Fish Department, 1992.

Parker, K. E., R. L. Miller and S. Isil. *Status of the Common Loon in New York State.* Delmar, New York: New York Department of Environmental Conservation, 1986.

Rimmer, C. C. "Population Status of Common Loons in the Northeastern United States." In: L. Morse, S. Stockwell, and M. Pokras, eds. *Proceedings of the 1992 Conference on the Loon and its Ecosystem.* Concord, New Hampshire: U.S. Fish and Wildlife Service, 1993.

Robinson, W. L. "Common Loon." In: Brewer, R. G., A. McPeek and R. J. Adams, eds. *The Atlas of Breeding Birds of Michigan.* East Lansing, Michigan: Michigan State University Press, 1991.

Semenchuk, G. P., ed. *The Atlas of Breeding Birds of Alberta.* Edmonton: Federation of Alberta Naturalists, 1992.

Strong, P. I. V. and R. Baker. "An Estimate of Minnesota's Summer Population of Adult Common Loons." B*iological Report Number 37.* Minnesota Department of Natural Resources, 1991.

Synder, L. L. *Ontario Birds.* Toronto: Clarke, Irwin & Co., 1951.

Tankersley, N. and A. K. Ruggles. "Status and Distribution of Common Loons in Alaska." In: L. Morse, S. Stockwell, and M. Pokras, eds. *Proceedings of the 1992 Conference on the Loon and its Ecosystem.* Concord, New Hampshire: U.S. Fish and Wildlife Service, 1993.

HUMAN DISTURBANCE

Caron, J. A. "Responses of Breeding Common Loons to Human Activity in the Western Upper Peninsula of Michigan." Master's Thesis. Northern Michigan University, 1991.

Christenson, B. L. "Reproductive Ecology and Response to Disturbance by Common Loons in Maine." Master's Thesis. Orono: University of Maine, 1981.

Heimberger, M. D. Euler and J. Barr. "The Impact of Cottage Development on Common Loon Reproductive Success in Central Ontario." *Wilson Bulletin* 95 (1983): 431-439.

Kelly, L. M. "The Effects of Human Disturbance on Common Loon Productivity in Northwestern Montana." Master's Thesis. Montana State University, 1992.

Ream, C. "Loon Productivity: Human Disturbance and Pesticide Residue in Northern Minnesota." *Wilson Bulletin* 88 (1976): 426-431.

Smith, E. L. "Effects of Canoeing on Common Loon Production and Survival on the Kenai National Wildlife Refuge." Master's Thesis. Colorado State University, 1981.

Titus, J. R. and L. W. VanDruff. "Response of the Common Loon (*Gavia immer*) to Recreational Pressure in the Boundary Waters Canoe Area, Northeastern Minnesota." *Wildlife Monograph* 79 (1981).

WINTERING AND MIGRATION

Alexander, L. L. "Patterns of Mortality among Common Loons Wintering in the Northeastern Gulf of Mexico." *Florida Field Naturalist* 19 (1991): 73-79.

Daub, B. C. "Behavior of Common Loons in Winter." Journal of Field Ornithology 60 (1989): 305-311.

Eberhardt, R. T. "Recent Recoveries of Common Loons Banded in Minnesota." Loon 56 (1984): 202-203.

Ewert, D. N. "Spring Migration of Loons at Whitefish Point, Michigan." *The Jack Pine Warbler* 60 (No. 4, 1982).

Haney, J. C. "Winter Habitat of Common Loons on the Continental Shelf of the Southeastern United States." *Wilson Bulletin* 102 (1990): 253-263.

Kerlinger, P. "The Migration of Common Loons Through Eastern New York." *Condor* 84 (1982): 97-100.

King, B. "Wintering Feeding Behavior of Great Northern Divers." *British Birds* 69 (1966): 468.

McIntyre, J. W. "Wintering Behavior of the Common Loon." *Auk* 95 (1978): 396-403.

McIntyre, J. W. and J. F. Barr. "Pre-migratory Behavior of Common Loons on the Autumn Staging Grounds." *Wilson Bulletin* 95 (1983): 121-125.

Powers, K. D. and J. Cherry. "Loon Migrations off the Coast of the Northeastern USA." *Wilson Bulletin* 95 (1983): 125-132.

Simons, M. M. "Beached Bird Survey Project on the Atlantic and Gulf Coasts." *American Birds* 39 (1985): 358-362.

Woolfenden, G. "Selection for a Delayed Simultaneous Wing Molt in Loons." *Wilson Bulletin* 79 (1967): 416-420.

BEHAVIOR

Barklow, W. E. "The Function of Variations in the Vocalizations of the Common Loon (*Gavia immer*)." Ph.D. Thesis. Tufts University, 1979.

Barr, J. F. "Feeding Biology of the Common Loon (*Gavia immer*) in Oligotrophic Lakes of the Canadian Shield." Ph.D. Dissertation. University of Guelph, 1973.

Croskery, P. "Flocking Behavior of Common Loons (*Gavia immer*) in Northwest Ontario: Early-Summer Sites." In: P. I. V. Strong, ed. *Papers from the 1987 Conference on Loon Research and Management.* Meredith, NH: North American Loon Fund, 1988.

Flick, W. A. "Observations on Loons as Predators on Brook Trout." *North American Journal of Fisheries Management* 3 (1983): 95-96.

Kirkham, I. R. and S. R. Johnson. "Interspecific Aggression in Loons." *Journal of Field Ornithology* 59 (1988): 3-6.

Miller, E. and T. Dring. "Territorial Defense of Multiple Lakes by Common Loons: A Preliminary Report." In: P. I. V. Strong, ed. *Proceedings of the 1987 Conference on Loon Research and Management*, Meredith, NH: North American Loon Fund, 1988.

Norberg, J. M. and R. A. "Take-off, Landing and Flight Speed During Fishing Flights of *Gavia stellata*." *Ornis Scandinavica*. 2 (1971): 5567.

Pittman, J. A. "Direct Observation of Flight Speed of the Common Loon." *Wilson Bulletin* 65 (1953): 213.

Rummel, L. and C. Goetzinger. "The Communication of Intraspecific Aggression in the Common Loon." *Auk* 92 (1975): 333-346.

Rummel, L. and C. Goetzinger. "Aggressive Display in the Common Loon." *Auk* 95 (1978): 183-186.

Stewart, P. "Diving Schedules of the Common Loon." *Auk* 84 (1967): 122-123.

Wentz, L. E. "Aspects of the Nocturnal Vocal Behavior of the Common Loon." Ph.D. Dissertation. Ohio State University, 1990.

DISEASE/CHEMICAL CONTAMINATION

Alvo, R, D. Hussell and M. Berrill. "The Breeding Success of Common Loons (*Gavia immer*) in Relation to Alkalinity and Other Lake Characteristics in Ontario." *Canadian Journal of Zoology* 66 (1988): 746-752.

Barr, J. F. "Population Dynamics of the Common Loon (*Gavia immer*) Associated With Mercury-contaminated Waters of the English-Wabigoon System in Northwestern Ontario." *Canadian Wildlife Service Occasional Paper* No. 56 (1986).

Brand, C. J. S. Schmitt, R. M. Duncas and T. M. Cooley. "An Outbreak of Type E Botulism Among Common Loons (*Gavia immer*) in Michigan's Upper Peninsula." *Journal of Wildlife Diseases* 24 (1988): 471-476.

Burger, J. M. P. "Heavy Metal Concentrations in Feathers of Common Loons (*Gavia immer*) in the Northeastern United States and Age Difference in Mercury Levels." *Environmental Monitoring and Assessment* 30 (1994): 1-7.

Ensor, K. L., D. D. Helwig and L. C. Wemmer. *Mercury and Lead in Minnesota Common Loons (Gavia immer)*. St. Paul: Minnesota Pollution Control Agency, 1992.

Field, R. M., R. North and J. Wells. "Nesting Activity of Yellow-billed Loons on the Colville River Delta, Alaska, After the Exxon Valdez Oil Spill." *Wilson Bulletin* 105 (1993): 325-332.

Frank, R. H. Lumsden, J. F. Barr and H. E. Braun. "Residues of Organochlorine Insecticides, Industrial Chemicals and Mercury in Eggs and in Tissues Taken from Healthy and Emaciated Loons, Ontario, Canada, 1968-1980." *Archives of Environmental Contamination and Toxicology* 12 (1983): 641-645.

Graham, F. "Mystery at Dog Island." *Audubon* (March 1984): 30-34.

Lange, R. and R. Stroud. *Information Summary of Common Loon Die-Off, Winter and Spring of 1983*. Madison, WI: U.S. Department of Interior, National Wildlife Health Laboratory, 1983.

Locke, L. N., S. M. Kerr and D. Zoromski. "Lead Poisoning in Common Loons." *Avian Diseases* 26 (No. 26 1981): 392-396.

Pokras, M. C. Press and S. Rohrbach. "The Mortality of Loons." *Massachusetts Wildlife* 42 (1992): 18-25.

Sutcliffe, S. A. "Pesticide Levels and Shell Thicknesses of Common Loon Eggs in New Hampshire." *Wilson Bulletin* 90 (1978): 637-640.

NATIVE AMERICAN CULTURE

Bierhorst, J. *Songs of the Chippewa*. New York: Farar, Straus and Giroux, 1974.

Clark, E. E. *Indian Legends of the Pacific Northwest*. Berkeley: University of California Press, 1953.

Garfield, V. and L. Forrest. *The Wolf and Raven Totem Poles of Southeastern Alaska*. Seattle: University of Washington Press, 1948.

Garber, C. *Stories and Legends of the Bering Strait Eskimos*. Boston: The Christopher Publishing House, 1940.

Gubser, N. J. *Nunamiut Eskimos: Hunters of the Caribou*. New Haven: Yale University Press, 1965.

Hantzsch, B. *My Life Among the Eskimos*. Edited by L. H. Neatby. University of Saskatchewan, 1977

D. Harper, F. *Caribou Eskimos of the Uyper Kazan River*. University of Kansas, Lawrence, 1964.

Warner, W. *History of Ojibway Nation*. Minneapolis: Ross and Haines, Inc., 1974.